A Management Approach to Database Applications

INFORMATION SYSTEMS SERIES

Consulting Editors

D. E. Avison
BA, MSc, PhD, FBCS

Professor of Information Systems
ESSEC Business School
Cergy-Pontoise, Near Paris, France

G. Fitzgerald
BA, MSc, MBCS

Professor of Information Systems
Department of Information Systems and Computing
Brunel University, Uxbridge, UK

This series of student and postgraduate texts covers a wide variety of topics relating to information systems. It is designed to fulfil the needs of the growing number of courses on, and interest in, computing and information systems, which do not focus on the purely technological aspects, but seek to relate to business and organisational context.

A Management Approach to Database Applications

David Avison
ESSEC Business School, France

Christine Cuthbertson
Templeton College, Oxford, UK

THE McGRAW-HILL COMPANIES

London Burr Ridge IL New York St Louis San Francisco Auckland Bogotá Caracas Lisbon Madrid Mexico Milan Montreal New Delhi Panama Paris San Juan São Paulo Singapore Sydney Tokyo Toronto

Published by McGraw-Hill Education
Shoppenhangers Road
Maidenhead
Berkshire
SL6 2QL
Telephone: +44(0) 1628 502500
Fax: +44(0) 1628 770224
Web site: http://www.mcgraw-hill.co.uk

British Library Cataloguing in Publication Data
A catalogue record for this book is available from the British Library

Library of Congress Cataloging in Publication Data
Library of Congress data for this book is available from the Library of Congress, Washington, D.C.

Web site address: http://www.mcgraw-hill.co.uk/textbooks/avison-cuthbertson

Acquisitions Editor: Conor Graham
Editorial Assistant: Paul Von Kesmark
Senior Marketing Manager: Jackie Harbor
Senior Production Manager: Max Elvey
Produced for McGraw-Hill by Steven Gardiner Ltd
Printed and bound in Great Britain by Bell and Bain Ltd., Glasgow

McGraw-Hill
A Division of The McGraw-Hill Companies

ISBN 0-07-709782-3

Table of contents

Preface

This book is a student text on databases from a management and information systems perspective. It is ideal for students taking MBA and management programs studying an IT course or students taking an undergraduate or postgraduate course in information systems. It is also suitable as a second text for computer science students taking database courses as it gives an organisational, management and human orientation to add other perspectives for databases on the one that is provided in their main technical text.

The book covers database modelling and development, the hardware and software environment, organisational, management and people issues and database applications. Technical material, such as SQL, UML, and modelling (e.g. relational and object modelling), is provided, but in easily assimilated chapters. The major database management systems, such as Oracle and Access, are described along with a discussion of software tools. The book is relevant to PC database applications development as well as large-scale database applications development. Discussions on database applications, such as data warehousing, data mining, client-server, geographical IS, enterprise resource planning, group database work, call centres, and e-commerce, are also provided to put database applications fully in their context.

David Avison has previously published the popular *Information Systems Development: A Database Approach* (second edition, 1992). This new book takes the best aspects of the earlier book (an information systems and management perspective to databases) but brings it up to date. The treatment of the technical material, which is necessary to a well-rounded course on databases, is nonmathematical and made palatable to all students. The new book should therefore appeal to those people who liked the old one. Some sections have been omitted so as to keep the text a reasonable size and up to date. The previous material is available on the companion web site. The web site also has case studies, PowerPoint slides, further exercises and discussion questions and the answers to the exercises that appear in the book. The address of the web site is:

http://mcgraw-hill.co.uk/textbooks/avison-cuthbertson/.

This book will also appeal to those students using Avison and Fitzgerald *Information Systems Development: Methodologies, Techniques and Tools* who are looking for a text giving more detail of the database approach to IS development.

In Part I we consider the database applications in the context of the organisation. We start in Chapter 1 by introducing databases, and argue for a database approach to information systems development. In Chapter 2 we look at the universe of discourse; in other words that part of the organisation that we will consider for modelling and implementing on our database. We also look at data, information and knowledge that we hope to exploit using the database applications. The goals of the organisation are identified to ensure that our strategy for information systems is aligned with business strategy. In Chapter 3 we look at the roles of the people involved, be they visionaries, managers or specialists.

In Part II we look at developing the various models, which can represent a stage towards developing the database. A model is a representation of the 'real world', the universe of discourse, for which we are developing our database applications. We look at entity-relationship modelling, relational modelling and object modelling in Chapters 4, 5 and 6 respectively. These are all conceptual models, and the mapping from this stage to a database model implemented on a database management system is feasible and commonly achieved. Definitions are given for the terminology used and, through the use of many examples we show how the modelling processes are carried out.

In Part III we look at how our database applications are implemented. A discussion of the commonly used data definition and manipulation language SQL is followed by PC databases using the Access database management system and another chapter on larger applications using Oracle. Further chapters are provided on the implementation environment, and, in particular, distributed databases and client-server computing and the Internet environment. Part III concludes with a chapter on tools that support database implementation and a chapter on security issues.

In Part IV we first look at data warehousing and data mining. These are very large database applications that became possible following the improvements in technology. We then look at enterprise resource planning systems, such as SAP, which enable an integration of the various applications (and their databases) in the organisation. Next we consider databases relating to e-commerce applications. Chapter 17 briefly describes a number of other database applications, such as public databases, geographic information systems, marketing information systems, computer supported co-operative working, document management systems, call centres and knowledge management systems.

Finally in Part V we provide a description of the process of developing a database application such as those described in Part IV. We suggest two general approaches, a formal information systems development methodology and then rapid application development. Finally we look at outsourcing, where the decision is made to develop and perhaps also run the application externally.

As we have mentioned, the companion web site has case studies, PowerPoint slides and other material, and will be a living site, one that is continually growing.

The authors would like to thank Paul Golder of Aston University and Hanifa Shah of Stafford University for their help in planning the book.

Part I: Introduction

In Part I we consider database applications in the context of the organisation. In Chapter 2 we look at the universe of discourse, in other words that part of the organisation that we will consider for modelling and implementing on our database. We also look at data, information and knowledge that we hope to exploit using the database applications. The goals of the organisation are identified to ensure that our strategy for information systems is aligned with business strategy. In Chapter 3 we look at the roles of the people involved, be they visionaries, managers or specialists. However, we start in Chapter 1 by introducing databases, and discuss why we argue for a database approach to information systems development and also outline the approach used in the book. It also discusses the motivation for the modelling approaches that we detail in Part II of the book.

1

Database approach

1.1 Introduction

The main objective for this chapter is to set the scene for the database approach. It shows the differences between the conventional file-based systems and database applications, discussing the advantages of the database approach. We also look at the difficulties of the database approach, and suggest that we need a strategy and methodology to develop database applications. Such an approach is outlined in this chapter and described in the rest of the book

With database systems, it is possible to hold the facts relating to parts of the organisation on an integrated set of computer files: a database. The 'organisation' in this context could be the whole business or, more likely, a part of it, such as a division or department. The various computer applications can use this as the data source. If the functions change, the data on the database will probably still be appropriate. If the facts change, then the database can be amended without redesigning the application systems. There is thus an element of **data independence** between the database and the applications that use it. The hardware and software can also be changed in order to reflect developments in the technology without requiring substantial changes in the application systems or the structure of the database.

Figure 1.1 illustrates three stages tracing the historical development of data processing. In Figure 1.1(a) the data is held on a document of some kind, the process carried out by the human being, and the result written down on paper. In Figure 1.1(b), the input source is the same but has been transferred to a medium that is suitable for computers to read. The process is performed by the computer, which puts the result on a laser printer, and is printed out. Although a computer application, the system reflects the previous clerical system. There may well be more stages, but data processing is likely to be quicker overall, due to the speed of the computer. Figure 1.1(c) represents something much more radical. The facts of interest to the business are modelled on the computer database, and the various applications use the database as required. If the process needs to be changed in some way to reflect changes in the environment, the database will still be appropriate. The third option is likely to be the most rewarding. This should provide real added value when compared to either a manual system or a conventional computer system not using a database.

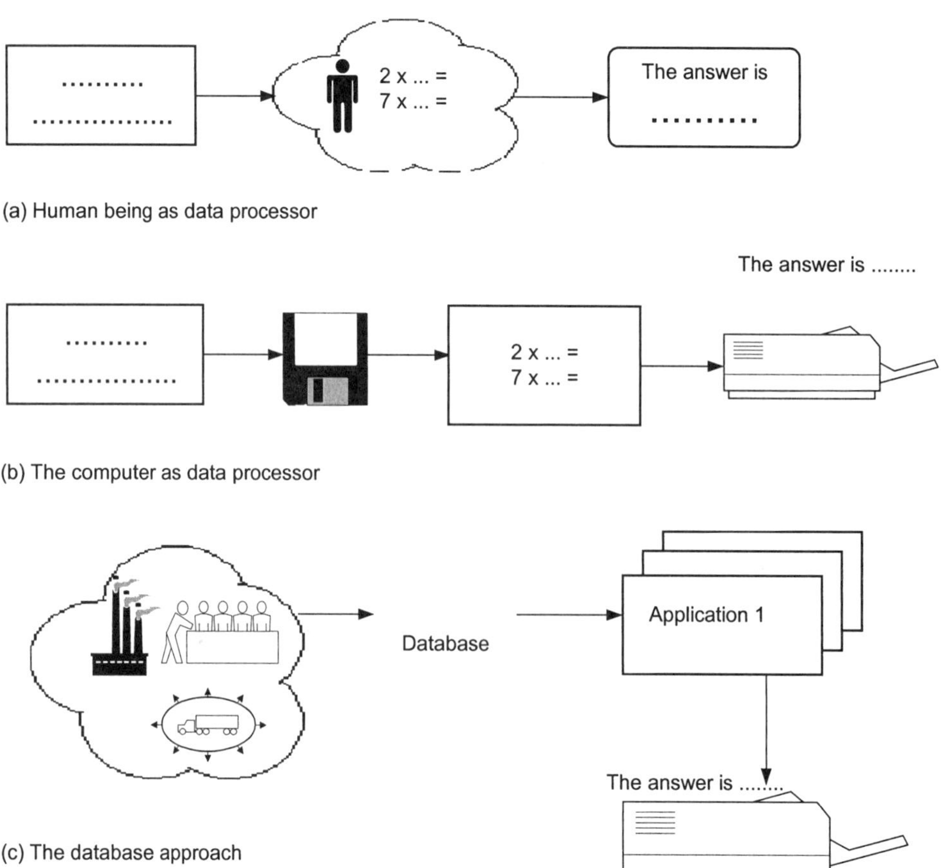

Figure 1.1: Three ways of data processing

However, constructing the database is a complex task. The real world is so complex that to model the organisation, or even part of it such as a department, is no easy task. This text proposes a methodology to help construct the database. In the next two chapters, which complete Part I of the book, we show how we can best understand the organisation – the environment of our task – and the roles of the various personnel who will be involved in developing the database applications.

With background knowledge of the organisation established, it is possible to develop a formal model of the organisation. We discuss three modelling approaches in Part II of the book. These are entity-relationship modelling, relational modelling and normalisation, and object modelling. All three modelling approaches are being used successfully; indeed, they are sometimes combined in the more flexible object-relational database management systems.

In Part III, we show how the model can be implemented on computer systems using database management systems (DBMS). We discuss implementation both on personal computers (PCs) and large computers. The well-used database language, Structured Query Language (SQL), is introduced, and we look in particular at two DBMS, Access and Oracle. Various issues are discussed, such as security and tool support in particular. We consider simple applications, implemented on PCs, as well as large corporate-wide distributed database applications.

In Part IV, we look at major database applications, including data warehousing, data mining, customer relationship management and Internet applications. Finally, Part V considers the issues relating to developing information systems that use a database as a source of information.

In the next section we look at the key factors for a database approach to business computer applications.

1.2 Motivations for the database approach

The database provides a major data resource for the organisation. It is an important asset of most organisations – just imagine if a company lost its customer or accounts data. The motivations for companies choosing a database approach for their data handling are many and include:

- Increase data shareability
- Increase data integrity
- Increase the speed in implementing applications
- Ease data access by programmers and users

- Increase data independence
- Reduce program maintenance
- Improve standards
- Provide a management view.

Increase data shareability: Large organisations, such as insurance companies, banks, local councils and manufacturing companies, have for some time been putting large amounts of data onto their computer systems. Frequently, the same data was being collected, validated, stored and accessed separately for a number of purposes. For example. there could be a file of customer details for sales order processing and another for sales ledger. This 'data redundancy' is costly and can be avoided by following a database approach.

In fact some data duplication is reasonable in a database environment, but it should be known, controlled and be there for a purpose, such as efficient response to some database queries. However, the underlying data should be collected only once, and verified only once, so that there is little chance of inconsistency. With conventional files, the data is often collected at different times and validated by different validation routines, and therefore the output produced by different systems could well be inconsistent. In such situations the data resource is not easily managed and this leads to a number of problems. With reduced redundancy, data can be managed and shared, but it is essential that good integrity and security features operate in such systems. In other words, there needs to be control of the data resource. Furthermore, each application should run 'unaware' of the existence of others using the database. Good shareability implies a ready availability of the data to all users. The computer system must therefore be powerful enough so that performance is good even when there are a large number of users concurrently accessing the database.

Increase data integrity: In a shared environment, it is crucial for the success of the database system to control the creation, deletion and update of data and to ensure its correctness and its 'up-to-dateness' – in general, ensure the quality of the data. Furthermore, with so many users accessing the database, there must be some control to prevent failed transactions leaving the database in an inconsistent state. However, this should be easier to effect in a database environment, because of the possibilities of central management of the data resource, than in an environment where each application sets up its own files. Standards need only be agreed and implemented once for all users.

Increase the speed of implementing applications: Applications ought to be implemented in less time, since systems development staff can largely concentrate on the processes involved in the application itself rather than on the collection, validation, sorting and storage of data. Much of the data required for a new application may already be held on the database, put there for another purpose. Accessing the data will also be easier because the data manipulation features of the database management system will handle this.

Ease data access by programmers and users: Early database management systems used well-known programming languages such as Cobol to access the database. Cobol, for example, was extended to include new instructions, which were used when it was necessary to access data on the database. However, we now have specific database query languages, such as SQL, and other software tools that ease the process of applications development in a database environment. Once the database had been set up, applications development time should be greatly reduced.

Increase data independence: There are many aspects to data independence. It is the ability to change the format of the data, the medium on which the data is held or the data structures, without having to change the programs that use the data. Conversely, it also means that it is possible to change the logic of the programs without having to change the file definitions, so that programmer productivity is increased. It also means that there can be different user views of the data even though it is stored only once. This separation of the issues concerning processes from the issues concerning data is a key reason for opting for the database solution. It provides far greater flexibility when compared to conventional file-based applications.

Reduce program maintenance: Stored data will need to be changed frequently as the real world, that it represents, changes. New data types need to be added, formats changed or new access methods introduced. The data independence of a database environment, discussed above, circumvents the necessity of changing each program with each change to the data structure or type.

Improve standards: Applications tend to be implemented by different project teams of systems analysts and programmers and it has been difficult to apply standards and conventions for all applications. Computer people are reputed to dislike adopting the norms of the firm, and it is difficult to impose standards where applications are developed piecemeal. With a central database, it is possible to impose standards for file creation, access and update, and to impose good controls, enabling unauthorised access to be restricted and providing adequate back-up and security features.

Provide a management view: This is a very important aspect in the context of this book. Managers have frequently complained that they do not get the benefits from the expensive computing resource that they have sanctioned. However, managers have become aware of the need for a corporate view of their organisation. Such a view requires data from a number of sections, departments, divisions and sometimes companies in a larger organisation. This corporate view cannot be gained if files are established on an application-by-application basis and not integrated as in a database. With decision-support systems using the database, it becomes possible for problems previously considered solvable only by intuition and judgement to be solved with an added ingredient, that of information, which is timely, accurate and presented at the required level of detail. Some of this information could be provided on a regular basis whilst some will be of a 'one-off' nature. Database systems should respond to both types of request.

1.3 Potential difficulties with the database approach

There are a number of problems with the database approach, but many have been largely overcome. The technology has improved out of all recognition, and this applies to both hardware and software. Costs have continued to go down, whilst both capacities and speed of access have improved. The technologist has learnt how to use the computer database environment to the good advantage of the organisation. User-friendly languages have been developed so that those users who are not computer experts may profitably access the database themselves. Managers are more involved with computing, partly as a result of their use of PCs, but also through their use of decision support systems, executive information systems and the like. A number of tools have been developed to support the user and developer and we are more aware of the importance of personnel in this success. All these aspects have played an important part in improving the likelihood of success for database projects.

However, a database project is large, expensive and long-term: there is a risk of failure, and it will be a most expensive failure. We need a methodology that supports the development process. Such a methodology need not be too prescriptive. It needs to be more like a framework to guide us in the process of modelling the organization onto the database and developing our applications. This text provides such a framework, and one that will harness some of the most sophisticated aspects of the new technology. It looks at the techniques, the role of the innovator, user and manager, for, without considering all aspects of the process and the people involved, the database project will fail. In the next section we outline our framework.

1.4 Database methodology

A major part of the process of developing our database is to derive a model of the area of discourse. This model aims to accurately represent the real world it is supposed to reflect. This book provides a modelling approach that guides this process. A **model** is a representation of the 'real world', often simplified, so that it represents only those aspects in which we are interested. Choosing and constructing appropriate models is difficult and the methodology described in this text uses a series of models and modelling techniques to derive the database.

This series of models begins with a very abstract model of the situation that is developed in the organisational analysis phase discussed in Chapter 2. It needs to be enhanced by understanding the roles of the personnel involved in the project. This includes users, managers and developers. These roles are discussed in Chapter 3. We can call this type of model 'coarse-grained', but it is a necessary first step to creating our more finely grained models later.

So the first phase of our approach is to understand that part of the organization that we are to model on the database. However, we cannot claim too much. It is impractical to represent the whole organisation on a database. The analyst aims to hold only that relatively small part which will be a good basis for most applications. More fundamentally, however, is that it can only be A and not THE model of the organisation. No model can reflect reality completely and accurately for all purposes. It may present a distorted picture for some purposes and even if the modelling process has 'gone according to plan', the resultant database cannot be perfect. We can never fully know reality; our perceptive process distorts our view of the real world.

In a database project, we are aiming to produce the most appropriate model of the organisation that we can, and transform this on to a computer database that can be used for the information systems applications. This is difficult. The coarse-grained modelling developed in the next two chapters is vital in this process because it is about choosing the most appropriate model for the organisation and people involved. It will be the basis for the finer-grained modelling approaches that follow.

Once we have created our coarse-grained model through the process of organisational analysis, we need to map this model into a form more suitable for database development. There are a number of potential models, but the most well used are entity-relationship, relational and object models. These are all described in Part II of the book. By mapping, we mean that the new model, though in a different form, accurately reflects the old model. In other words, everything on the old model that we want to represent in our database is contained in the new model, albeit in a different way.

Entity-relationship and relational models are the result of applying data analysis to our coarse-grained model. Object modelling is an alternative approach which models data and processes using one representation form. Each modelling approach has its supporters, but whichever is followed there are a series of well-defined steps to achieving the model. Indeed many aspects of this process are mechanistic and rule-based. This cannot be said of the organisational modelling which preceded this stage.

The model derived at this stage is not arranged for particular users or applications. It is a general model. But it is still not yet our database model. There is a further mapping process, described in Part III of the book, to our database management system. This is the software that manages the database. This mapping process can be even more mechanistic. Indeed, there are software tools that automate some of the task (described in Chapter 12). Many database management systems are based on the relational or object model (or indeed both).

Once the database has been modelled on to a database management system, and we look in particular at Access and Oracle in Part III, we can then develop applications that use the database. These applications are described in Part IV and the process of developing such applications described in Part V. But first we consider in the next two chapters how we form our coarse-grained model, which starts the process.

Summary

- Through the database approach, we have data independence, that is, a separation of the database and the applications that use it.
- The database approach represents a much more fundamental change than ‘computerising’ manual systems.

- The database approach provides many advantages, such as, increased data shareability, data integrity, speed of developing applications, easing the access of data, reducing program maintenance, improving standards as well as supporting management in its decision-making role.
- Developing a database, which accurately reflects the organisation it is meant to represent, is complex and it is necessary to follow an appropriate methodological framework.
- The modelling process, in particular, is complex, long term, costly and risky. One approach is to implement the database through a series of modelling steps, from coarse-grained to fine-grained.

Exercises

1. Distinguish between data independence and data redundancy. How are they both keys to the database approach? When might some data redundancy be appropriate?
2. What is the difference between conventional file and database applications?
3. In what ways might a database be a model of an organisation?
4. What difficulties do you envisage in developing a database for a university or other organisation of your choice?

Further reading

Beynon-Davies, P. (2000) *Database Systems,* Macmillan, Basingstoke.

Connolly, T. and Begg, C. (2002) *Database Systems: A Practical Approach to Design, Implementation and Management,* Addison-Wesley, Harlow.

Date, C. J. (2000) *An Introduction to Database Systems,* 6th edn, Addison-Wesley, Reading, Ma.

Elmasri, R. and Navathe, S. (2000) *Fundamentals of Database Systems,* Addison-Wesley, New York.

McFadden, F. R., Hoffer, J. A. and Prescott, M. B. (1999) *Modern Database Management,* 5th edn, Addison-Wesley, Reading, Ma.

These books provide alternatives to the present book. There are a number available and they tend to emphasise the technical aspects of database systems. Wc stress the management, organization and human aspects.

2

Organisational analysis

2.1 Introduction

A computer database is a model on a computer of part of the real world – an organisation of some kind. Examples include the section in a company dealing with sales orders, a personnel department or the local branch of a government's social security department. However, before we can create the model, we need to go through a number of stages. The first stage is an attempt to understand the part of the real world we are dealing with and which we want to model. This is sometimes called the **universe of discourse**. If we do not understand the real world well, then the model cannot be a reasonable approximation of it, and therefore our database would not be very useful. This initial stage of understanding the organisation is called **organisational analysis**. The objective of this chapter is to discuss the process of organisational analysis and, in doing so we describe many of the techniques used and some of the issues that need to be considered at this time.

During this stage, the analysts will need to gain a general appreciation of the business as well as more detailed information concerning the universe of discourse. Background information will include an examination of the goals of the organisation, the company structure and the roles of key personnel. We will discuss the latter in detail in Chapter 3, but we will need to know something about these roles at this stage, as it will help the analysts construct an interview plan. Following preliminary interviews, they will be able to construct models and attempt to find out in outline the information needs of the organisation. Sometimes this analysis may suggest altering business practices rather than reveal a need for a computer information system supported by a database. But in this text we will assume that there will be a need for a computer database of some sort to help the organisation. The information supplied by the database might help managers make better decisions, help them improve the organisation's cost structure and, perhaps, thereby gain competitive advantage.

2.2 Data, information and knowledge

Of course the information provided will only be as good as the data that has been entered into the database. The terms information and data represent different things. **Data** elements represent facts. These facts may concern people, objects, events, products and so on. **Information** comes from selecting this data and presenting it in such a way that is meaningful and useful to the users. Information needs to be accurate, relevant, complete, timely and to the correct level of detail. Sometimes its value comes from its rareness or unexpectedness (for example, a product whose sales suddenly fall sharply), although more frequently its value comes from the database system's power to summarise the data, providing total product sales, or provide the user with information about exceptional conditions, such as users ordering unusual quantities of product.

Data may not appear at first sight to be an important resource of the organisation. But it certainly is a resource, for data is essential for the organisation to operate effectively. If the company 'lost' its accounts data, for instance, this would represent a serious loss and one from which it would be difficult to recover. Indeed, some firms sell data such as the names and addresses of their customers. These can be used by other companies to create mailing lists that are relevant to them. Data is costly to collect, store, keep up to date, and validate. It is also costly to transform data into information.

Information systems access data using the database and transform it into a readily usable form, that is information. The value of information can be readily appreciated. For example, accurate information about future weather conditions will help the manager of a grocery store or shop to determine whether to buy stocks of ice cream or stocks of soup. Here, information has the key role of reducing uncertainty. Poor information is likely to prove very costly for the shop owner as he builds up unsold stocks of ice cream or misses sales opportunities. Decisions, such as where and when to build a new warehouse, whether to buy out competitors or whether to change product structure, may have very long-term consequences and involve huge investments of money. Thus it is very important that the information on which such a decision is based is the best available.

Knowledge is the ability to use information effectively. It is the know-how that enables decision-makers to use the information to decide where to build the new factory, what products to develop or stop producing and which markets to enter. No computer system can take the place of the human decision makers, but information systems can provide support through the provision of the best available information. There are now computer applications based on databases that manage and diffuse knowledge throughout the organisation. These **knowledge management** applications are usually based on Intranet sites, that is, the use of the Internet within the organisation. An example occurs where a manufacturing company wishes to inform its outside workforce or customers about a change in the parts required for a product and how to install those parts.

2.3 A simplified model of an information system

Figure 2.1 represents a simplified model of an information system using a database. The model assumes that managers can specify their information requirements. The system then has to transform these requirements for information into requirements for data. The data will be retrieved from the database, assuming that it has already been collected and stored. If this is not the case, a data collection exercise is necessary to capture the data and store it into the database. Having retrieved this raw data, it can be transformed into the required information, perhaps by some preceding analysis work. Information can then be presented to the manager who now has the opportunity to make good or at least better decisions because the information is available. The effectiveness of the decision will depend on the manager's knowledge to use the information to best effect. The information system is unlikely to be very useful without the decision-makers' 'know-how'.

The database system needs to be flexible. Some types of information might be regularly required and be fairly predictable. Managers will require regular information about how the organisation is or is not meeting its targets. Some decisions can even be made automatically by the information system. These decisions will be structured, rule-based and routine. A common example occurs in a stock control system that checks stock levels and prints purchase order requests automatically when stocks are too low. But other information requirements may be more difficult to predict, indeed form 'one off' requests for information. Some enquiries will only be addressed through combining data from a number of different areas in the database – sales, product, and employee data, for example, or using external databases supplied by the government or consultancy companies. This makes such information systems complex to analyse, design and implement.

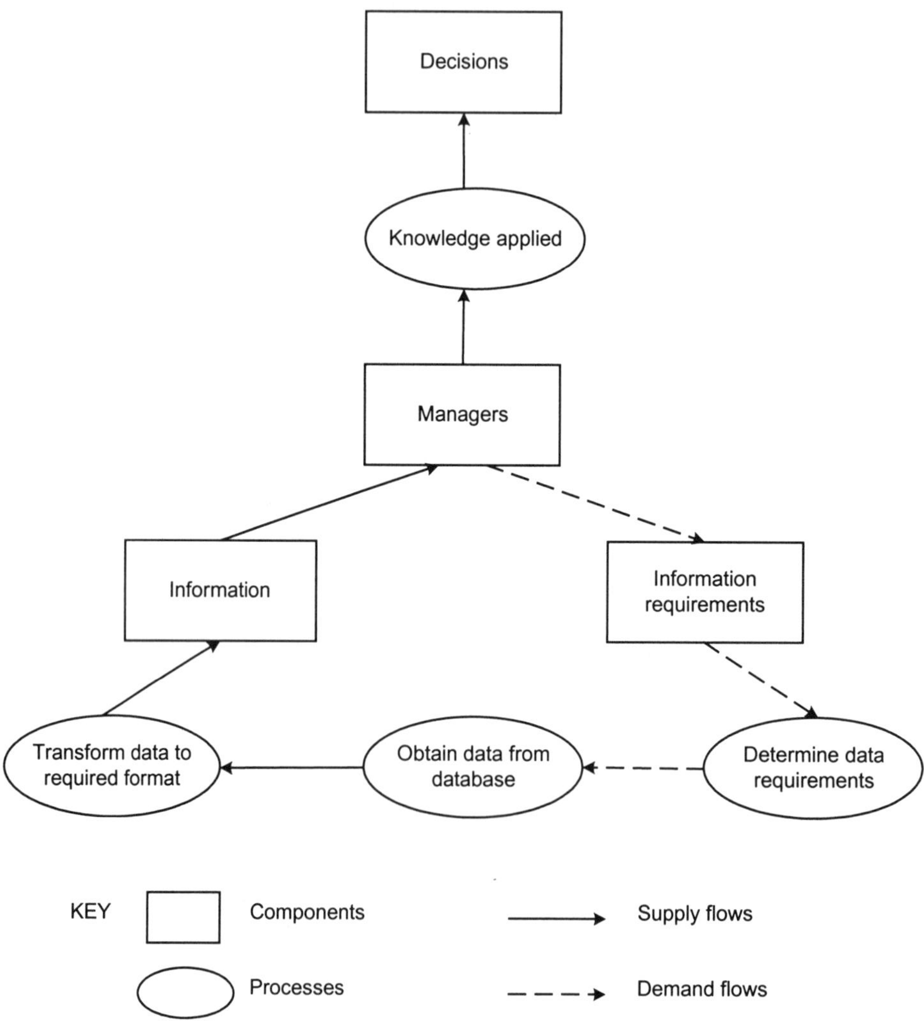

Figure 2.1: A simplified information system using a database

One of the most important tasks is to determine the boundaries of the database application. This may encompass a whole company, a department or a function. If it is the latter case, the design should be such that other applications and associated databases can be integrated with this one. The priority for developing each application area will depend on potential benefits, the urgency of need, probability of success or natural precedence, that is, the next 'piece of the jigsaw'. The plan for developing applications will also need to coincide with organisational goals.

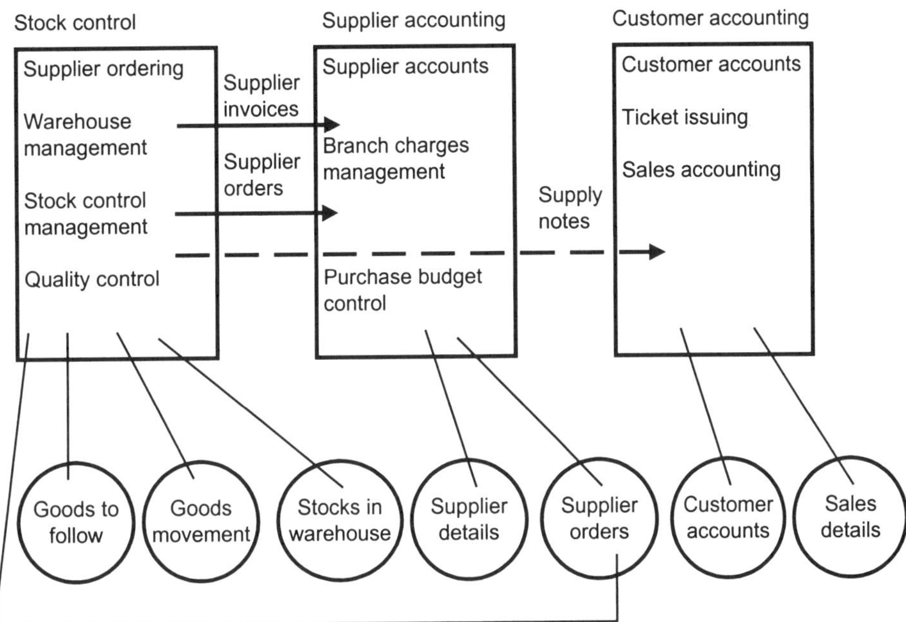

Figure 2.2: Developing the information model

The analyst may draft an information model such as that shown as Figure 2.2. The information model is largely a pictorial representation of part of the organisation in outline and it can be used as the basis for discussions with management. It combines a process-oriented view of the organisation (supplier ordering, warehouse management and stock control) with a data-oriented view (goods to follow, warehouse stocks and supplier orders). It will show the major applications systems for part of the organisation and the flows of resources between them. It might be particularly useful in providing some boundaries and interfaces. We have grouped data into logical files. These give the analyst ideas on what sort of data would be needed to support the information systems. The detail about processes, database design and data storage is not mapped out at this stage.

2.4 Understanding the organisation

The analysts cannot understand current and future information requirements unless they know something more about the organisation. It is best to start with a broad brush and then find out more about the particular area they will be modelling. In this way, it should be possible to avoid a data model that has only one or at least a limited perspective or one that will remain applicable only in the short term. Database applications are likely to be expensive and so they need to have a long-term payoff. It is useful, therefore, to look first at the **goals** of the organisation.

Texts used to talk about organisations having just one goal. This was frequently said to be profit maximisation. According to this view, an organisation was tuned to maximise this one goal. The truth is that even commercial businesses have a number of goals. These might include increasing the size of the market, increasing return on capital, increasing turnover, ensuring long-term survival, improving the welfare of employees and improving public image, as well as increasing profits. An information system supported by a database can inform managers on their progress in achieving these goals. Goals may conflict. For example, in a retail organisation, a goal to increase sales may conflict with one to reduce staffing levels.

Many organisations have a corporate **mission statement** or **vision statement**. This is a declaration of the company's 'reason for being'. It reveals a long-term vision of the organisation in terms of what it wants to be. The mission statement of a health authority may be to promote the health and hygiene of the people in its catchment area. Those of a church, hospital, business or charity are likely to be very different. This type of information may well be gleaned from interviewing members of the directorate or its equivalent, that is the chief executive, vice-president, general managers and, perhaps, divisional managers. A mission statement may even be displayed for visitors to see. Other sources of information include the written company review and accounts. These are usually published annually as part of the statement to the shareholders or governors. Recruitment brochures may also be interesting. These may well stress long-term objectives such as growth in assets, profitability, the degree and nature of diversification, earnings-per-share and social responsibility. Analysts will also need to look outside at the environment of the organisation, for instance, competitors, suppliers and customers.

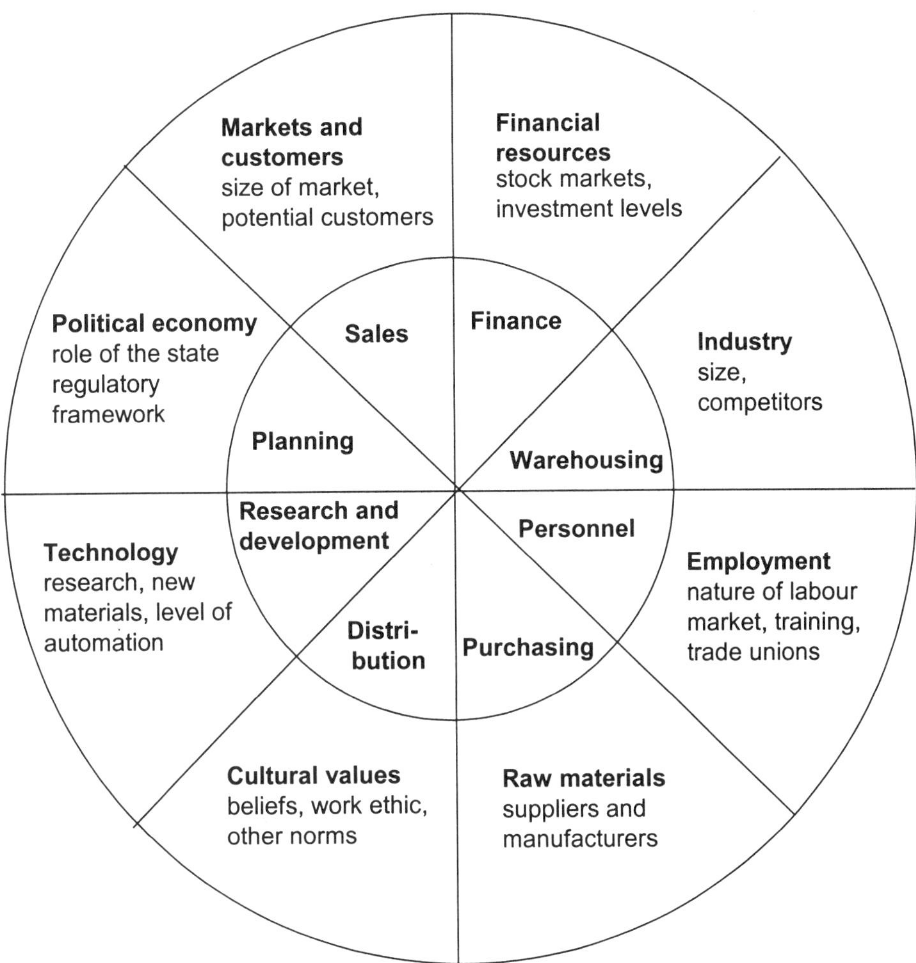

Figure 2.3: The business universe

Figure 2.3 represents the organisation and its environment. The inner circle encloses those subsystems that are part of a typical business. The outer circle encloses the environment of the company – markets, role of the state and so on.

Medium and short-term **objective** setting is usually the concern of individual managers. These will be used as a basis for allocating resources, evaluating the performance of managers, monitoring progress towards achieving long-term goals and establishing divisional and departmental **priorities**.

All this company background can help the analysts get a 'feel' for the organisation and the relevant universe of discourse, particularly if they are from outside the company. Information systems work is frequently carried out by external consultants or people only recently recruited from outside because they have relevant skills gained from their previous positions.

Some readers may be surprised that we have included **organisational culture** as an important element of the universe of discourse in this context. However, the success of the database and information systems project is likely to depend more on these aspects than state-of-the-art technology. Yet frequently only lip service is paid to these aspects or they are ignored altogether. It is important to recognise key individuals in the universe of discourse. It might be crucial to the project's success to position a 'hero' in charge of the project, make transition rituals the pivotal elements of change and highlight the importance of job security in any transition. Analysts need to explore these factors in the organisational analysis stage. We explore the roles of people in such large projects in Chapter 3.

2.5 Techniques for investigation and analysis

In the organisational analysis stage we are not looking for solutions but an understanding of the organisation. We will later move away from understanding the real world towards improving the problem situation through our database applications. Analysis of the problem situation will only require access to part of the database, that part relevant to the situation.

Analysts will use a number of techniques to help in this investigation. Some techniques can be described as formal and reasoned. But others are more creative and informal. Some of these techniques stimulate the identification and representation of as many views and perspectives on the problem situation as possible. In order to find out more about the area of discourse, the analyst will be asking 'who-what-where-when-why and how'. These questions might include:

- What should be happening here?
- Who or what are involved and how are they affected?
- What seems to be preventing the desired results?
- Why might this be happening?
- What associated problems might be connected?
- Why might this be a symptom of a more fundamental and deeper problem?

When looking at a problem situation, there are a number of techniques that we can use to help us. One of the most obvious is to define the situation in terms of higher and lower levels of **abstraction**. As Figure 2.4 shows, we can use this approach to obtain more and more detail.

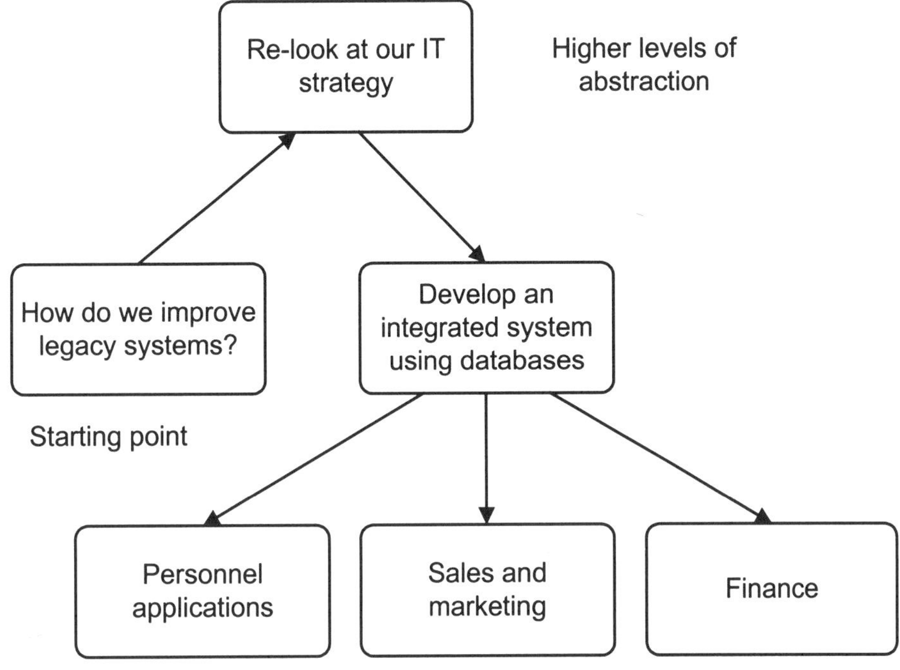

Figure 2.4: Successive abstractions

We may also use **analogies** and **metaphors** as these redefine the problem situation in an imaginative, and none literal fashion. The original problem definition 'how do we improve the sales team?' could be re-expressed as an analogy: 'how can we get the sales team performing like those of the leading football club?'. This might suggest better training or a new look at tactics. The use of the metaphor 'how do we address corporate turbulence' may prompt ideas that might improve inter-departmental conflict.

Other imaginative techniques might include **wishful thinking**. The statement 'if I could play God, I would implant the standards in their brains' may spark off more realistic ideas such as that to start a course to explain standards to the group (perhaps in a country hotel that tells us to make it a pleasant experience). Another approach is to think of all the **barriers** to achieving the various goals for a project. In this way, it might be possible to redefine the situations in ways that are more useful. Analysts may use **non-logical stimuli**. Looking at a pot plant, for instance, may suggest a better environment or (plant) food to improve employee morale.

More well-known approaches include **brainstorming** where a group of people, often with different backgrounds and experiences, suggest all sorts of ways to deal with a problem and **lateral thinking** where the analyst goes back a step or two and develops ideas in a different direction than previous.

Drawing a **rich picture** can help to map out aspects such as the organisational structure, roles of personnel, organisational goals, employee needs, issues, problems and concerns. A rich picture is a pictorial caricature of an organisation and is an invaluable tool for helping to explain what the organisation is 'about'. It should be fairly self-explanatory and easy to understand. Although drawing packages can help in constructing this pictorial representation of the universe of discourse, a satisfactory version may use a pencil as the basic tool.

We can start to construct a rich picture by looking for elements of structure in the problem domain. These might include things like departmental boundaries, activity types, physical or geographical layout and product types. Having looked for elements of structure, the next stage is to look for elements of process, that is, 'what is going on'. These might include the fast-changing aspects of the situation, the information flow, flows of goods and so on.

The relationship between structure and process represents some aspects of the **climate** of the situation. Very often an organisational problem can be tracked down to a mismatch between the established structure and new processes.

The rich picture may include all the important hard facts of an organisational situation, and the examples so far have been of this nature. However, these are not all the important facts. There are many **soft** or subjective 'facts', which should also be represented. The process of creating the rich picture serves to tease out the concerns of the people in that situation. These soft facts include the sorts of things that the people in the problem domain are worried about, the social roles that the people within the situation think are important, the sorts of behaviour that are expected of people in these roles, and the problems that people have, including communication difficulties.

Figure 2.5 shows a rich picture of a district health authority. None of the symbols depicted are 'standard': a rich picture is not like an entity-relationship diagram, for example. These have standard symbols and we will look at these in Chapter 4. But the symbols in Figure 2.5 are meant to represent aspects of the problem domain that we are looking at. The people, house and other symbols are obvious. In the think bubbles we represent problems and it is worth representing these because hopefully we will address these later. The eye symbol represents external people or bodies that have a controlling responsibility. The tank symbol here represents conflict of some kind.

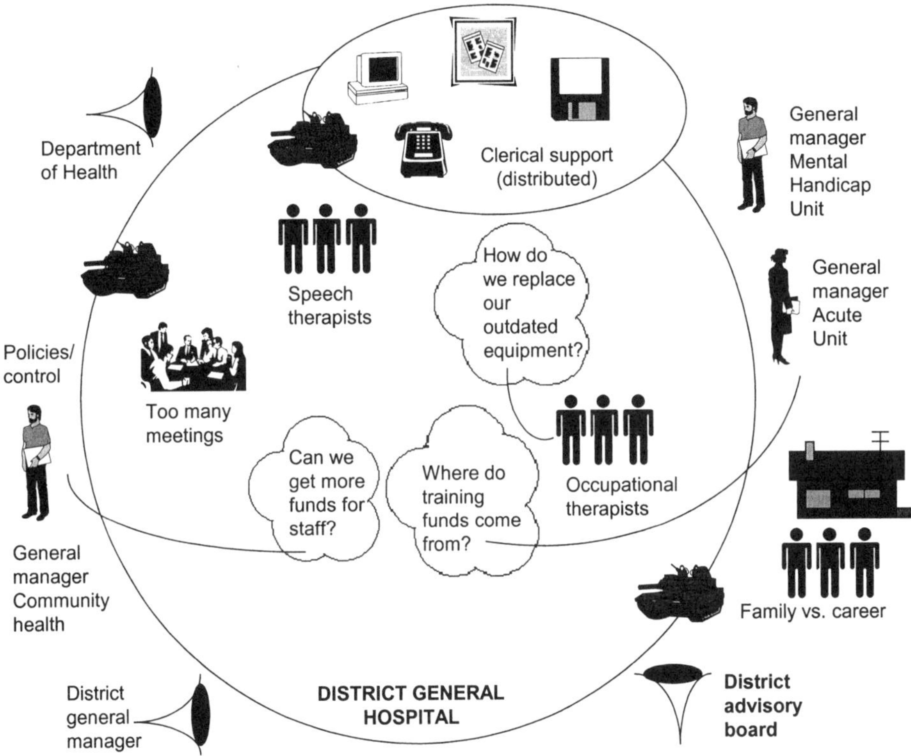

Figure 2.5: Rich picture of a district health authority

Typically, a rich picture is constructed first by putting the name of the organisation into a large bubble, perhaps at the centre of the page. Other symbols are sketched to represent the people and things that interrelate within and outside that organisation. A standard drawing package can help us in constructing a rich picture, because most have icons that represent people and other elements that we wish to represent. Of course a standard drawing package will not verify the correctness of any diagram. Some of the tools discussed in Chapter 12 will perform more sophisticated tasks appropriate to the particular technique used.

2.6 Strategy for developing a database application

There are a number of alternative strategies that we may adopt. We need to evaluate which might be the most appropriate strategy or combination of strategies for the particular organisation. Information technology and information systems need to be aligned with business needs, which were established through analysis of the mission statement and goals of the organisation. The particular strategy appropriate to the organisation will depend to a large extent on its political and financial circumstances. Attempts in the past to implement change may have left scars, and the spirit of trust, confidence and co-operation necessary to implement radical change is going to be difficult to achieve in these circumstances.

Much will depend on factors related to deciding on the boundary of the problem domain. If the organisation is organised into departments, then an **organisation chart approach** might be appropriate. The analyst looks at each department in turn. Thus we may start with the sales office, then production, warehousing, buying, accounting and finance, and human resource management. Other organisations are organised into **projects** or **processes**. Again it may be appropriate to examine each in turn with a view to **integrating later**. An opportunity will certainly be lost if the analyst looks at these separate parts of the organisation without regard to integration. It is normal for a database application to access data that relates to different departments, processor or whatever. Unfortunately applications have in the past been developed in a piecemeal fashion and these **legacy systems** are often difficult to integrate using a database. However, Enterprise Resource Planning (ERP) systems such as SAP, attempt to absorb these systems using common databases. These systems are discussed in Chapter 15.

An alternative strategy is to base the database on management needs, a sort of **top-down approach**. Alternatively the design could be **bottom-up**. This stresses the importance of operational **data collection**. We will see in Part II how data collected in this way can be organised and structured. Frequently, the approach actually adopted is some sort of combination of these 'ideal types'.

Whichever strategy is used, it is important that close attention is paid to people factors. This means that managers need to show their support for this potentially costly and long-term project. It also means that employees feel secure in the change process. At the extreme, they need to know that they will keep their jobs. However, equally important is that they feel they will not lose status because of the change or perceive the change as negative in other ways. It is unlikely that such a major change will be successful without the support of the main body of people within the organisation. We look at the role of people in Chapter 3. This is crucial to the success of the database.

IS projects are frequently very expensive and difficult to justify in tangible terms. The major product is information, not tangible objects like stocks of goods, which are easier to evaluate. What is the value of information? There are obvious advantages of the information and these could include better costing, better cash flow, improved customer relations, and it should lead to better decisions being made by management. But it is still difficult to put a monetary value on these. Unless management is convinced about these gains, the project is unlikely to be successful.

Many of the techniques discussed in this chapter are as much about providing an opportunity to inform, help and convince, than an opportunity to find out about the organisation. However, we have broadly decide on our universe of discourse which will be the basis of future models, we have also identified the people concerned in the problem domain, found out about the functions of the business in outline, and decided on a strategy for future development. In short we have a coarse-grained model from which we can develop a finer model in later stages.

Summary

- The universe of discourse is that part of the real world that we will model and implement on our database system.
- Organisational analysis is the process of understanding the organisation and represents the first stage in the modelling process. It includes establishing goals for the organisation, and thereby the information systems that support reaching these goals through strategic alignment.
- We distinguish between the raw facts, that are data, and information, which is the presentation of these data in a way that is useful and meaningful to decision makers.
- Information is relevant, complete, timely, appropriately detailed and accurate.
- Knowledge is the ability to use information effectively, and knowledge systems (also supported by databases) support that process.
- The use of analogies, metaphors, brainstorming and lateral thinking techniques along with drawing tools such as information models, rich pictures and abstraction hierarchies, support organisational analysis.

- Organisational analysis needs to identify hard facts, such as technology presently used, problems identified and formal hierarchy, and soft facts, such as concerns, conflicts and social roles.
- There are various strategies for developing a database application, such as an organisation chart approach, integrating later, top-down, bottom-up and data collection strategies.

Exercises

1. How can organisational analysis help define the universe of discourse for the database application.
2. Distinguish between data, information and knowledge.
3. Distinguish between the techniques and tools available for organisational analysis stating where they might be appropriate.
4. Distinguish between vision, mission, goals, objectives and priorities.
5. For an organisation of your choice such as a university, hospital or business:
   a) Suggest or obtain a mission statement
   b) Identify goals to meet that mission
   c) Suggest information requirements for management to help meet these goals
   d) Suggest information requirements for management to ascertain whether these goals are being met
   e) Use the structure of Figure 2.1, but be explicit about the decisions to be made, the appropriate managers, the actual information and data required.
   f) Construct an information model
   g) Construct a draft rich picture for your organisation.

Further reading

Avison, D. E. and Wood-Harper, A. T. (1990) *Multiview: An Exploration in Information Systems Development,* McGraw-Hill, Maidenhead.

Checkland, P. B. (1981) *Systems Thinking, Systems Practice,* Wiley, New York.

Marchand, D. A., Davenport, T. H. and Dickson, T (2000) *Mastering Information Management,* Prentice Hall, London.

Walsham, G. (1993) *Interpreting Information Systems in Organizations,* Wiley & Sons, Chichester.

3

Roles of personnel

3.1 Introduction

It is an important requirement of a database approach that the business and technical requirements are complementary. It is, of course, foolish to develop systems with no business benefit. However, there may be benefits to the organisation in looking at the business from an IS perspective and exploiting technological advancements for business benefit. Therefore, the personnel required to adopt a database approach includes members from the business as well as members of the information systems group. The objective of this chapter is to discuss the roles of the various personnel in this major project to developing a database.

It may be thought that there is a set of IT roles for the development and a different set for the operation of a database. This is certainly true in smaller database projects where the application is developed and completed but then only occasionally reviewed for enhancement. However, in adopting a database approach, both the business and technical roles in the organisation are in a state of constant enquiry, looking for technical developments and business initiatives that might provide opportunity for competitive advantage, enhancement, efficiencies and diversification.

Figure 3.1 shows the roles and their interaction. The arrow along the bottom of the figure shows the movement from initiation through to realisation. As we have seen, a database approach suggests a strategic outlook and therefore it is necessary for the initiation to evolve from collaboration between the business and IS visionaries. The development proceeds from a liaison between IS management and the business client, to be realised by a close association between the business user and the IS staff responsible for implementation. The vision, first shared by senior management, is translated through these roles to realisation. However, it is important to remember that these are roles and not people. For example, the business client may also be the user and IS implementation is likely to be conducted by a team.

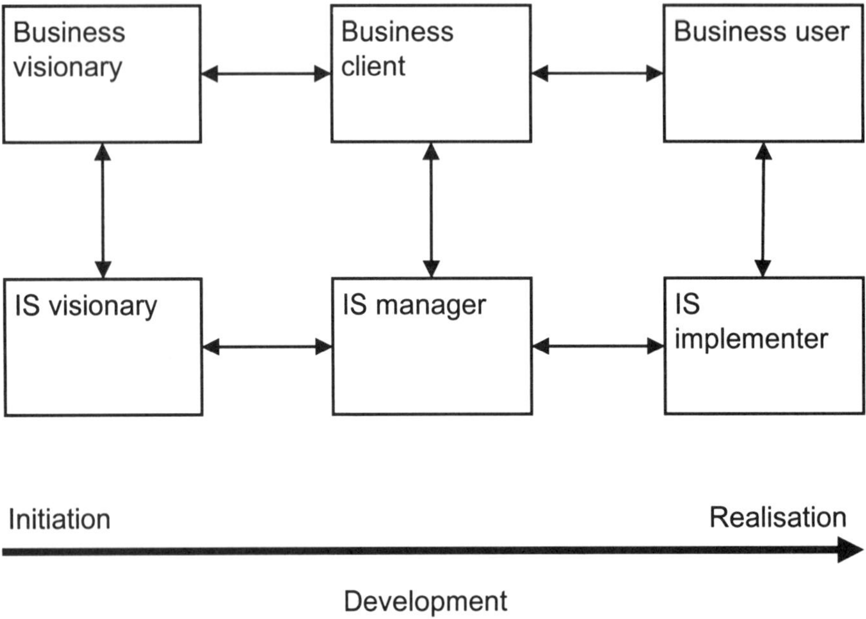

Figure 3.1: Roles of personnel and their interaction

In this chapter, we consider each role in turn. It is not intended to provide a series of job descriptions for personnel in a database environment. For readers requiring further details, the British Computer Society Industry Structure Model (ISM) includes a thorough description of each IS position. In this chapter, the roles are considered in outline, with some of the more important aspects elaborated.

3.2 Visionaries

We usually consider a visionary to be someone from the business side of the organisation, with the technical requirements satisfied by IT personnel. However, as Figure 3.2 shows, the database approach accepts a blurring of these distinctions, and indeed the trend within large organisations has been towards appointing information systems professionals at executive levels with no management responsibilities in the information systems function.

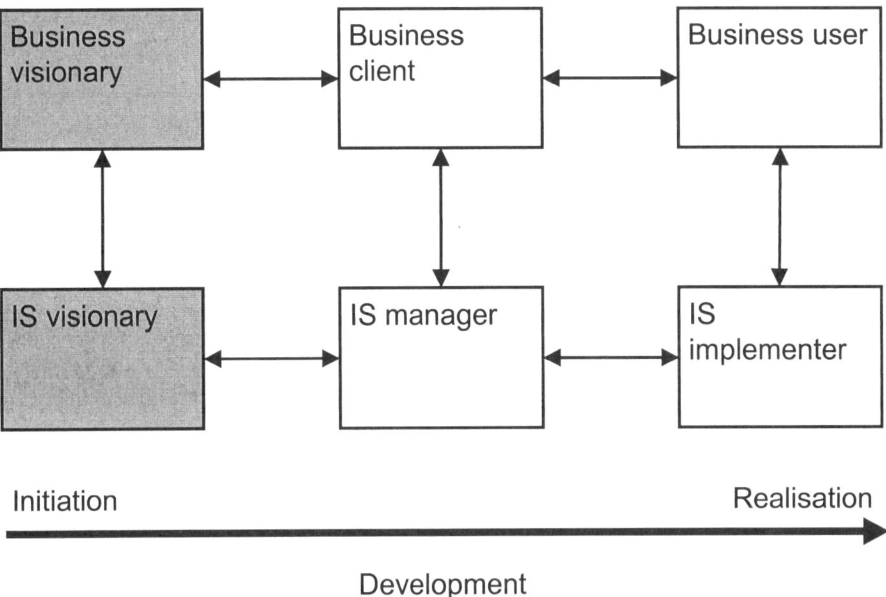

Figure 3.2: The visionaries

Many members of the IS group have, of necessity, an internal focus. That is, an IS manager or implementer is primarily concerned with methods of working within the organisation. The prime goals of IS managers and implementers are generally related to service quality and productivity. However, organisations benefit from an external focus to IS that includes evaluating the emerging technologies in a business context, and the role of the **IS visionary** is to investigate the emerging technologies and seek innovations that the organisation can exploit. In recent years, business ideas such as customer relationship management, virtual organisations, knowledge management, and b2b and b2c electronic commerce have all been realised using, for example, Internet technology and database concepts.

Much research has been conducted into the critical success factors (CSF) for information systems development, and consistently the importance of champions has been recognised. A champion is a **business visionary** who initiates and supports the project from a senior level, giving it authority and a high profile. Some further discussion on this issue is found in Chapter 2 in the context of business goals. However, a business visionary is extremely important if the benefits of a database approach are to be realised.

3.3 Managers

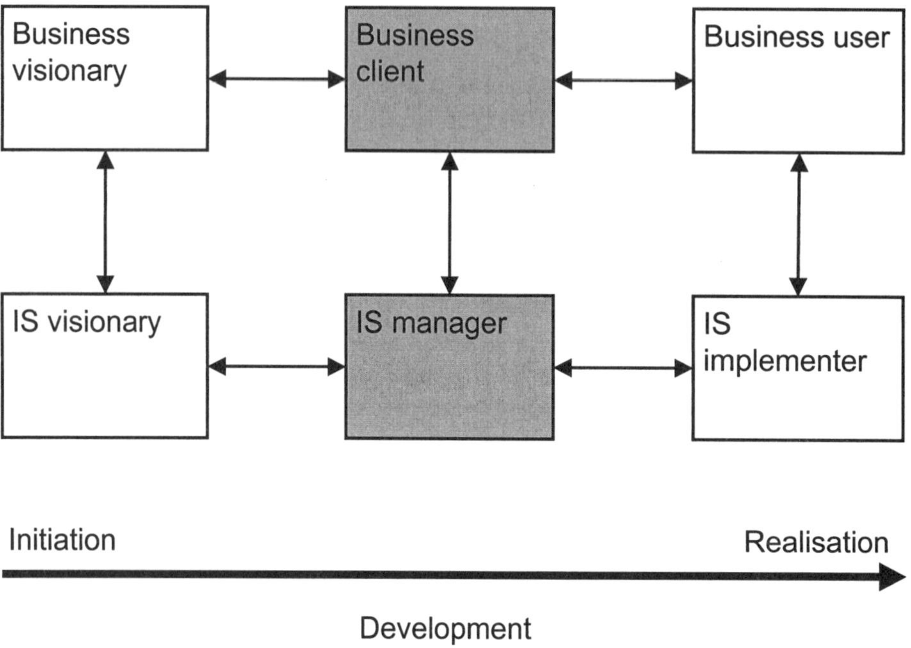

Figure 3.3: The managers

Since the 1980s, the term 'hybrid manager' has been used to describe a manager with both business insight and IS 'know-how'. Nowadays we can increasingly expect staff at all levels throughout the organisation to have an understanding of the use and potential of IS in their business area, and we would expect IS professionals to be able to develop IS within the context of their organisation. Therefore, the concept of the 'hybrid manager' is possibly less important in more recent times. Nevertheless, the business client and the IS manager must develop a common understanding to shape and manage the database development. This is shown by the arrow between the business client and the IS manager in Figure 3.3.

IS strategy and planning is usually carried out through a team approach and we now discuss the role of the **systems planning team** whose main function is to co-ordinate and control the information systems project and ensure that information systems are closely aligned with the goals of the organisation. With an emphasis on the use of information technology to gain and/or sustain competitive advantage, systems planning may to some extent govern and certainly influence business plans. The Internet, broad bandwidth and WAP technologies provide the most recent examples of technology influencing business planning.

However, it is important that the systems planning team is not dominated by technologists. A synthesis of corporate and sector knowledge with technological exploitation is the ideal. The information systems project will affect the whole organisation and, as we have seen, it is necessary to include user management in the team. This would suggest that the chair of the systems planning team would be the 'executive responsible', who would carry the required status. Other business representatives of the systems planning team could include the production manager, marketing manager and other department heads. Such a high-powered team should ensure that the project has the authority and contextual appreciation necessary to carry its proposals through the organisation. It should also help to gain and retain management commitment for the project, and therefore significantly increase the likelihood of success. The business representatives of the systems planning team represent the business client in a database development. The business client has the role of understanding the vision of senior management and communicating that vision to the IS management team.

The information systems project will cause changes to the roles of employees and in working relationships. An important role of the systems planning team is to try and anticipate problems that may occur. It is therefore necessary to include the personnel manager and a trade union representative in the team. It is important to keep employees fully informed of the project. Many systems may be excellent from a technological or systemic point of view but fail because of a lack of consideration given to 'people' issues. The new system may be seen as a threat to status and job. Frequently, staff will resist the change in ways that may be less dramatic than sabotage but equally effective. Once the trust of the workforce has been lost, it is difficult to regain, even if future change is perceived to be in the interest of employees.

Two of the most important representatives from the innovating group will be the **database administrator (DBA)** and the senior analyst. The senior analyst will have both organisational and technical skills, and is seen as a link between the business client and the implementers. The need for a database administrator is clearly recognised, although the role is often filled late in the life of the project, perhaps sometimes when it is too late. The database administrator can help the systems planning team decide on standards for communication, documentation, project development and evaluation, and help to implement these standards. The project leader is likely to be either the senior analyst or the database administrator. The role of the database administrator is crucial to the success of the database project. One of the main objectives of the database approach is to facilitate the sharing of data between many users. However, users may well resist both the DBA taking control of 'their' data, and other users having access to it. For example, though a minute-by-minute relaying of production output may be invaluable to the production manager in production scheduling, the production manager may not want this data available to the operations executive or to the sales force, however useful they might find the data for their own decision making. This may lead to conflict.

The DBA needs to have the necessary status and tact to apply an organisation-wide perspective to mediate in such a conflict. Hopefully this will be achieved by facilitating communication between departments rather than by 'rule of law'. The DBA is likely to play a large part in decisions relating to rival application candidates according to some priority that reflects the objectives of the visionaries. The DBA will need the strong backing of management to succeed in this task. Otherwise there will be no authority to back up the decisions. In order to make recommendations, the DBA also needs to have good communications with the business and technical specialists.

The DBA has responsibility for:

- Establishing technical standards and guidelines
- Application support through internal schema definition
- Physical and logical database definitions
- Implementing access rights
- Developing backup, recovery and security procedures
- Investigating security breaches
- Monitoring and optimising performance levels
- Maintaining the integrity of the database
- General maintenance and upgrade of the database and the software supporting the database.

Many of the database management tasks are assisted by the database management system (DBMS). Modern DBMS provide management tools for auditing, backup and recovery procedures, job scheduling, schema management and security management. For example, Oracle8 has the Oracle Enterprise Manager (OEM) to support these and other management tasks. The DBA may also be a marketer, a trouble-shooter and an educator. In practice, a team carries out the role of the DBA. The director of the DBA team should have sufficient standing in the organisation to remain independent of pressure groups of database users.

Frequently, the systems planning team might also include an outside consultant. This person will not have a background in the organisation, and a perceived lack of departmental bias may be useful when arbitrating on differences of opinion. The consultant is likely, however, to have experience from similar projects, perhaps in organisations in the same sector, and is valuable in sharing expertise and best practice. Consultants may also be used to plug gaps in internal expertise or provide short-term commitment in highly specialised areas.

3.4 Specialists

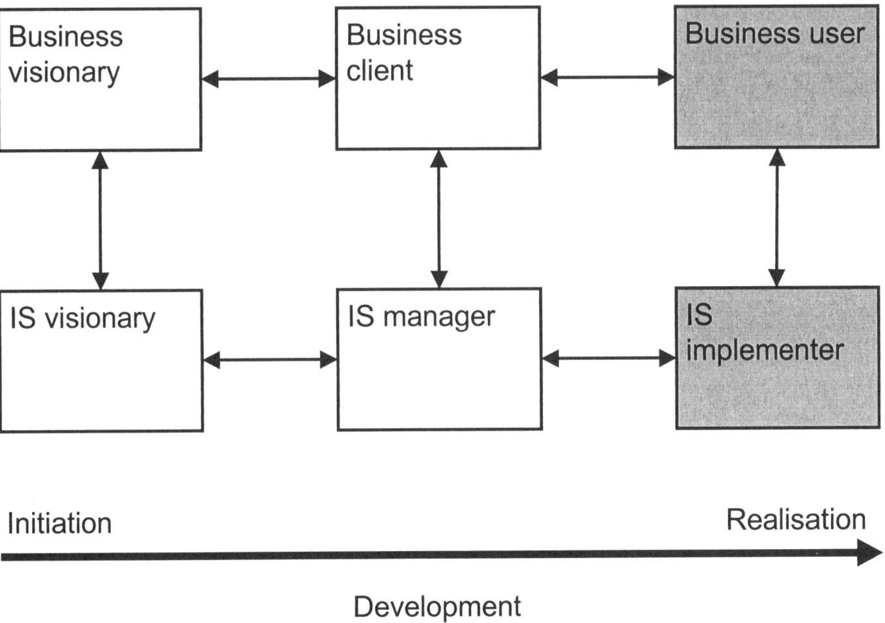

Figure 3.4: The business and information systems specialists

The systems planning team, as described above, will oversee the development of the project, although they will appoint a **systems development team** to control the day-to-day development. The composition of the systems development team will depend on the degree of user participation adopted, although it is usual, if not always desirable, that it is biased towards the technologists. The systems development team will include the chief analyst and the database administrator who are both likely to be members of the systems planning team, as described above. The project leader, who will be one of those two representatives, is likely to act as chair of the development team. Other likely members of the systems development team will be the data analysts who will be involved in developing the data model, and systems analysts, systems designers, programmers and hardware specialists who will identify the needs of users, and design and develop the various applications and querying capabilities.

It would be incorrect to consider that the only specialists in a database development are the IS professionals. In Figure 3.4 we highlight the role of the business user and IS implementer. The business user is a specialist in the business area, and the success of the project depends as much on the participation of the users as on the technical specialist. The final members of the systems development team are the users. Several individuals may together fulfil the role of 'user', and sometimes identifying a representative group of users is a difficulty. Business users may have different experience and expectations, and user groups are as subject to issues such as domination, coalition and coercion as any other social group. Users also have issues of time and motivation, as the IS development takes them away from their 'real' job.

Therefore, the identification of a 'representative user group' is not prescriptive. The partnership between IS specialists and business specialists is critical, equal and mutually beneficial. However, unless this is recognised in, for example, individual and organisational objectives, accounting systems and evaluation criteria, the relationship between a business user and an IS professional may be seen as that between a customer and provider or between a client and expert rather than between team members.

3.5 Application service providers

A combination of Internet and mobile technologies, IS skills shortage and growing application size and complexity has encouraged the development of a new kind of outsourcing, provided by application service providers (ASP). ASPs are sometimes formed from an alliance between a hardware vendor and a software provider such as Hewlett-Packard and SAP or IBM and Oracle, or may be third party providers such as the large consultancy groups. There may sometimes seem to be more ASPs than ASP customers. However, there is a trend in all organisations toward outsourcing their databases to ASPs. An ASP will build the data pool, develop applications, ensure the appropriate level of security, allow access, monitor usage, tune, upgrade and enhance the database. Such databases might be used for customer relationship management, enterprise resource planning or e-business. The relationship between an ASP and its client organisation is critical, since an ASP places a further layer between the organisation and its data.

3.6 Conclusions

If the benefits of an integrated approach to information systems planning and development are to be realised, then the development must be a response to both business and technological pressures and opportunities. To ensure that a vision is communicated from the strategic level through to the specialists, it is necessary not only to encourage communication between user and specialist, or client and IS manager but also from the initiators through to realisation by the developers.

Summary

- The roles of the people involved in a database application are crucial to the success of the project.
- Key personnel include those from the business and technical teams.
- Both the business and technical teams will include visionaries, managers and specialists.
- Most organisations follow a team approach, including the systems planning team, systems development team and the database administration team.
- Database administration concerns standards, data definition, security, privacy, access rights and performance issues.
- Some organisations go to outside organisations, such as application service providers, to help develop the database project.

Exercises

1. Discuss the relationships between technical and non-technical people during the development of a database application.

2. Who do you think ought to be designated 'leader' of a database project?
3. What are the different personal goals of an IS implementer, such as the user interface designer, and a business user, such as a member of the accounting department?
4. For an organisation of your choice such as a university, hospital or business:
   a) Suggest detailed roles for the personnel in the development of a database project.
   b) Discuss the potential relationship between the organisation's staff involved in a database project and those of an application service provider.

Further reading

Dench, S. (1998) *Keeping IT Together,* Institute for Employment Studies, Brighton.

Hoch, D. J., Roeding, C. C., Purkert, G. and Lindner, S. K. (1999) *Secrets of Software Success,* Harvard Business School Press, Cambridge

Yardley, D. (2001) *Getting a Top Job in IT*, The Times/Kogan Page, London.

The British Computer Society (BCS) have a Professional Development Scheme (PDS) that uses the Industry Structure Model (ISM) developed by BCS and now in version 3.2. The ISM defines over 250 roles in IS, and provides performance, training and development standards. Although the adoption of the PDS is low and restricted to the UK, the ISM is an interesting and well-researched model and is used by some UK organisations to predict staffing requirements, write job descriptions, set objectives and evaluate staff. Further details can be obtained from www.bcs.org.uk.

Part II: Modelling

In Chapter 2, amongst other things, we discussed how we might agree on a problem domain for our database applications. In Part II, we now develop a further model, which is a representation of this universe of discourse. This intermediary model is often referred to as a conceptual model.

A model is a simplified version of reality. The conceptual model provides a description of the data and is not arranged for a particular user or application. Nor does it describe a specific technological architecture. These ideas are developed in Part III.

Conceptual modelling is independent, therefore, of the database management system, any computing requirements and any individual user. It is a way of representing the data in our universe of discourse and is a preparatory stage in the design and implementation of a database application. As an aside, conceptual modelling can also be of interest to management as a way of understanding their organisation.

Here, we look at entity-relationship modelling, relational modelling and object modelling in Chapters 4, 5 and 6 respectively. These are all conceptual models, and the mapping from this stage to a database model implemented on a database management system is feasible and commonly achieved. Definitions are given for the terminology used and through the use of many examples we show how the modelling processes are carried out.

Conceptual modelling, however, has its limitations. A conceptual model can only ever represent part of the 'real world' and organisations can be modelled in a variety of other ways including knowledge profiling, socio-political modelling, cultural modelling and so on.

It is important to recognise that in modelling an organisation based on its objects, data structure or data flow, the modeller is choosing to focus on a particular aspect of the system, and is ignoring other aspects that may be equally important in other contexts. They are chosen in the context of this book because they prove to be an appropriate middle stage between organizational analysis and implementation on a database management system. We might like to consider the underlying data structure of an organisation as value-free and fairly stable. However, the model is as open to influence from dominant groups or analyst bias as any other modelling technique.

In a sense, then, conceptual modelling is about making choices, and those choices are of necessity based on implementation factors, previous experience and unchallenged assumptions. It is important to appreciate the level of interpretation in even a 'hard' technique like the methods described in these three chapters, and to make the choices both intelligent and explicit. However, we have found these modelling techniques a useful intermediary between the organizational model of Part I and the database management models of Part III.

4

Entity-relationship modelling

4.1 Introduction to entity-relationship modelling

Many methodologies for information systems development adopt a 'data driven' approach. Data driven approaches assume that data is fairly stable and that processes are more likely to change. Therefore, basing a design on the structure of the data rather than the business activities seems sensible. The most used approach that achieves this is known as entity-relationship modelling and the objective of this chapter is to describe this modelling approach

Let us illustrate this with an example. A university stores data on STUDENTs, COURSEs and MODULEs. One process is to enrol STUDENTs in September and another is for STUDENTs to choose MODULEs. If the university changes its mission and goals to become a distance and flexible learning institution, the processes would need a lot of changing, with STUDENTs enrolling at any time, and doing unusual combinations of MODULEs over varying time periods. However, the university would still need to store data on STUDENTs, MODULEs and COURSEs – the data model remains largely unchanged.

Entity-relationship modelling is a popular top-down method of mapping the underlying data structure of an organisation. A top-down method begins at a high level of abstraction and moves closer to the detail. Entity-relationship modelling is often used in conjunction with other methods. These may take a 'bottom-up' approach of data collection, for example, through studying various forms used in the application domain or modelling processes. By using these approaches alongside entity-relationship modelling, they can be used to verify the model and a more accurate and detailed representation of the 'real world' should result.

4.2 Definitions

An **entity** is a thing of interest to the organisation. It is anything about which the organisation wishes to hold data. It could include all the resources of the business, such as the people of interest, for example, EMPLOYEEs, and it can be extended to cover such things as a PART, a CUSTOMER or ORDERDETAILS.

An entity is not data itself but something about which data is kept. For example, John Smith is an **occurrence** of EMPLOYEE, and the EMPLOYEE entity will have many such occurrences, all with different 'names', 'addresses' and so on. An entity has its own identity and is given a unique name so that it can be distinguished from other entities. In creating an entity model, the aim should be to identify and describe entities that define the data structure of the problem domain.

Entities are not processes. For example, PRODUCT is an entity but 'inventory management' is not. Documents are not entities either. Documents usually contain data from a variety of entities. For example, an order contains CUSTOMER details, such as name and account number; ORDERDETAILS such as delivery address and total amount payable; PRODUCT details such as price and description; and ORDERLINE details that give the quantities required and perhaps the discount applied.

A **relationship** in an entity model represents an association between two entities. For example, a PRODUCT is 'sourced' from a SUPPLIER and a SUPPLIER 'supplies' a PRODUCT. The relationship is 'supplying', though notice that it is a two-way relationship and any description of it tends to support one particular view. Entities may have more than one relationship between them. For example, a LECTURER may 'supervise' a STUDENT, and may also 'tutor' a STUDENT. So the relationships of 'supervision' and 'tutoring' both exist between LECTURER and STUDENT.

The **cardinality** of a relationship could be one-to-one, one-to-many or many-to-many. A MEMBER of parliament in the UK can only 'represent' one CONSTITUENCY, and a CONSTITUENCY can only have one MEMBER of parliament. The relationship of 'representation' is one-to-one. Notice that the relationship is considered both ways before the cardinality can be determined. As Figure 4.1 shows, a single line between the two entities denotes a one-to-one relationship.

Figure 4.1: One-to-one relationship

The relationship between an ORDERLINE and ITEM is one-to-many, as shown in Figure 4.2, because although an ITEM will appear on many ORDERLINEs, an ORDERLINE will only ever be for one particular ITEM. The relationship here might be described as 'fulfilling'. Notice that a one-to-many relationship implies something about frequency. In other words, there are more ORDERLINEs than there are ITEMs. Notice also the use of the singular term to identify an entity, thus we use ITEM rather than ITEMS. It is far clearer to describe an entity and to understand the relationship between occurrences when the singular term is reserved for identifying entities. As seen in Figure 4.2, there is a 'crow's foot' at the 'MANY' end of the one-to-many relationship, so that here one ITEM appears on many ORDERLINEs.

Figure 4.2: One-to-many relationship

A many-to-many relationship is one in which a one-to-many relationship exists both ways. For example, a SUPPLIER can 'supply' many ITEMs and an ITEM can be 'supplied' by many SUPPLIERs. The relationship of 'supplying' is many-to-many. For example, when considering individual occurrences of the entities SUPPLIER and ITEM, supplier 000001 might supply items a, b and c, supplier 000002 might supply items a, c, d and e, and supplier 000005 might supply items a, e and f. As Figure 4.3 shows, a many-to-many relationship is denoted as having a line with crow's feet at both ends.

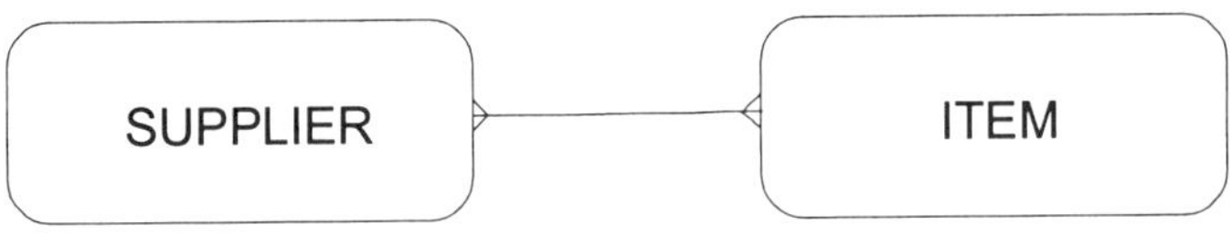

Figure 4.3: Many-to-many relationship

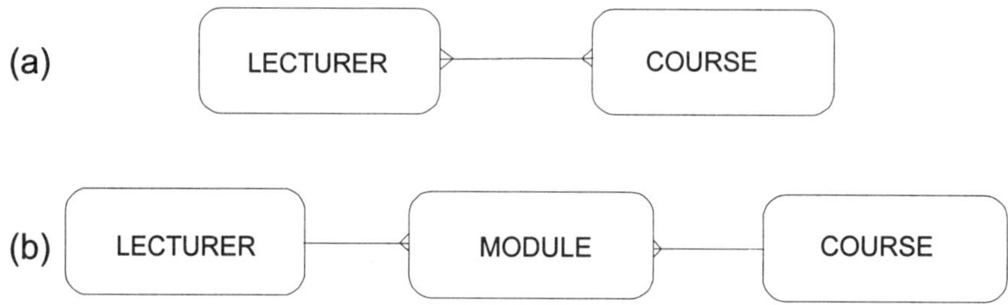

Figure 4.4: A many-to-many relationship (a) resolved as two one-to-many relationships (b)

Conceptually, it may be necessary to resolve a many-to-many relationship into two one-to-many relationships with a third entity created to link these together, as sometimes the relationship itself has attributes. For example, the relationship shown as Figure 4.4 (a), between COURSE and LECTURER, is many-to-many, that is, one LECTURER lectures on many COURSEs, and one COURSE is given by many LECTURERs.

As shown in Figure 4.4 (b), a new entity, MODULE, can be indicated to describe the relationship between LECTURER and COURSE. This resolves the many-to-many relationship by creating two one-to-many relationships: that between lecturer and module and that between course and module. In the creation of this new entity we find that it has attributes of its own, including 'module name' and 'recommended textbook'. We will see later that resolving many-to-many relationships is also important for implementation considerations.

There are further distinctions and greater sophistications to describe relationships in more detail. Sometimes a one-to-many or a many-to-many relationship is a **fixed relationship**. For example, the many-to-many relationship between PARENT and CHILD is two-to-many because although a parent may have many children, a child has only two natural parents. While some relationships are **mandatory**, others are **optional**. A MALE and a FEMALE may be joined by the relationship 'marriage', optional in both directions. Notice, however, that for the entities HUSBAND and WIFE, the relationship 'marriage' is mandatory in both directions. Given the entities FEMALE and HUSBAND we might describe a relationship of 'marriage', which is optional for the FEMALE but mandatory for the HUSBAND. This is shown in Figure 4.5. Here, the 0 indicates the relationship is optional for a FEMALE to have a HUSBAND, and the | indicates that it is mandatory for a HUSBAND to have a FEMALE.

Other structures include **exclusivity**, where participation in one relationship excludes participation in another and **inclusivity**, where participation in one relationship automatically includes participation in another.

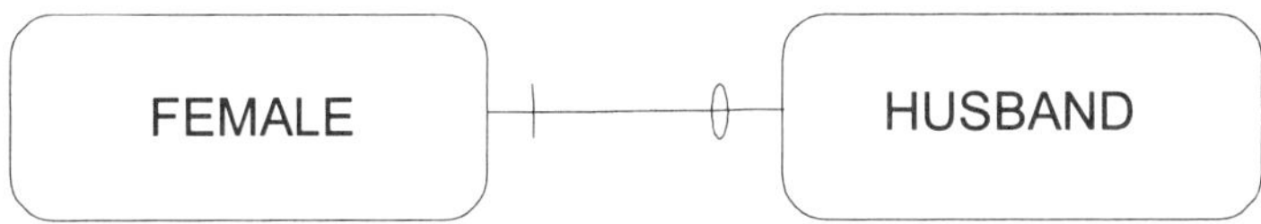

Figure 4.5: Optional and mandatory relationships

A relationship may also be **involuted** (also termed **recursive** or **reflexive**), where entity occurrences relate to other occurrences of the same entity. For example, as Figure 4.6 illustrates, an EMPLOYEE may have another EMPLOYEE as a mentor or manager.

Figure 4.6: Involuted relationship

The number of entities involved in a relationship describes the **degree** of the relationship. Any relationship is necessarily linked to at least one entity. If it is linked to only one entity, it is involuted, as described above. Where a relationship is linked to two entities it is said to be **binary**, and when linked to three it is **ternary**. Otherwise it is ***n*-ary**, with *n* being the number of entities.

Each entity has an **entity description** that details the entity's **attributes**. Attributes are data items that have a one-to-one relationship with the entity, and each occurrence of that entity has its own set of values associated with it. For example, a CUSTOMER entity is likely to have attributes including 'name', 'address', 'credit limit' and 'account balance'. Each occurrence of the entity needs to have a unique element, known as the **key attribute**, to distinguish it from other occurrences in the same entity. For a CUSTOMER this may be a 'customer number', and each occurrence of the customer will have its own unique 'customer number'.

Entity descriptions are identified in this book by an entity name with the full description, that is the attributes, between parentheses. All attributes are in lower case, with the key attribute underlined.

CUSTOMER (customer number, customer name, address, postcode, credit rating)

The entity descriptions do more than simply list the attributes for each entity in the problem domain; they also provide the link between entities that share a relationship. For example, the relationship between STUDENT and COURSE entities may be described as one-to-many as shown in Figure 4.7, since although one STUDENT may only be enrolled on one COURSE, each COURSE will have many students enrolled.

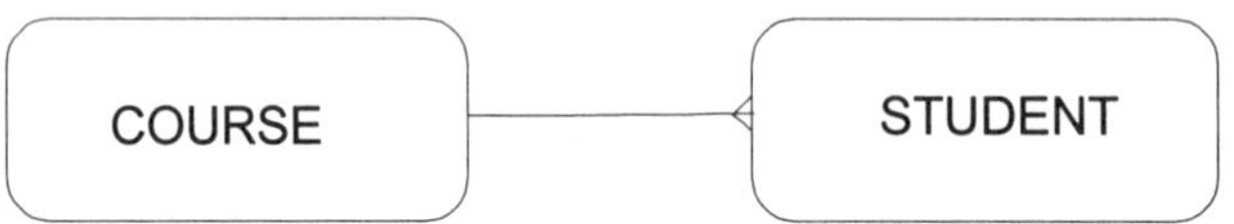

Figure 4.7: Relationship between COURSE and STUDENT

STUDENT (student number, student name, address, postcode, points score, local education authority)

COURSE (course ID, course name, entry requirements)

In looking at the two entity descriptions, we can see that there is nothing linking students to courses. The relationship of 'enrolment' is implemented using a common attribute. In this case, we place a special attribute, that of course_ID, known as a **foreign key**, in the STUDENT entity, as shown below:

STUDENT (student number, student name, address, postcode, points score, local education authority, course_ID)

COURSE (course ID, course name, entry requirements)

A foreign key, denoted by a non-continuous underline, is an attribute that is not a unique identifier in the entity in which it occurs, but is unique in another entity with which it has a relationship; thus providing a link between one entity and another. Here, any single occurrence of the entity STUDENT, for example a student named Fabienne Maes together with her details, can be linked with the details for a particular course, perhaps Persian Studies. This is because, given any particular student number in

STUDENT, the course ID is also listed and the course details found in the COURSE entity, using the course ID as the unique identifier.

In entities that share a relationship such as STUDENT and COURSE, it is always clear in which entity description the foreign key should appear because, if we are tempted to include the student number in the COURSE description we can see that we would need to include many student numbers – as many as we have students on the course. Since a student is enrolled on only one course, the solution is to include the course ID in the STUDENT entity description, where it need appear only once. The foreign key, then, always appears at the 'many' end of a relationship.

Entity-relationship modelling is a technique adopted by many methodologies for information systems analysis and design (see Chapter 18), including Information Engineering and Structured Systems Analysis and Design Method (SSADM). However, a variety of **notations** are used to express entities and their relationships. In the notation used above, entities appear in soft boxes (rectangles with curved corners) with lines between them to represent a relationship and its cardinality. Entity names appear in upper case. (Note that in the large example shown as Figure 4.16 at the end of the chapter, we use another convention for comparison purposes. In this example, the entities are shown as hard boxes and an arrow pointing to the 'many' entity denotes the one-to-many relationships).

4.3 Creating an entity-relationship model

The first stage of entity analysis requires the definition of an area for analysis. This was discussed in Chapter 2, and is frequently referred to as the **universe of discourse**. Sometimes this will be the organisation, but this is usually too ambitious for a detailed study and, as we have seen, the organisation will normally be divided into local areas for separate analysis. However, if a consistent approach is used, the resultant conceptual model will naturally integrate as, for example, data about STUDENTS link processes for 'enrolment' and 'awards' and data about PRODUCTS link procedures for 'buying' and 'despatch'.

As already stated, entity-relationship modelling is a top-down approach. The entities are identified first, then the relationships between them, with the attributes following as the study progresses. The data for entity-relationship modelling is generally gathered and enhanced through interviewing key personnel (see Chapters 3 and 18). Supporting documents can be used to provide the detail – about data items, for example – and this information is completed later in the study when more detail is known.

The obvious and major entities are identified first. The analyst attempts to name the fundamental things of interest to the domain of study. All the entities identified as being a part of the area under investigation must be related to one another, either directly or indirectly. For example, a LECTURER is an entity in a university timetabling system, and is related to the other entities of STUDENT, COURSE, MODULE and ROOM to a greater or lesser extent.

We might be tempted to link all entities to each other by a many-to-many relationship, since the resulting model would accommodate all possible access requirements. However, considering the degree and cardinality of each relationship with regard to the events and operations that need to be supported develops a more flexible and less complex model. For example, though we know that a LECTURER teaches a particular STUDENT, the query 'which LECTURER teaches which STUDENT' may never be made and the more common query might be to discover which LECTURER teaches which MODULE. Therefore, the relationship between LECTURER and STUDENT is seen as indirect and can be represented as shown in Figure 4.8.

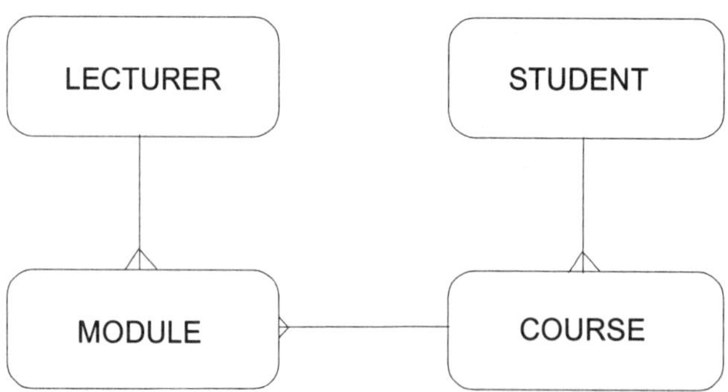

Figure 4.8: Building an entity-relationship model

The relationship between LECTURER and STUDENT has not been lost, since for a given STUDENT, the LECTURER for a particular MODULE on a COURSE can be determined transitively. It can be seen that the choices made in developing the entity-relationship model are dependent on the requirements of all users.

The developing model becomes useful as a communication tool between the analysts and the business users, with the users highlighting errors and omissions and making additions to the model. Though an entity-relationship model might be considered by some to be difficult to construct, they are fairly easy for business users to understand as they describe data with which they are familiar in terms used in the application areas (sometimes referred to as the environment).

The analyst has now constructed the model in outline and is in a position to fill in the detail. This means establishing the attributes for each item. Each attribute will say something about the entity. Both entities and attributes are usually identified during interviewing and document reading. Further into the analysis, the attributes will be refined to include properties, such as the data type, length and range.

There often arises the problem of distinguishing between an entity and an attribute. For example, for an organisation retailing plastic barbecue plates, the colour would be an attribute of the stock item. However, for a manufacturer of artists' paints, any particular colour may have attributes of its own that are important to the organisation such as the variety of pigments and their percentages. In the former case, therefore, colour of paint may be an attribute; in the latter example, colour itself will need to be an entity.

In practice, many of these ambiguities are settled in the process of **normalisation**, described in Chapter 5. However, in general, entities participate in functions carried out within the organisation and the attributes are those elements that are required to support the functions.

The analyst has to ensure that any **synonyms** and **homonyms** are detected. Synonyms occur when a single data item is known by more than one name. For example, a 'part number' might be known as an 'item number', 'part ID' or a 'finished product number' depending on the department. Homonyms are different data items with the same name. For example, a 'project code' might be the identifier for a project in one department and a task in another. The identification of synonyms and homonyms is no easy task, as users may well be unaware of the inconsistencies. However, synonyms and homonyms are very common and confuse analysis unless identified, reconciled and recorded in the **data dictionary**, which is the overall description of data in the database.

Sometimes, the attributes identified are included on the entity-relationship diagram, as illustrated in Figure 4.9.

Alternatively, the entity descriptions might appear in a list enclosed by parentheses and given the entity name as a label, as in the following example:

COURSE (<u>course-ID</u>, course-name, administrator)

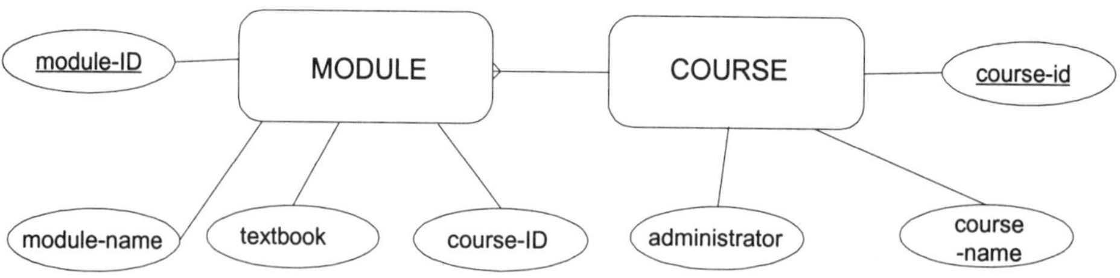

Figure 4.9: Adding the attributes

Alternatively, the entity descriptions might appear in a list enclosed by parentheses and given the entity name as a label, as in the following example:

COURSE (course-ID, course-name, administrator)

The description begins with the entity name, and the description within parentheses opens with the key attribute. As already described, the key attribute is the unique identifier for a particular occurrence of the entity so that, for example, although two COURSES may have the course-name 'information systems' they would each have their own unique module-ID and therefore be easily distinguished.

The final stage of creating an entity-relationship model is to look at all the **events** within the area and the **operations** that need to be performed following an event, and ensure that the model supports these events and operations.

Events are frequently referred to as transactions. An event might be 'customer makes an order', 'employee joins the organisation' or 'raw materials are purchased from the supplier'. If, for example, a customer makes an order, this event will be followed by a number of operations. The operations will be carried out so that it is possible to find out how much the order will cost, whether the product is in stock or how long the order might take to fulfil, and to determine the customer's credit rating. The entities such as PRODUCT and CUSTOMER will be examined. Some attribute values will need to be adjusted following the event, for example, the product stock level might need to be updated. The process of examining events and their associated operations frequently helps identify further attributes, and sometimes entities, that need to be added to the model.

4.4 Documenting the model

TITLE: Entity Type Specification Form			
DATE 19/01/2002	**TIME** 22:18:24	**PAGE** 1 OF 1	DEA/ CC
Entity Name The standard name for the entity			
Description A brief description of the entity type			
Synonyms Other names by which the entity is known			
Identifier(s) Name of the key attribute(s) which uniquely identify the entity occurrence			
Minimum Occurrences expected Maximum Occurrences expected			
Average Occurrences expected Growth Rate % over time			
Create Authority Names of users who are allowed to create entity occurrences			
Delete Authority Names of users who are allowed to delete entity occurrences			
Access Authority Names of users who are allowed to read entity occurrences			
Relationships involved cross reference as shown in the entity-relationship diagram			
Attributes involved cross reference attributes which are found in other entities (to cross reference different entities for access)			
Functions involved cross reference applications that require data contained in these and other entities			
Comments			

Figure 4.10: Entity type specification form

Entity-relationship modelling has documentation aids like other methods of systems analysis. It is possible to obtain forms on which to specify all the elements of the data analysis process. The separate documents will enable the specification of entities, attributes, relationships, events and operations (see Figures 4.10 to 4.14).

Development tools, such as Computer Associates' ERwin, and Popkin's System Architect 2001 assist in the drawing and integration of entity-relationship models with the rest of the design, including automatically creating a data dictionary using the information on the forms.

TITLE: Attribute Type Specification Form
DATE 19/01/2002 **TIME** 22:29:27 **PAGE** 1 OF 1 DEA/ CC
Attribute Name The standard name for the attribute
Description A brief description of the attribute
Synonyms Other names by which the attribute is known
Entity Cross Reference Entities that include the attribute, including those where the attribute is a key or part of the key
Create Authority Names of users who are allowed to create attributes
Delete Authority Names of users who are allowed to delete attributes
Access Authority Names of users who are allowed to read attributes
Relationships involved cross reference as shown in the entity-relationship diagram
Functions involved cross reference uses of the attribute in the function of the organisation
Format the type and length of the attribute
Values the values that the attributes may have
Comments

Figure 4.11: Attribute type specification form

TITLE: Relationship Type Specification Form	
DATE 19/01/2002 **TIME** 22:39:25 **PAGE** 1 OF 1	DEA/ CC
Relationship Name The standard name for the relationship	
Description A brief description of the relationship	
Synonyms Other names by which the relationship is known	
Entities Involved (Owner) The owner and member entity(ies) **(Members)**	
Create Authority Names of users who are allowed to create relationships	
Delete Authority Names of users who are allowed to delete relationships	
Access Authority Names of users who are allowed to read relationships	
Occurrences The numbers of each entity type involved in an occurrence of a relationship and the occurrence of that relationship	
Cardinality (1:1, 1:m, m:n) Optional Mandatory Conditions governing the existence of a relationship	
If exclusive state paired relationship name	
If inclusive state paired relationship name and first existence relationship name	
Comments	

Figure 4.12: Relationship type specification form

TITLE: Event Type Specification Form	
DATE 19/01/2002 **TIME** 22:49:22 **PAGE** 1 OF 1	DEA/ CC
Event Name The standard name for the event	
Description A brief description of the event	
Frequency of the event	
Operations following event The procedures that are triggered by an event	
Create Authority Names of users who are allowed to create relationships	
Delete Authority Names of users who are allowed to delete relationships	
Access Authority Names of users who are allowed to read relationships	
Synchronisation The conditions of an event that effects the trigger	
Pathway following event A diagrammatic representation of the processes following the event through the entity types accessed	
Comments	

Figure 4.13: Event type specification form

TITLE: Operation Type Specification Form
DATE 19/01/2002 **TIME** 22:58:54 **PAGE** 1 OF 1 DEA/ CC
Operation Name The standard name for the operation
Description A brief description of the operation
Access Key
Entities Involved Entity names and processing carried out on those entities
Create Authority Names of users who are allowed to create operations
Delete Authority Names of users who are allowed to delete operations
Access Authority Names of users who are allowed to read operations
Events preceding operation Events caused by operation
Response time required
Frequency
Privacy Level
Comments

Figure 4.14: Operation type specification form

4.5 Developing and enhancing the model

Conceptual modelling is an iterative process: the final model will not be obtained until after a number of tries. Indeed, it may be considered that the final model is never reached, as enhancements and new applications and querying capabilities cause the data model to adapt and expand to fulfil user requirements. The time spent on developing and enhancing the data model should not be seen as inefficiency, but worthwhile care for accuracy. If the entity model is inaccurate, the database applications that use it will also be inaccurate ('garbage-in, garbage-out'). On the other hand, the process should not be too long or there will be 'diminishing returns'.

The entity-relationship diagram seen in Figure 4.15 shows the entities for part of an Internet book retailer. We have checked that customer order processing is supported. This is a very common data structure, applicable to customer orders, invoices, statements, delivery notes and purchase orders in many business environments. We have also started to fill in our attributes for each entity, including the key attribute in each case.

Note that the attribute 'customer number' in the ORDER DETAIL entity is underlined with dashes, indicating a **foreign key**. Foreign keys are explained in more detail in Chapter 5, where the detail of entity descriptions is used as the starting point for the modelling technique known as normalisation. Note also that *both* 'order number' and 'book number' are underlined and form the key to the ORDER ITEM entity. This means that to identify every occurrence of the entity requires more than one attribute. Such a key is known as a **composite key**. The creation of composite keys also receives more attention in Chapter 5.

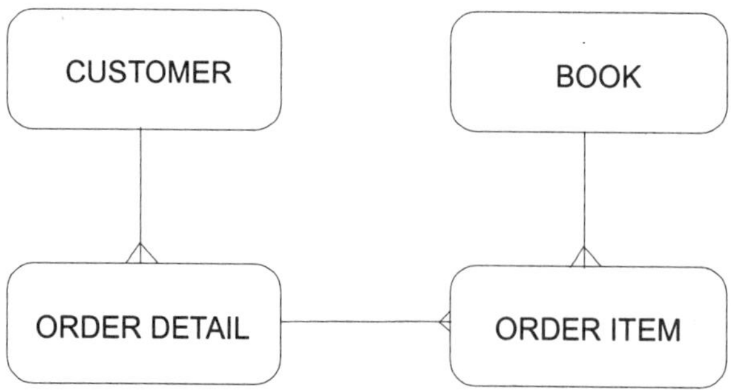

Figure 4.15: Building the model

CUSTOMER (<u>customer number</u>, customer name, customer address, postcode, credit rating)

ORDER DETAIL (order number, customer number, delivery address, delivery postcode, discount percentage)

ORDER ITEM (order number, book number, quantity)

BOOK (book number, title, number in stock, publisher, price)

By identifying the entities, relationships and attributes to form our data structure in an entity-relationship diagram, along with our entity descriptions, we have a fair representation of the data aspects of that part of the real world that we are modelling.

A more realistically large model is shown as Figure 4.16. We show it to give an idea of the complexity of entity-relationship models in some situations. Even so, it has been greatly simplified to make it readable (and fit into a page of a book). We have used another convention for comparison purposes. In this example, the entities are shown as hard boxes and an arrow pointing to the 'many' entity denotes the one-to-many relationships.

Summary

- The main components of entity-relationship models are entities, attributes, and relationships. An entity is a thing of interest in the organisation about which the organisation wishes to hold data. Attributes give detail about the entity. A relationship represents the association between entities.
- Occurrences of an entity are examples of each entity, for example, each book in our list of further reading are occurrences of the BOOK entity. Each will be identified by the value of the key attribute.
- Relationships can be one-to-one, one-to-many or many-to-many.
- Entity-relationship models can be checked by following operations that might be implemented for each event (or transaction) that occur in the application domain.

Exercises

1. Use the entity-relationship technique to describe the relationship between a project and its team members, all dedicated to that single project.

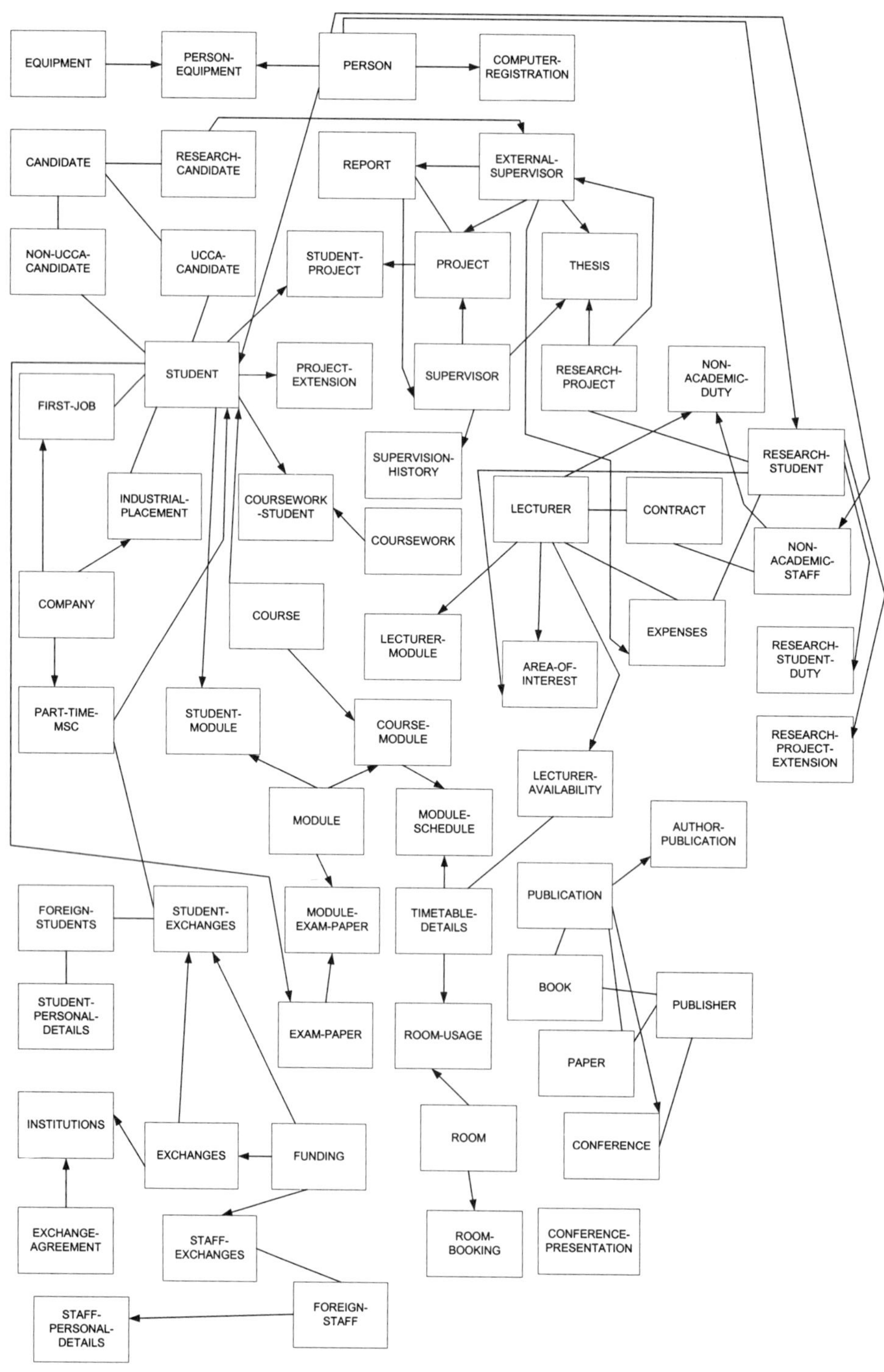

Figure 4.16: Entity-relationship model of an academic department

2. Use the same technique to describe the relationship between an ambassador and an interpreter, assigned for his or her sole use.
3. Describe the situation where a given make and model of car can have up to 20,000 components and each component can be used in many makes and models of car.
4. Draw an entity relationship diagram to describe the relationship between thoroughbred horses in a pedigree. You may need to know the terms 'sire' and 'dam'!
5. Draw an entity-relationship diagram for the delivery process for a clothes manufacturer described below:

   'We need to know which customer it is going to, and the delivery address, which is sometimes different from the customer address. We need to know what items we are delivering and how many. We have to get the customer to sign for the items on delivery. The price is included, so that the customer agrees that too when they sign.'
6. Draw an entity-relationship diagram for the creation of a statement of account for a beauty parlour described below:

   'Clients usually pay for treatment as they go along but every quarter we send a statement. It includes all the treatments that they have had in that quarter and in the unusual case of any payments being outstanding, it shows that too. Sometimes treatments are bought as gifts and so the statement goes to the 'gift-giver', rather than the actual client.
7. Compare the results from your modelling of exercises 2 and 3. They should have the same pattern. However, the entities may have different names as a result of the different terminology used. Imagine that you have modelled the delivery process and the statement of account for the same organisation, for example the clothes manufacturer. You may well get different entity names as well. Does it matter? And if so, how would you resolve the apparent conflict?
8. Discuss and criticise the entity-relationship model presented as Figure 4.16.
9. Where does the foreign key appear if entities share a one-to-one relationship? In considering the maintenance of relationships through keys in many-to-many relationships, can you see why many-to-many relationships need to be 'resolved into two one-to-many relationships?
10. For part of an organisation of your choice, such as a university, hospital or business department, create the conceptual model in terms of an entity-relationship model.

Further reading

Avison, D. E. and Fitzgerald, G. (2002) *Information Systems Development: Methodologies, Techniques and Tools,* 3rd edn, McGraw-Hill, Maidenhead.

Codd, E. F. (1970) A Relational Model of Data for Large Shared Data Banks, *Communications of the ACM,* **13**, 6.

Date, C.J. (2000) *An Introduction to Database Systems* 7th edn., Addison Wesley, Harlow.

Silverston, L., Inmon, W. H. and Graziano, K. (1997) *The Data Model Resource Book,* John Wiley, Chichester.

5

Relational model and normalisation

5.1 Definitions

The objective of this chapter is to discuss relational modelling and the rules of normalisation. Many database management systems are relational (even those such as Oracle, Informix and DB2 that accommodate object implementation as well) so that the mapping of this model on to those of most database management systems is relatively easy. Further, relational modelling proves to integrate well with entity-relationship modelling described in Chapter 4. You will notice many similarities in our descriptions of the two models. As we progress towards implementing a database, relational modelling frequently follows or is conducted in parallel with entity-relationship modelling.

The building block of the relational model is a **relation**. We have mentioned the similarities between the two models, but relations should not be confused with relationships! A relation is a two-dimensional table and represents an entity in entity-relationship modelling. A relational model consists of a number of relations.

Each row in a relation is a **tuple**, described as an occurrence in entity-relationship modelling. The order of tuples is immaterial in the model, although they will normally be shown in this text in a logical sequence so that it is easier for the reader to follow the contents of the relation. No two tuples can be identical in the relation.

A tuple will have a number of **attributes**. For example, in a relation named STUDENT the tuples each have attributes that might include 'name', 'term time address' and 'local education authority'. The attribute names, therefore, form the columns of the table. All items in a column are in the same **domain**, and there are circumstances where the contents of two or more columns are in the same domain. The number of attributes in a relation is called the **degree** of the relation. The number of tuples in a relation defines its **cardinality**.

Each tuple in a relation is distinguished from another because one or more attributes in a relation are designated **key attributes**. In a CUSTOMER relation, for example, 'customer name' is unlikely to be unique and so a 'customer number' or 'customer code' can be used to provide a unique identifier. There may be more than one possible key. These are known as **candidate keys**. For example 'product ID' and 'product description' might both be unique in a PRODUCT relation. In this circumstance, one of the candidate keys is chosen as a **primary key**. An attribute that is a primary key (or another candidate key) in one relation and included in another relation where it is not a candidate key is known as a **foreign key** in that second relation. As explained in Chapter 4 on entity-relationship modelling, it is the keys that describe the relationship between entities. If there is no common attribute between two entities, then there is no way of linking one set of details with details in another entity and unless the common attribute uniquely identifies a particular row of a table in at least one of the entities, then there is no way of relating the details usefully.

The structure of a relation is commonly expressed as in the following example.

CLIENT (client ID, client name, client postcode, credit rating)

QUOTE (quote number, client ID, agent code, description, value)

AGENT (agent code, agent name, area, mobile number)

Examples of possible tuples in the CLIENT relation are illustrated in Figure 5.1.

client ID	client name	client postcode	credit rating
A0001	CDF CONSULTING	RG6 8JY	3
A0003	RAMPAGE	DT4 9IL	4
S0017	BAILEY & CROSS	OX12 4HN	7

Figure 5.1: CLIENT relation

5.2 Normalisation: creating a relational model

Given a document, for example an order form, most analysts would be able to distinguish the different *types* of data it contains. There will be data about the CUSTOMER, including the name and address, credit rating and account balance. There will be data about the ITEMS that they have ordered, including the item price and description. There will be something peculiar to the ORDER itself, perhaps a delivery address for that particular order or a discount applied in this case. There is some further data that seems to relate to this particular order *together with* the items that have been ordered, an ORDER LINE, which will include the quantities of product ordered.

In grouping together the data items logically into data groups, the analyst is generating a data model. The process of **normalisation** is the formalised application of rules to the data items that will generate the relations in just the way described above. This set of rules proves to be a useful guideline, because we are dealing with large sets of data and the relations formed by the normalisation process will make the data easier to understand and manipulate. The model so formed is appropriate for the further stages of the methodology and the database will have the data independence, integrity and therefore the flexibility required of the database approach.

We will use three nested levels of normalisation, and the third and final stage is known as **third normal form** (3NF). It is this level of normalisation that is usually used as the basis for the design of the data model and for mapping onto a database. Normalisation is the process of transforming data into well-formed or natural groupings. The grouping ensures that data redundancy is minimised, data availability is maximised and security is increased. The relations formed by the normalisation process will make the data easier to understand and manipulate. As well as simplifying the relations, normalisation also reduces anomalies that may otherwise occur when manipulating the relations in a relational database. Normalised data is stable and a good foundation for any future growth. It is a mechanical process, and the process can be automated. The difficult part lies in understanding the meaning, that is, the semantics, of the data. This is only discovered through extensive and careful conceptual modelling. Thorough organisational analysis, which was discussed in Chapter 2, will also help here.

Although the process of normalisation is normally described as a series of steps, it is much more likely that an experienced analyst will assemble the data items into relations, decide whether they are in an appropriate normal form and adjust them if necessary. However, it is important to appreciate the steps and the underlying principles in order to reach such a level of understanding.

There are three stages of normalisation. We will describe these briefly and formally first and then explain these steps. The purpose of **first normal form** (1NF) is to ensure that all the attributes are atomic. All the attributes must have a one-to-one relationship with the key attribute. This is often expressed as the fact that relations must not contain any repeating groups or that the relations should be 'flat'; that is of fixed length with one row per 'record'. The rules of **second normal form** (2NF) ensure that each non-key attribute is functionally dependent on the whole of the key. Once in **third normal form** (3NF), all the non-key attributes are functionally independent of each other, that is, there are no transitive dependencies.

A rather flippant but more memorable definition of normalisation can be given, as 'the non-key attributes in a relation must depend on the key, the whole key, and nothing but the key'. This is an oversimplification but it is essentially true and could be kept in mind during the process of normalisation.

A key concept of normalisation is **functional dependency**, sometimes referred to as **determinacy**. The dependency is of one data item on another, and a functional dependency is a one-to-one relationship. So 'customer name' is functionally dependent on 'customer number' in the relation CUSTOMER, since for every 'customer number' there is only one relevant 'customer name'. Functional dependency is frequently illustrated by an arrow, as shown in Figure 5.2.

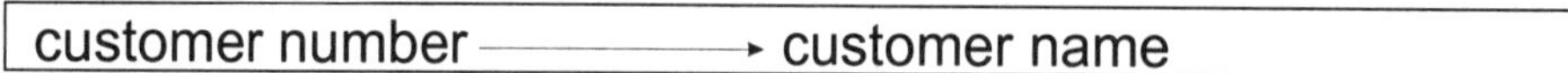

Figure 5.2: Functional dependency

Before normalising the unnormalised relation below, it is necessary to analyse the meaning of the relation. Knowledge of the application area gained from organisational analysis (Chapter 2) and entity-relationship modelling (Chapter 4) will provide this information. It is possible to make assumptions about the inter-relationships between data, but it is obviously better to base these assumptions on thorough analysis.

This is the kind of data that is gathered through document reading. As we have shown, the analyst when presented with a document, for example an order form in this case, is able to identify the individual data items and begin to identify their logical groupings.

5.3 Zero normal form (0NF)

The list of data items, perhaps taken from a document, is unnormalised, or in zero normal form (0NF). In unnormalised form, the data items are listed with the key attribute at the beginning. Repeating groups are placed within curly brackets, as shown below.

ORDER (order number, customer ID, customer name, customer address, discount, {item code, description, quantity, price})

A relation with some data included might look like the table in Figure 5.3.

A look at the table confirms some of the difficulties of unnormalised data. There is data redundancy, the customer address, for example, is stored each time an order is made. The record is not of a fixed length. This makes it difficult to update the data with any changes that are made, and makes it difficult to use the data for other applications.

order number	cust-ID	cust-name	cust address	dis-count	item code	description	qty	price
000342	AS12	Brogan	1 Temple Close Scunthorpe	10%	Z02	Blue spotted	2	49.99
					X05	Red striped	4	49.99
000367	AS12	Brogan	1 Temple Close Scunthorpe	12%	Z02	Blue spotted	2	49.99
					Y11	Yellow self-patterned	1	54.99
000453	AT14	Lovell	16 Stanford Road Matlock	5%	Z02	Blue spotted	3	49.99
					Z04	Red spotted	3	49.99

Figure 5.3: Zero normal form

5.4 First normal form (1NF)

The first step to first normal form does not really improve the situation from a design perspective, and it would make a very bad design if the analyst simply stopped at first normal form. However, the step makes the table 'flat', satisfies the first requirement of relational modelling, that the order of tuples should not be significant, and makes the next steps, which *are* an improvement, much easier. In our example, first normal form requires an elimination of the repeating groups by making the 'item number' a key attribute.

ORDERDETAILS (order number, customer ID, customer name, customer address, discount, item code, description, quantity, price)

We have now gone from having just three records to having six completed tuples, as can be seen in Figure 5.4. All the tuples are distinct, as they have different key attributes. This has been achieved by including 'item code' as a key attribute. Together with 'order number', it makes a **composite key**.

order number	cus-ID	cust-name	cust-address	dis-count	item code	description	qty	price
000342	AS12	Brogan	1 Temple Close Scunthorpe	10%	Z02	Blue spotted	2	49.99
000342	AS12	Brogan	1 Temple Close Scunthorpe	10%	X05	Red striped	4	49.99
000367	AS12	Brogan	1 Temple Close Scunthorpe	12%	Z02	Blue spotted	2	49.99
000367	AS12	Brogan	1 Temple Close Scunthorpe	12%	Y11	Yellow self-patterned	1	54.99
000453	AT14	Lovell	16 Stanford Road Matlock	5%	Z02	Blue spotted	3	49.99
000453	AT14	Lovell	16 Stanford Road Matlock	5%	Z04	Red spotted	3	49.99

Figure 5.4: First normal form

5.5 Second normal form (2NF)

Second normal form is achieved if all the relations are in first normal form and all the non-key attributes are fully functionally dependent on the whole of the key. The relation ORDER is in first normal form but by considering each non-key attribute in turn we can see that while 'quantity' is dependent on both of the components of the composite key, the other attributes are functionally dependent on one or other of the key attributes. The functional dependencies are illustrated in figure 5.5.

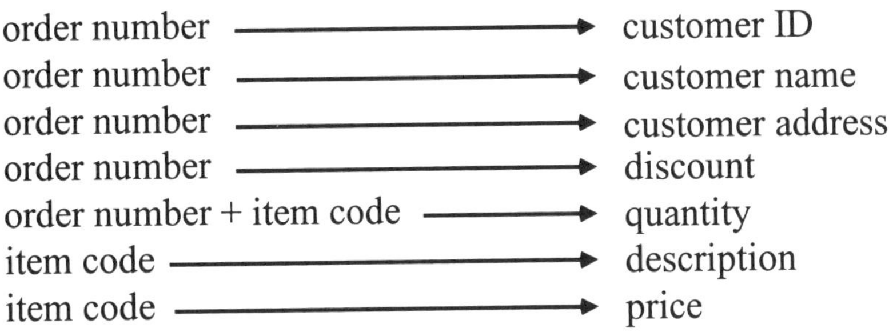

Figure 5.5: Functional dependencies

Identifying the functional dependencies has created two new relations, ORDER LINE and ITEM.

ORDER DETAILS (<u>order number</u>, customer ID, customer name, customer address, discount)

ORDER LINE (<u>order number, item code</u>, quantity)

ITEM (<u>item code</u>, description, price)

5.6 Third normal form (3NF)

Second normal form may cause problems where non-key attributes are functionally dependent on each other. In our example, although 'customer name' is dependent on 'order number', it is dependent *through* 'customer ID'. The same is true of 'customer address'. This is known as **transitive dependency**. This means that each time a customer placed an order, the customer name and address would be recorded. This unnecessary inclusion of data is known as **data redundancy**. While storage capacity may very often not be a consideration, processing time, accuracy and integrity are all compromised by redundant data. The solution is to eliminate the transitive dependencies by creating new relations. In this example the new relation is CUSTOMER, which has the attributes 'customer name' and 'customer address', and has 'customer ID' as its key attribute. However, the relationship between customer and order must be maintained, and so 'customer ID' remains in the ORDER DETAILS relation, and given a dashed underline to show it is a foreign key; that is, it is not a key attribute in this relation but is a key in another relation.

The relations in third normal form are shown below.

ORDER DETAILS (order number, discount, customer ID)

ORDER LINE (order number, item code, quantity)

ITEM (item code, description, price)

CUSTOMER (customer ID, customer name, customer address)

You might think an alternative is to include the 'order number' as a foreign key in the CUSTOMER relation. However, since the CUSTOMER can have many ORDER DETAILS, 'order number' would have to be a repeating group in the CUSTOMER relation and the resulting relation would not be in first normal form. The foreign key goes at the many end of a one-to-many relationship, that is, one customer may have many ORDER DETAILS and second normal form ensured that each ORDER DETAIL is for only one customer.

Normalisation may sometimes seem difficult to learn. You may find it useful to review the beginning of this chapter where we gave the common-sense approach to data modelling that is used by IT professionals with experience that makes them familiar with the concepts of good design and acutely aware of the problems caused by bad design. A good design is one that, while maintaining good performance, allows for ease of maintenance and enhancement. Normalisation ensures that all the data is arranged in tightly associated bundles with minimal unnecessary repetition of data making the data easy to update, easy to enhance and easy to use for new applications. The whole design is flexible, integrated and extensible.

Non-normalised relations form a poor basis for the model. For example, if we used the first normal form relation shown as Figure 5.4 as one of the relations in the final model, and we added a new order from customer Brogan, we would have to key in again the customer address and other details that we already have in the database (all the information must be completed for each attribute in a tuple). There is evidently a lot of redundant data in the relation. If customer Lovell cancelled order 453, as it is the only order from that customer, we would have to delete those tuples and lose information that we would want to keep, such as that customer's name and address details. Furthermore, if we were in contact with a new customer who had not placed an order yet, we could not complete customer information, such as name and address details, because we do not have an order number. We also gave reasons at the beginning of this section showing why the second normal form model gives rise to redundancy.

The third and final stage of normalisation described in this chapter is usually used as the basis for the design of the data model. However, some circumstances may arise when data redundancy is caused by hidden dependencies, and academics have discussed 'Boyce-Codd', fourth and fifth normal forms for situations that rarely arise in practice. Our practical approach ensures a sensible, composite data design that satisfies user requirements *and* provides simple, flexible relations. For a detailed discussion on these further refinements to the normalisation process, see Date (2000).

Chapter 8 about the Access database management system implemented on PCs follows through an example of relational modelling.

Summary

- Relational modelling frequently follows or is undertaken in parallel with entity-relationship modelling. A relation can represent an entity, with each row being called a tuple and a column a domain.
- The process of normalisation is the formalised application of rules to make the model easy to understand and manipulate. We apply three rules leading to third normal form. At this stage, 'the non-key attributes in a relation depend on the key, the whole key, and nothing but the key'.
- Further rules of normalisation can be followed, but third normal form rarely gives rise to major anomalies in practice.

Exercises

1. Discuss the advantages and disadvantages of a bottom-up approach to conceptual modelling. How does it differ from a top-down approach? Show how the two approaches may be used to compliment each other.
2. Under what circumstances might analysts not fully normalise a set of relations?
3. Explain what is meant by the expression 'the key, the whole key and nothing but the key'.
4. Normalise the following unnormalised relation:
   WARD (ward name, head nurse {nurse number, nurse name} {bed number, patient, GP number, GP name, GP address, consultant number})

5. Normalise the following unnormalised relation:
   DEPARTMENT (department name, head of department, administrator, {Project number, project name, project leader {team member, role} client, client contact, client address})
6. Normalise the following unnormalised relation:
   HORSE (registration number, birthdate, sex, owner name, owner address {race track, track manager, race date, race time, race length, position})
7. Normalise the data to be found in the following online flight booking confirmation:

Confirmation

Book date: 15th August
Confirmation Number: C6T8DA
NB: you will need to provide this confirmation number and your passport/photo ID and visas (where applicable) at check-in to receive your boarding card.

Going out

From London Stanstead (STN) to Brussels S. Charleroi (CRL)
Tuesday 2nd July 2002 Flight HG1097 Depart: STN 20:10
Arrive: CRL 22:10

Coming back

From Brussels S. Charleroi (CRL) to London Stanstead (STN)
Wednesday 3rd July Flight HG1097 Depart: CRL 22:20
Arrive: CRL 22:20

Billing Address

Timms, Laura
44 Portsmouth Drive
Kings Heath
Birmingham
BR15 4TG

Passenger Details

2 Passengers:	Addresses
1: Timms, Laura.	Same as billing
2: Timms, Annie.	29 Boxer Court Pimlico London SW1A 4FR

8. For part of an organisation of your choice, such as a university, hospital or business department, create the conceptual model in terms to a set of normalised relations.

Further reading

Avison, D. E. and Fitzgerald, G. (2002) *Information Systems Development: Methodologies, Techniques and Tools,* McGraw-Hill, Maidenhead, 3rd edn.

Codd, E. F. (1970) A relational model of data for large shared data banks, *Communications of the ACM,* **13**, 6.

Date, C. J. (2000) *An Introduction to Database Systems,* 7th edn, Addison Wesley, Harlow.

Silverston, L., Inmon, W. H. and Graziano, K. (1997) *The Data Model Resource Book,* John Wiley, Chichester.

Teorey, T.J. (1998) *Database Modelling and Design: The Fundamental Principles,* Morgan Kaufman.

6

Object modelling

6.1 Introduction

The proponents of object-oriented development suggest that human understanding is more object-oriented than process-oriented or even data oriented. For example, a course administrator in a university thinks of a student together with their enrolment, academic progress and graduation. Thus we tend to think of the data (such as the student data) and the operations on that data (the enrolment, recording examination grades, the final award) as a single entity or object. Object-oriented development uses this concept to analyse, design and implement a generation of object-oriented applications that, it is claimed, are easier to understand, build and use. In addition, objects are reusable, that is, able to be used later by these or other applications. This is a characteristic that can help minimise maintenance and provide flexibility for future enhancement.

In the early 1990s, it seemed that object-orientation was going to replace the data-driven approach to applications development. However, despite the advantages, object-oriented development accounts for only a small percentage of overall systems development. In computing, as in other domains, there is an in-built conservatism due to the costs of changing approaches and technology.

This chapter begins with definitions of the terms used in an object-oriented environment. Then, the three perspectives of a system: what the system is; what the system does; and how the system behaves, are illustrated using the Unified Modelling Language (UML) notation.

6.2 Definitions

Object-oriented design takes a different view of the organisation from the data-oriented view described in Chapters 4 and 5. An **object** is, unlike an entity, a combination of both data *and* activity. For example, a library has a MEMBER. Taking a data-structure view, the MEMBER would be an entity that consists of attributes including name, address and membership details. However, taking an object-oriented perspective, a MEMBER would be an object that comprised the data *and* some operations, such as 'reserve a copy of a book' or 'return a copy of a book'.

An object exhibits **behaviour** depending upon its **state**. For example, a library MEMBER can only 'lend a copy of a book' if the *membership is active*. Other states that a MEMBER might be in include *loan entitlement full* and *membership lapsed*. An object interacts with other objects, having data input and data output. For example, a library MEMBER loans a copy of a BOOK. An object has a boundary and can be named; that is, given a unique identifier. The naming of an object gives it an **identity**.

Objects are grouped into **classes**. Though a class may have a similar name to that given to an entity in data modelling, they are quite different concepts. Members of a class have a core of the same attributes and behaviour. Classes can have **sub-classes**. For example, CAR could be a sub-class of VEHICLE in a vehicle hire company. Sub-classes **inherit** the attributes and operations of the class so that, for example, all VEHICLEs have a 'chassis number', a 'registration number' and a 'cubic capacity'. However, sub-classes can have extra attributes of their own. For example, a CAR has the property of 'seating capacity', which might not be appropriate to another sub-class of VEHICLE such as a TRACTOR, and so cannot be inherited from the **super-class**. An object is said to be an **instance** of class.

An object communicates with other objects and manages its own internal communication by sending and receiving **messages**. The coupling between objects, known as the **public interface**, is loose or low and the **private interface** used by an object ensures that it is highly cohesive. The *high cohesion* within an object is known as **encapsulation** and the *low coupling* between objects is **abstraction**. The two concepts are closely linked, since a highly cohesive object will have low coupling. For example, if we chose FAMILY as a class, within a particular FAMILY object the communications would be many and varied. The large amount of messages passed between FAMILY components would form a private interface that reflected the high cohesion within the FAMILY unit. If we then looked at the FAMILY's interaction with the LOCAL GOVERNMENT, for example, we would find the communication, or public interface, fewer and more formalised; thus demonstrating low coupling. If we went on to take the same individuals and class them as MALE or FEMALE rather than FAMILY and LOCAL GOVERNMENT some components of the two objects would be involved in lengthy communications across objects and yet within the object there would be little communication. It is a class grouping that makes little sense. Low coupling and high cohesion between classes helps reduce complexity and increases the flexibility of the system overall.

Relationships between objects are known as **associations**. For example, an association between the classes of STUDENT and LECTURER is 'supervision', when a LECTURER monitors the progress of a STUDENT project. Further associations might include 'interviewing', when a LECTURER might create a new STUDENT, or 'calculating pay' when the number of STUDENTs a LECTURER assesses might be important. Associations may be one way or the other, or both ways. All associations cause changes in the objects involved because they invoke **methods**. A method is a program or a set of instructions.

The **attributes** or properties of an object are similar to the attributes of an entity. An attribute is a data item with a value that may change over time, changing the state of the object. Some attributes may never change. For example a unique identifier for a STOCK ITEM never changes in its lifetime but attributes such as 'price' and 'stock level' have different values over a period of time.

It may be confusing to the reader when first presented with the concepts of object-orientation and its particular terminology. However, the following sections explain the concept within the context of conceptual modelling.

6.3 UML and object modelling method

An object-oriented conceptual model includes expressions of what the system *is*, what the system *does* and how the system *behaves* over time.

The explanation and examples given here are based on the **Unified Modelling Language (UML)**. UML brings together the ideas of three people who have been important in the development of object-oriented concepts, Grady Booch (and his method OOD), Jim Rumbaugh (with OMT) and Ivar Jacobson (OOSE). There are a number of different methods that may be employed to model a system using objects, but the flexibility of UML and the software support available has made UML very popular and many other approaches have fallen into disuse. The Object Management Group (OMG) (a non-profit-making organisation that exists to promote object-oriented tools, techniques and technologies) has adopted UML, and so the trend towards UML as a standard continues. However, we do not provide a definitive guide to UML and the many reference manuals, guides and textbooks should be consulted for further detail.

UML provides a non-proprietary notation for describing the systems from a variety of perspectives. UML does not provide a method or methodology for modelling systems. There is no prescriptive way of modelling the system correctly, and the development of a useful model is contingent upon many factors including the type of organisation, the context within which the development takes place, the type of objects and their volatility, the type of tasks and their complexity and so on. For example, it is of no benefit to model the behaviour of a simple enquiry system such as an online catalogue. Therefore, the following sections outline some of the diagrams used to create an object-oriented model from the three perspectives of system objectives, use and behaviour.

6.4 What the system *is*

Usually, the first step in object modelling is to identify classes and their associations. Statements from the real world such as 'customers own pets' and 'the pet has an appointment with the veterinary surgeon' are used to identify candidate classes. As seen in Figure 6.1, in the example of a veterinary surgery, two classes, CUSTOMER and PET are identified, with the association 'is owner of'.

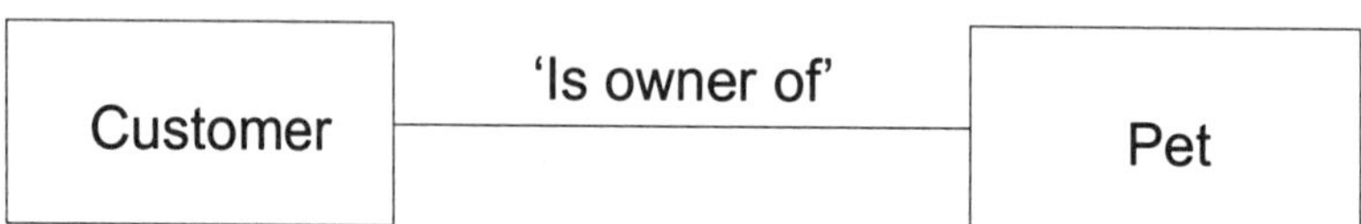

Figure 6.1: Classes and associations

There is nothing here about how many PETs a CUSTOMER can 'own', how many CUSTOMERs a PET has as 'owner' or which direction the association flows (beyond the implication in the association name). In Figure 6.2 below, it is made clear that a CUSTOMER 'owns' at least one pet, and can have an infinite number. However, one PET is always 'owned' by just one CUSTOMER.

There may be more than one association between classes. For example, between CUSTOMER and PET we might include 'cares for' and 'loans' as associations. The different associations may involve different objects of the classes CUSTOMER and PET. From the identification of the main classes and their associations, an outline class diagram is developed.

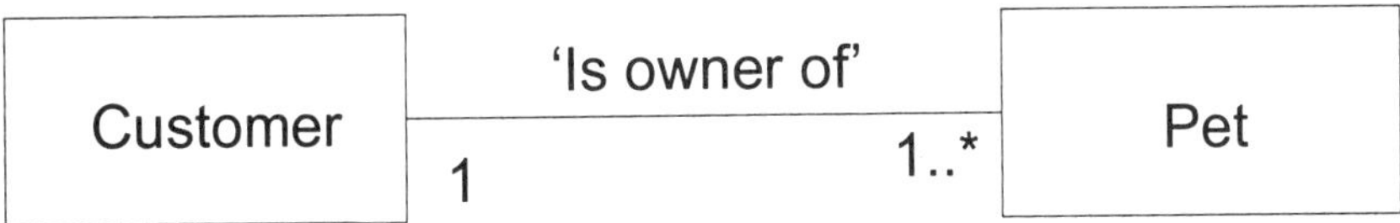

Figure 6.2: Adding further information

The next step is to identify the attributes and operations of each object. Each association implies a series of operations. For example, we may want to know how many PETs a CUSTOMER 'owns', or allow the CUSTOMER to register a new PET. The class model shown as Figure 6.3 includes these operations.

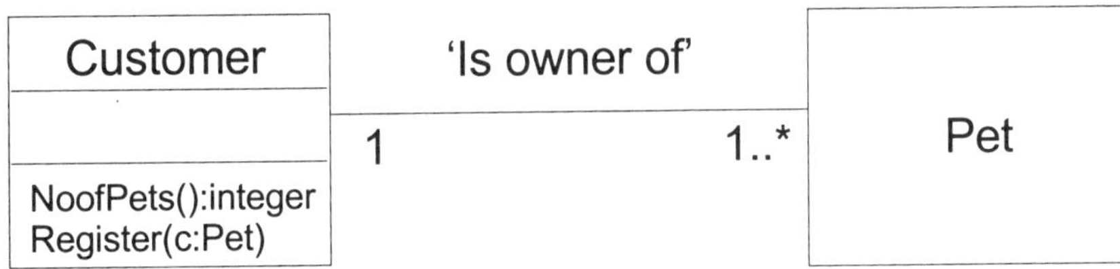

Figure 6.3: Identifying operations

The attributes are included on the diagram in the middle portion of the class box. In the enhanced diagram (Figure 6.4), the CUSTOMER is given a name of type 'string'.

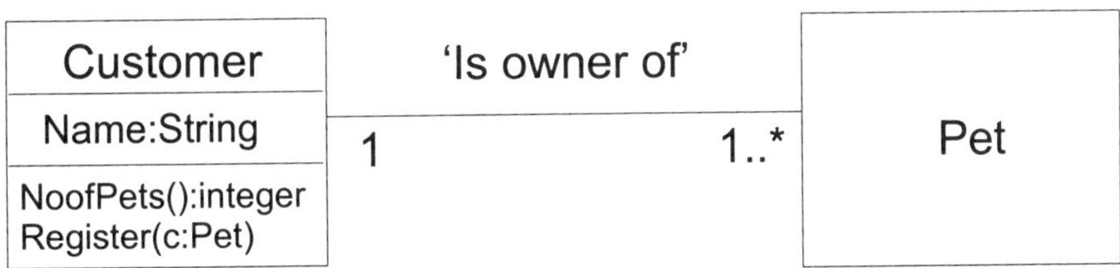

Figure 6.4: Adding attributes

In UML, this model is known as the static structural model. Although any class in a system will appear only once in a model of the system, it may be clearer to separate the developing model into a series of diagrams depicting the whole design. In Figure 6.5, some further classes have been identified and added to form an outline class model.

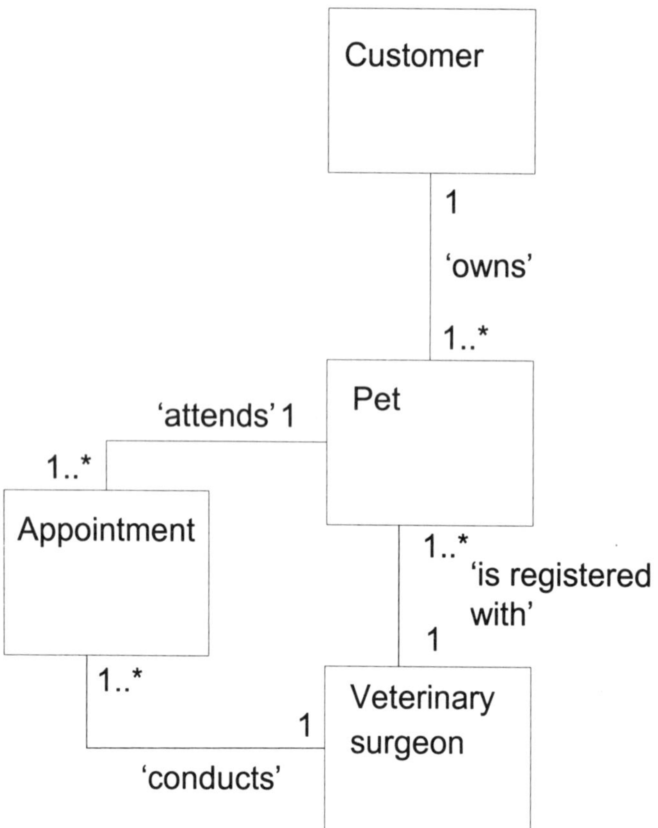

Figure 6.5: Outline class model

Further steps might add more information about dependencies and constraints on associations between classes. However, the discussion is not appropriate here, and a more detailed explanation can be found in the seminal work of Booch (1991). It can also be found in more general books on the object-oriented approach, for example, Bennet *et al.* (1999), Martin and Odell (1997) and Page-Jones (1999), and handbooks such as Stevens and Pooley (2000) and Rumbaugh *et al.* (1999).

6.5 What the system *does*

The modelling of what a system does takes a user perspective in **use case diagrams**. The process of modelling begins by identifying the roles. In UML, the user in a role is known as an **actor**, so a university lecturer may act in the role of ACADEMIC TUTOR and an employee may act in the role of RECEPTION. In differentiating between the person and their role, we can see that a user may have more than one actor role, so a lecturer may be both an ACADEMIC TUTOR and a RESEARCH CO-ORDINATOR. Actors may be individuals or, more likely, groups of people. For example, CLIENT is an actor, and so are MARKETING DEPARTMENT and HELP DESK and even software systems such as the LEDGER.

Let us look at an example. The actors in a veterinary practice clearly include the VETERINARY SURGEON and the CUSTOMER. These are also classes, as shown in the class diagram (Figure 6.5). When considering the activities that go on in the surgery, we might come to the conclusion that the RECEPTIONIST has a role, and also the NURSE. The PET must at least be a candidate actor; that is to say, we may or may not want to include the PET as an actor in the final use case diagram. If we continue the example of an appointments system, we have identified the roles shown in Figure 6.6.

Figure 6.6: Identifying the actors

The process continues with the identification of the tasks that the users undertake. In UML, tasks are known as **use cases**. For example, a CLIENT might ‘request an appointment’ or ‘make a payment’; a HELP DESK might ‘log a query’ or ‘place a request’. The use cases can be high level, that is, a single use case may describe many steps.

The example shown as Figure 6.7 includes a relationship between use cases, in this case an <<include>>. UML has notation for three different relationships between use cases: <<include>> to ‘insert’ one use case inside another; <<extend>> to add one use case to another; and generalisation for a specialised variation of a particular use case. Whether to insert, extend or generalise a use case is often decided when it becomes obvious that a use case includes a series of steps that are repeated in another use case, or if the use case contains many steps. This emerges in the development of the **use case descriptions**.

Each use case is described in a use case description. The use case description may be either a formal documentation of steps or a narrative. The example seen as Figure 6.8 shows an informal description of the use case ‘prescribe for pet’.

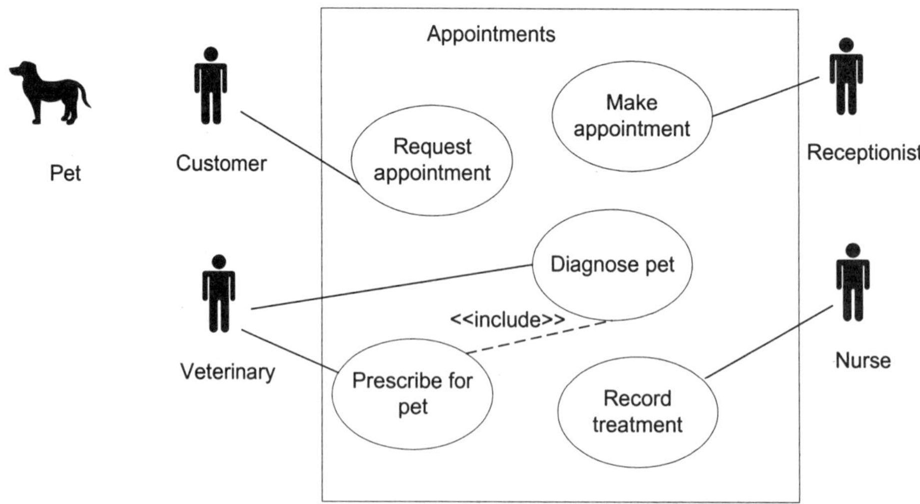

Figure 6.7: Identifying the use cases

Title	Prescribe for pet
Actors	Veterinary surgeon
Description	Prescribe for pet begins when the pet attends an appointment. This initiates the 'diagnose pet' use case. The vet refers to the pet's record. If diagnosis does not require a prescription, the appointment ends. However, if the pet needs treatment, the required drugs are removed from stock and issued, subject to any side effects or contraindications identified.

Figure 6.8: Use case description

The initial use case diagram describes the usual system activity. However, exceptions occur, and these are described in **scenarios** – adjuncts to the main use case descriptions. For example, although a CUSTOMER may attempt to 'make an appointment', they may be prevented from doing so because they failed to 'make a payment' last time and a different set of tasks are initiated.

6.6 How the system *behaves*

Interaction diagrams bring together the objects and the use cases. In other words, the model of the behaviour of the system provides the link between what a system is and what it does. In UML, **sequence diagrams** are used to order the method calls between objects, and **collaboration diagrams** show how the method calls use the structure of the relationships between objects. Since either one can be generated from the other, it is only the sequence diagram that is explained here.

A sequence diagram takes a use case and provides a chronological view of the messages that pass between objects. In Figure 6.9, it is the use case 'request appointment' that is modelled.

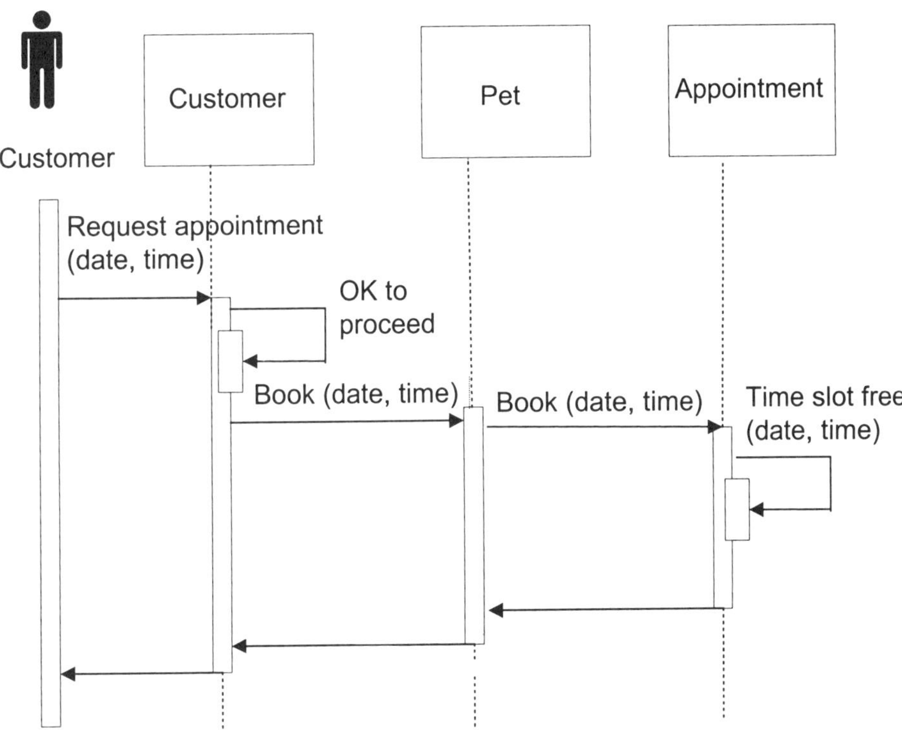

Figure 6.9: Example of a sequence diagram

In a sequence diagram, time moves from top to bottom and the involvement of objects is shown from left to right. Thus the diagram shows the involvement of objects through time. The lines between objects represent messages.

The same information can be represented in a collaboration diagram, although the emphasis is on the use of the static relationships between objects. State diagrams also model behaviour, and show how the objects in a system change over time. For example, during his or her 'lifetime' with the university, a student can be either proceeding, referred or graduating. Activity diagrams extend the model further by adding details that will be useful at implementation, such as dependencies between tasks and steps, and general workflow. However, these further modelling techniques are not explored here, as the intention is only to give an appreciation of the concepts of object modelling and an idea of object model creation.

UML also provides notation to model system implementation issues using **component diagrams** and **deployment diagrams**. However, Part II has been concerned with conceptual modelling and is not intended to be a definitive guide to UML.

As with any successful modelling approach, object modelling is an iterative process and the set of diagrams that comprise the model are refined and enhanced, as more information becomes available. It is self-evident that all the diagrams that make up the model should be consistent. Modelling tools such as Rational Software's Rational Rose aid consistency, and provide speed and integration in object-oriented model development.

Summary

- Object modelling represents an alternative modelling approach to entity-relationship and relational modelling.
- Object modelling models data and activity.
- The unified modelling language (UML) represents a well-adopted modelling language and has software support.
- Through object modelling, we can see what the system is, what the system does and how the system behaves.

Exercises

1. Do you find it easier to view the business world in terms of objects or data structures? Explain your preference.
2. Draw an outline class model for a university timetabling system.
3. Draw an outline class model for a library.
4. Draw a use case diagram for a university enrolment system. Add a use case description for one of the use cases.
5. Draw a use case diagram for taking out a loan. Add a use case description for one of the use cases. What exceptions may be described in further scenarios?
6. Draw a sequence diagram for registering a new customer for a bank.

7. Draw a sequence diagram for accepting an academic paper for publication.
8. For part of an organisation of your choice, such as a university, hospital or business department, create an object model comprising an outline class diagram, two or three use case diagrams, use case descriptions and a sequence diagram for each use case. Ensure that your diagrams are consistent. Compare and contrast the object model with a data structure model.

Further reading

Bennet, S., McRob, S. and Farmer, R. (1999) *Object Oriented Systems Analysis and Design,* McGraw Hill, Maidenhead.

Booch, G. (1991) *Object Oriented Design with Applications,* Benjamin Cummings, Menlo Park.

Martin, J. and Odell, J. (1997) *Object Oriented Methods,* Prentice Hall

Page-Jones, M. (1999) *Fundamentals of Object Oriented Design in UML,* Longman, London.

Rumbaugh, J., Jacobson, I. and Booch, G. (1999) *Unified Modelling Language Reference Manual,* Addison Wesley, London.

Stevens, P. and Pooley, R. (2000) *Using UML: Software Engineering with Objects and Components,* Addison Wesley, Harlow.

Part III: Implementation

In Part I we looked at the database approach as a whole and considered in particular the importance of organisational analysis and the roles of personnel in this approach. In Part II we looked at developing the various data models, which represent a stage towards developing the database. We examined, in particular, entity-relationship modelling, relational modelling and object modelling. A model is a representation of the 'real world', the universe of discourse, for which we are developing our database applications.

In Part III we look at how our database applications are implemented. A discussion of the commonly used database language SQL begins Part III. SQL can be used to create the database structure designed through relational modelling. It can also be used to add the data populating the tables and query the database to produce reports. We then look at two database management systems. In Chapter 8 PC databases are discussed using the Access database management system and this is followed in Chapter 9 by a discussion of corporate database applications using Oracle on larger computers.

Further chapters are provided on the implementation environment, which discusses in particular distributed databases and client-server computing. We then consider database applications in an Internet environment. Part III concludes with a chapter on tools that support database implementation, and again we use Oracle as exemplar, and one on security issues, which are a major concern in an environment where data is shared.

7

Structured Query Language (SQL)

7.1 Introduction

In Part II we looked at relational modelling and normalisation. SQL provides a standard data definition language and data manipulation language for use with all relational database management systems (DBMS) and therefore it conforms to the relational data model. All access to the database is through SQL, whether for ad hoc user queries, those embedded in an application or a web-based enquiry. Therefore, it is important to understand how SQL operates in order to make good design decisions. This chapter demonstrates standard SQL for both data manipulation and data definition, and goes on to discuss extended and embedded SQL.

7.2 Standard SQL operations for user queries

(a) Database model

In this section we discuss the way in which SQL is used to manipulate data in the database. Using the notation introduced in Chapters 4 and 5, the demonstration that follows is based on the Entity-Relationship diagram shown as Figure 7.1.

The tables from the diagram have the following entity descriptions:

STUDENT (STUDENTID, STUDENTNAME, DATEOFBIRTH, COURSEID)

COURSE (<u>COURSEID</u>, COURSENAME, LEVEL)

MODULE-GROUP (<u>COURSEID, MODULEID</u>, WEIGHTING)

MODULE (<u>MODULEID</u>, MODULENAME, MODULEMANAGER, RECOMMENDEDTEXT)

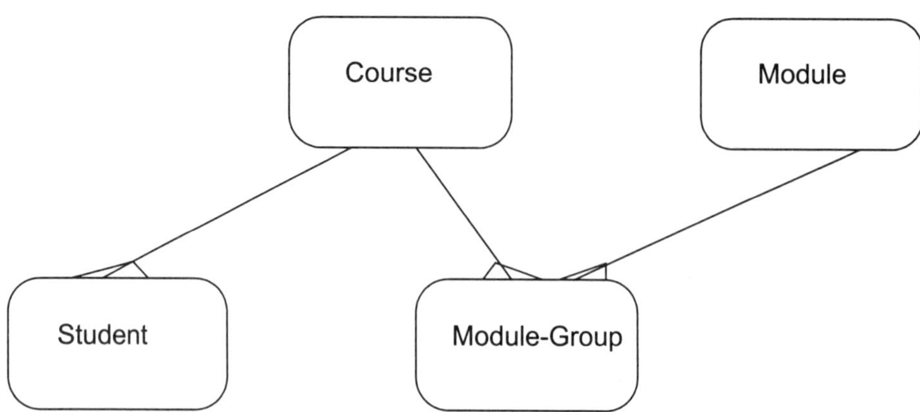

Figure 7.1: A simplified information system using a database

The tables have been populated below with examples of data.

STUDENT

STUDENTID	STUDENTNAME	DATEOFBIRTH	COURSEID
123	Biggs	06-06-1982	AM6
124	Trafford	23-04-1980	AM5
125	Hughes	28-03-1981	AM7
127	Wilson	06-02-1978	AM6
129	Ashton	30-07-1980	AM5
130	Brundell	15-07-1981	AM6
132	Pearce	03-10-1980	AM6

COURSE

COURSEID	COURSENAME	LEVEL
AM5	MBA	4
AM6	MSc IS	4
AM7	MBA PS	4

MODULE-GROUP

COURSEID	MODULEID	WEIGHTINGS
AM5	125	30/70
AM5	142	30/70
AM5	201	50/50
AM5	218	100
AM5	324	30/70
AM5	516	50/50
AM5	518	100
AM5	637	40/60
AM6	125	50/50
AM6	144	30/70
AM6	201	30/70
AM6	220	100
AM6	337	100
AM6	510	50/50
AM7	142	50/50
AM7	144	50/50
AM7	201	40/60
AM7	218	100
AM7	638	30/70

MODULE

MODULEID	MODULENAME	MODULEMANAGER	RECOMMENDEDTEXT
125	Corporate Strategy	Jenkinson	Stein & Mortimer
142	Law	Taylor	Henderson
144	Human Resource Management	Gilles	Edwards & Hunter
201	Information Management	Arinze	Jacobs
218	Management Accounting	Talbot	Smith & Koskinen

220	Data Management	Bailey	Avison & Cuthbertson
324	Information Systems	Day	Avison & Fitzgerald
337	Knowledge Management	O'Keefe	Farringdon
510	IS Security	Williamson	Warman
516	Marketing	Goldfield	Barrington & Leven
518	Organisational Behaviour	Morgan	Dibble
637	Organisational Design	Newington	Gaban-Tino
638	Public Sector Management	Tansey	Rose & Chapman
712	Politics	Tansey	Barnaby

(b) Manipulating single tables

SQL, like Access (see Chapter 8), uses the more inexact but more popular language of table, row and column, rather than relation, tuple and attribute, and therefore this chapter adopts the same terminology. The data design described above allows a variety of operations. For example, given a student identifier it is possible to discover the main recommended texts for a particular student by first determining the course, then the set of modules on that course and then finally determining the recommended text for each module.

The simplest operations can be executed on single tables. These operations allow the user to add, delete, amend and display data in a wide variety of formats.

To add a row, for example a new student to the student table, the insert operation is used. The VALUE clause must have, as parameters, the value of the individual data items. The example below adds student 134 to the table. Her name is Plowright, her birthday is on 18th May and she has enrolled on course AM6.

```
INSERT   INTO STUDENT     VALUES (134,PLOWRIGHT,18-05-1983,AM6)
```

Partial rows can be added to the table. For example, if the DATEOFBIRTH was not known, the remaining data elements could be added, as shown below.

```
INSERT   INTO STUDENT     (STUDENTID,STUDENTNAME,COURSEID)
                          VALUES (134,PLOWRIGHT,AM6)
```

Notice that the required columns have to be identified if values are not being added to every element of a row. The unknown elements will have a null value.

Rows are deleted by using conditional statements. The following SQL statement removes a single student record.

```
DELETE          STUDENT
WHERE           STUDENT.STUDENTID = '124'
```

This statement removes the student whose name is 'Trafford' in the STUDENT table.

Groups of rows can be removed, as follows:

```
DELETE          STUDENT
WHERE           STUDENT.COURSEID = 'AM6'
```

The SQL statement above removes all students with a COURSEID 'AM6'. In the example tables, this would remove four student records: Biggs, Wilson, Brundell and Pearce.

As with INSERT and DELETE, changes can be made to data elements in a row or group of rows using the UPDATE statement. For example, the following SQL statement changes the course on which Wilson is enrolled from 'AM6' to 'AM5'.

```
UPDATE          STUDENT
SET             COURSEID = 'AM5'
WHERE           STUDENTID = '127'
```

Alternatively, all 'AM6' student records could be altered to read 'AM5' by the following statement:

```
UPDATE          STUDENT
SET             COURSEID = 'AM5'
WHERE           COURSEID = 'AM6'
```

Notice that although the SQL commands are easy to construct and understand, they do require the user to know the SQL syntax, and the structure and identity of the data in the database.

(c) Manipulating a subset of a table and the SELECT statement

Many queries require the display of a sub-set of a table, sometimes known as a projection in relational algebra (see our companion web site for a description of this relational language). The sub-set may be a sub-set of rows, a sub-set of columns or a combination of some rows and columns. For example, the query may be on STUDENTNAME and DATEOFBIRTH for STUDENTID with a particular COURSEID (projecting a sub-set of rows).

```
SELECT      STUDENTID, STUDENTNAME, DATEOFBIRTH, COURSEID
FROM        STUDENT
WHERE       COURSEID = 'AM6'
```

This query results in the table below:

STUDENTID	STUDENTNAME	DATEOFBIRTH	COURSEID
123	Biggs	06-06-1982	AM6
127	Wilson	06-02-1978	AM6
130	Brundell	15-07-1981	AM6
132	Pearce	03-10-1980	AM6

Instead of listing all the column names, an asterisk (*) can be used in the SELECT command where all the attributes in the table are required, so that the following example has the same result as the preceding example. Note that the original table of data is unaltered by any projection.

```
SELECT  *
FROM    STUDENT
WHERE   COURSEID = 'AM6'
```

Alternatively, the query may ask for a projection of just DATEOFBIRTH for all STUDENTID. The result is a sub-set of columns.

```
SELECT  DATEOFBIRTH
FROM    STUDENT
```

This query results in the table below.

DATEOFBIRTH

06-06-1982
23-04-1980
28-03-1981
06-02-1978
30-07-1980
15-07-1981
03-10-1980

A combination of a sub-set of rows and columns can be projected giving, for example, the DATEOFBIRTH of all students on a particular COURSEID.

```
SELECT  DATEOFBIRTH
FROM    STUDENT
WHERE   COURSEID = 'AM5'
```

The following table represents the projection of the date of birth of students Trafford and Ashton.

DATEOFBIRTH
23-04-1980
30-07-1980

The SQL SELECT command allows duplicate rows, and so does not necessarily project normalised data. In the example above, displaying the list of student dates of birth, duplicate rows are acceptable. However, consider a query to discover the range of courses studied.

The following SQL command delivers the table below:

```
SELECT  COURSEID
FROM    STUDENT
```

COURSEID
AM6
AM5
AM7

AM6
AM5
AM6
AM6

The duplicate rows here are unacceptable, since only the range of courses is required. In SQL, using the DISTINCT qualifier solves this problem, as shown below.

```
SELECT   DISTINCT COURSEID
FROM     STUDENT
```

The command now returns the table below.

COURSEID
AM6
AM7
AM5

More than one condition can be used in the SELECT statement.

```
SELECT   STUDENTID
FROM     STUDENT
WHERE    COURSEID = 'AM6' AND DATEOFBIRTH > 01-01-1981
```

For example, the above statement results in the table shown below. Notice that it is possible to use arithmetic operations on dates, provided they have been stored in a date format, and not as character strings.

STUDENTID
123
130

In addition, multiple values can be accepted, as in the example shown below.

```
SELECT   STUDENTID
```

```
FROM     STUDENT
WHERE    COURSEID IN ['AM6', 'AM5'] AND DATEOFBIRTH > 01-01-1981
```

Here, the resulting table would contain the STUDENTID for all the students in the example STUDENT table on courses AM6 or AM5 and with a birth date greater than 1st January 1981.

The operands <, > and = can be used, as can the key words AND, OR, NOT and IN in a variety of combinations. So, by selecting and projecting sub-sets of columns and rows based on a variety of conditions it is possible to view the table from a number of perspectives. The better the design of the data in the database, the greater the number of querying options.

One or more attributes can be chosen to sequence the table resulting from a query by adding the ORDER BY clause. In the following example, the list of students is arranged in ascending date of birth order.

```
SELECT      STUDENTNAME
FROM        STUDENT
WHERE       COURSEID = 'AM6'
ORDER BY    DATEOFBIRTH
```

The delivered table is shown below.

STUDENTNAME
Wilson
Pearce
Brundell
Biggs

Standard SQL has five functions built-in, shown in the following table.

Function	*Returns*
AVG	Mean average value of a numeric column
COUNT	Number of rows in a table
MAX	Maximum value in a numeric column

MIN	Minimum value in a numeric column
SUM	Calculated total value of a numeric column

```
SELECT  COUNT(*)
FROM    STUDENT
```

For example, the above statement returns the value ‘7’, and that below gives ‘06-06-1982’ as the answer.

```
SELECT  MAX(DATEOFBIRTH)
FROM    STUDENT
```

The built-in functions can be applied to groups of rows by using the GROUP BY clause. An example is given below.

```
SELECT          COURSEID, COUNT(*)
FROM            STUDENT
GROUP BY        COURSEID
```

The example above returns the table

COURSEID	COUNT
AM6	4
AM5	2
AM7	1

(d) Manipulating more than one table

Some queries need to access more than one table to retrieve the desired data. For example, taking the tables introduced at the beginning of the chapter, it is possible to find a list of MODULEMANAGERS given a COURSEID. The data could be requested by the following series of SELECT statements:

```
SELECT  MODULEID
FROM    MODULE-GROUP
WHERE   COURSEID = ‘AM7’
```

MODULEID
142
144
201
218
638
712

```
SELECT  MODULEMANAGER
FROM    MODULE
WHERE   MODULEID IN[142,144,201,218,638,712]
```

MODULEMANAGER
Taylor
Gilles
Arinze
Talbot
Tansey
Tansey

However, the query can be made in a single statement, thus:

```
SELECT  MODULE.MODULEMANAGER
FROM    MODULE
WHERE   MODULE.MODULEID IN
                (SELECT  MODULE-GROUP.MODULEID
                 FROM    MODULE-GROUP
                 WHERE   MODULE-GROUP.COURSEID = 'AM7')
```

Here, the table name is stated, and separated from the attribute name by a full stop. The use of the table name may not always be necessary. However, the use of the table name makes the example easy to read.

Nested SELECTS, like those demonstrated above, project data from a single table. However, some queries may require a join of tables. The result of any SQL operation is a single table that comprises all the data requested, even when the data requested is derived from a number of tables, as in the examples below.

For example, the following SQL SELECT statement delivers the STUDENTNAME and COURSENAME by joining the STUDENT and COURSE tables.

```
SELECT  STUDENT.STUDENTNAME, COURSE.COURSENAME
FROM    STUDENT, COURSE
WHERE   STUDENT.COURSEID = COURSE.COURSEID
```

The result is as follows:

STUDENTNAME	COURSENAME
Biggs	MSc IS
Trafford	MBA
Hughes	MBA PS
Wilson	MSc IS
Ashton	MBA
Brundell	MSc IS
Pearce	MSc IS

For an example delivering data from three tables, the following statement displays STUDENTNAME, WEIGHTING and MODULENAME for a particular STUDENTID.

```
SELECT  STUDENT.STUDENTNAME, MODULE-GROUP.WEIGHTING, MODULE.MODULENAME
FROM    STUDENT, MODULE-GROUP, MODULE
WHERE   STUDENT.STUDENTID = 125
        AND
        STUDENT.COURSEID = MODULE-GROUP.COURSEID
        AND
        MODULE-GROUP.MODULEID = MODULE.MODULEID
```

The resulting table is as follows:

STUDENTNAME	WEIGHTING	MODULENAME
Biggs	50/50	Law

Biggs	50/50	Human Resource Management
Biggs	40/60	Information Management
Biggs	100	Management Accounting
Biggs	30/70	Public Sector Management
Biggs	30/70	Politics

This short introduction to SQL is intended to convey the power and flexibility of SQL as a data manipulation language. For a more in-depth tutorial, the reader needs to turn to one of the texts suggested at the end of this chapter.

7.3 Data definition

In this section, we discuss the use of SQL as a data definition language. There are three basic commands for data definition: CREATE, ALTER and DROP. These commands can be used for tables, views and indexes.

The CREATE command specifies a new table, view or index by giving it an identity and detailing its columns. Each column is given a name, a data type and sometimes some constraints on possible values. The data type may be one of those listed in the table below, although some SQL derivatives allow different data types to be specified.

Key Word	Data Type	Description
DATE	Date	Calendar date in variety of formats
INTEGER	Numeric	Whole number
SMALLINT	Numeric	Small integer
FLOAT	Numeric	Floating point
DECIMAL(i,j)	Numeric	Decimal i digits & j decimal places
CHAR(n)	Character	n number of characters
VARCHAR(n)	Character	Variable length, not exceeding n characters

The tables derived from CREATE statements are known as base tables. The following statement creates the base table for STUDENT, as used in the data manipulation example in Section 7.2 above.

```
CREATE  TABLE STUDENT
```

```
(STUDENTID CHAR(3) NOT NULL
STUDENTNAME CHAR(30) NOT NULL
DATEOFBIRTH DATE
COURSEID CHAR(3)
PRIMARY KEY (STUDENTID))
```

It may sometimes be necessary to restrict the data that is available to specified users. For example in the STUDENT data, it may be that the senior administrator is able to view some of the data for all the students. This restriction represents a sub-set of columns in the STUDENT table. The course administrator may only be allowed access to the data for a particular course. A course is a sub-set of rows in the STUDENT table. It may be appropriate, however, for the student counsellor to have only partial data on some students. The student counsellor view is a sub-set of rows and columns. The varying requirements are achieved in SQL using the keyword VIEW. To create a view that is a sub-set of columns, a SELECT command is used, as in the example below.

```
CREATE VIEW ENROLMENT
        AS SELECT STUDENTNAME, STUDENTID
        FROM STUDENT
```

For a view of a sub-set of rows, the WHERE clause is added.

```
CREATE VIEW COURSELIST
        AS SELECT *
        FROM STUDENT
        WHERE COURSEID = 'AM5'
```

Sub-sets of rows and columns combined require both the attribute list and the WHERE clause:

```
CREATE VIEW MATURELIST
        AS SELECT STUDENTNAME
        FROM STUDENT
        WHERE DATEOFBIRTH < 01-01-80
```

Tables are usually accessed either sequentially or through the use of indexes. Using indexes to retrieve data is usually quicker, as less data is stored in an index. Indexes are also built using CREATE. For example, STUDENTID can be made unique by the SQL command creating an index called STUDIND below.

```
CREATE  UNIQUE INDEX STUDIND
        ON STUDENT(STUDENTID)
```

Indexes can be created using non-key attributes and are not required to use only unique values. The following statement uses COURSEID in STUDENT.

```
CREATE  INDEX   COURSEIND
                ON STUDENT(COURSEID)
```

The ALTER TABLE command is used to add or change columns in a table. Any alterations to a table structure may corrupt the data in the table. Although most DBMS have facilities to recover data following structural changes, it is safer to first create the new table. Data can then be moved from the old table into the newly created table before finally deleting the old table, together with its views and indexes. The ALTER command has the format shown in the example below that adds a new column, ALEVELSCORE to the STUDENT table.

```
ALTER   TABLE   STUDENT
        ADD     ALEVELSCORE     INTEGER
```

DROP TABLE is used for deleting a table, and removes all the views and indexes associated with the named table. The following example deletes the STUDENT table.

```
DROP    TABLE   STUDENT
```

Individual views and indexes can be removed, leaving the table intact. Therefore the following two SQL statements delete a view and an index for the STUDENT table while leaving the STUDENT table unaltered.

```
DROP    VIEW    MATURESTUDENT
DROP    INDEX   XCOURSE
```

All of the commands in the data definition repertoire have the power to restructure the database, and the responsibility for the creation, alteration and deletion of tables, views and indexes normally rests with the database administrator (DBA), as discussed in Chapter 3.

7.4 Extending SQL

SQL has an ANSI standard, that is, it has been accepted by the American National Standards Institute as a United States standard. In the computing context, this usually implies an international standard. Partly as a consequence, one of the benefits of SQL is its portability. However, DBMS such as Oracle have extended SQL, and these extensions are peculiar to the proprietary software, providing tools for special circumstances. Extensions can add greater power and flexibility to SQL, with each supplier producing a version that is 'better than standard'. Extensions may cause problems with portability. However, since portability is so desirable, providers of DBMS such as Oracle allow data and applications in other DBMS, such as DB2 and Sybase, to be used through the use of translating software between non-standard SQLs.

Extensions may add extra data types to data definition, or new clauses and constraints to data manipulation allowing the use of SQL for object-oriented development or web-based applications, for example. SQL was originally developed for use with relational databases. However, the interest in an object-oriented approach has led many DBMS providers to develop extensions to SQL to allow for the definition and manipulation of objects. For example Oracle's new data types, CLOB, NCLOB and BLOB are used to store large objects, and a BFILE is used as a pointer to non-Oracle data. In addition, some DBMS allow users to define new data types.

Many of the extensions, such as Oracle's Cluster or Function-based indexes, are intended to increase efficiency in certain circumstances. Oracle8 also allows for partitioning of tables and materialised views, a form of data warehousing (see Chapter 14). A DBMS may come with tools for tuning SQL statements to improve their efficiency. The criteria for improvement lie with the database administrator who understands the whole of the database and whose job it is to enforce priorities. Oracle's SQL Analyze utility is an example of SQL tuning. Optimisation is discussed further in Chapter 12.

Oracle's PL/SQL is an example of a procedural language extension to SQL that adds the programming constructs of sequence, iteration and selection to a series of SQL statements for data manipulation. PL/SQL procedures are compiled and stored in the database. The latest version of PL/SQL also provides a toolkit for web-based development. The advantage of PL/SQL over another host language is that it has been created around SQL, and is therefore fully compatible with SQL methods of data manipulation. PL/SQL is further discussed, with examples, in Chapter 9.

7.5 Embedded SQL

SQL statements can be embedded into a host language such as Visual Basic, C++ or Java. Any SQL statement, such as those used for demonstration above, can be embedded in the program. The full power of the SQL data manipulation statements already discussed, such as the SELECT statement, is maintained in the host language version. Such statements will be prefixed with a special character or characters that enable identification by the DBMS precompiler as being SQL, and different from the host language. A fragment of a program written in VBScript, a development from Visual Basic for an Internet environment, and incorporating SQL statements is shown below.

```
<%@LANGUAGE="VBSCRIPT"%>
<%
set Recordset1 = Server.CreateObject("ADODB.Recordset")
set oConn = Server.createobject("ADODB.Connection")
oConn.ConnectionString = "DRIVER=SQL Server;SERVER=JKL-
SCUN;UID=gs;APP=Microsoft Development Environment;WSID=ITS87-
TEMP;DATABASE=clippings;Regional=Yes;PWD=gs"
oConn.open
Recordset1.ActiveConnection = oConn
Recordset1.CursorType = 0
Recordset1.CursorLocation = 2
Recordset1.LockType = 3
Recordset1_numRows = 0
if request("SubjectArea") <> "" then
 Recordset1.Open "SELECT * FROM articles where
 OfInterest like '%" & right("0" & request("Subject Area"),2) & "%'", oConn
elseif request("FreeSearch") <> "" then
 strSQL = "SELECT *,DATEDIFF(day, getdate(),dateadded) AS DaysSinceCurrent
FROM articles where " & Request("searchby") & " like '%"
& request("FreeSearch") & "%'"
 Recordset1.Open strSQL, oConn
else
 Recordset1.open "SELECT top 20 * FROM articles where Top20Flag > 0 order by
Top20Flag ", oConn
end if
%>
```

The statements are checked for correct SQL syntax and translated into the call statement of the host language. An alternative is to use subroutines to the DBMS library. However, this method takes time and may be subject to programmer error and is only adopted where there are significant efficiency gains to be made.

7.6 Conclusion

To conclude, it is worth reflecting on the importance of good SQL formulation with respect to issues already raised in this book. For example, the order in which SQL statements are executed has repercussions for integrity and speed, the power of SQL means that an apparently simple statement can have dramatic results. This is unlikely to be evident to an inexperienced user. Despite, therefore, its claims to be an easy language, good SQL code is more likely to be created by IS and IT people than business users.

Summary

- Although it was designed originally for DBMS based on the relational model, SQL provides a standard data definition language and data manipulation language for use with all database management systems.
- Although the SQL commands are easy to construct and understand, they do require the user to know the SQL syntax, and the structure and identity of the data in the database.
- The SQL SELECT statement in its various forms proves very effective for queries.
- There are three basic commands for data definition: CREATE, ALTER and DROP.
- Some DBMS, such as Oracle, have extended SQL to include commands not in the ANSI SQL command set.
- SQL statements can be embedded into a host language such as Visual Basic, C++ or Java

Exercises

1. Distinguish between data independence and data redundancy. How are they both keys to the database approach? When might some data redundancy be appropriate?

2. What is the difference between conventional file and database applications?
3. In what ways might a database be a model of an organisation?
4. Given the following entity-relationship diagram and the associated entity descriptions, write the SQL statements to create each table:

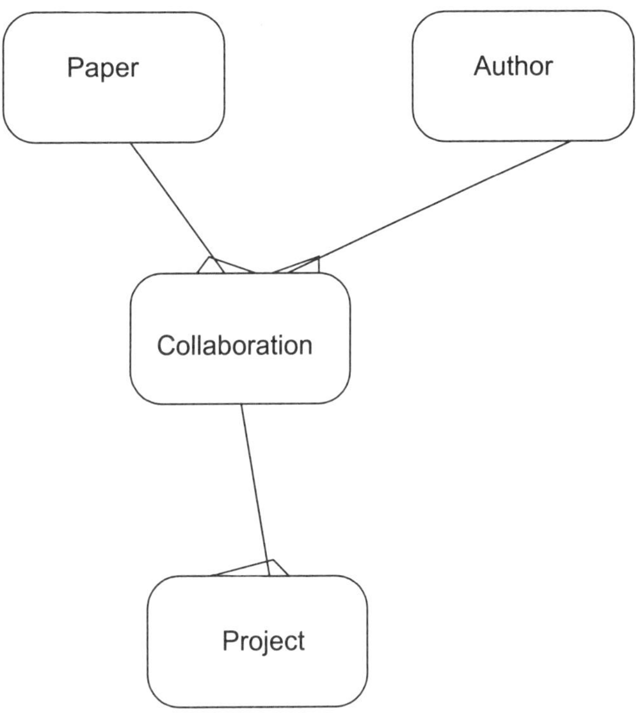

AUTHOR (<u>AuthorID</u>, LastName, FirstName, Qualifications, Institution)
COLLABORATION (<u>AuthorID, PaperID</u>, ProjectID, Remuneration)
PAPER (<u>PaperID</u>, Title, Journal, Volume, Issue, Pages)
PROJECT (<u>ProjectID</u>, ProjectName)

5. Alter the PROJECT table to include the attribute 'sponsor'.
6. Write the SQL statements to add data to populate the tables as shown below:

AUTHOR

AUTHORID	LASTNAME	FIRSTNAME	QUALIFICATIONS	INSTITUTION
U001	Rose	Derek	BA, MA	Ulster
E005	New	Frank	BSc, MBA	Edinburgh
N013	Ind	Paula	BA, PhD	Nottingham
C017	Barrett	Katrina	Beng, MSc	Cardiff

COLLABORATION

AUTHORID	PAPERID	PROJECTID	REMUNERATION
U001	LK001	E12003	£150
E005	LK001	E12003	£50
N013	PJ001	T67	£100
C017	PJ001	T67	£50
U001	LK002	E12003	£150
E005	PJ001	T67	£50
N013	LK002	E12003	£50
C017	PJ002	T69	£200

PAPER

PAPERID	TITLE	JOURNAL	VOLUME	ISSUE	PAGES
LK001	Next Steps for eGovernments	JGHI	12	3	333-340
LK002	eSolutions for eGovernments	JGHI	12	6	567-574
PJ001	Cross Border eCommerce	EJOP	5	1	86-98
PJ002	Food Safety & eCommerce	EJOP	6	2	110-123

PROJECT

PROJECTID	PROJECTNAME	SPONSOR
E12003	GLOOP	Roberts
T67	MINX	Williams
T68	POOKIE	James
T69	SOCKS	Martin
E12003a	GLOOP2	Martin

7. Perform the following data manipulations in SQL, adding your own IDs as required:
   a) Add a new author, Pekka Laine, BSc PhD from Jyvaskyla.
   b) Add Pekka's new paper with Frank New entitled 'The Finnish eExperience' for the GLOOP project, published in EJHI, Vol 2, Issue 1, pages 12-20.
   c) Delete the POOKIE project.
   d) Change all the references to E12003 in the COLLABORATION table to be E12003a.
8. Write SQL statements to return the following data:
   a) The ProjectName and Sponsor for all the PROJECTS

b) The PaperID, journal, volume, issue and pages for the PAPER entitled 'eSolutions for eGovernments'.
c) Title, LastName and FirstName for PaperID PJ001.
d) All the AUTHORS writing papers on the MINX project.

Further reading

Gruber, M. (2000) *Mastering SQL*, Sybex International.
Kline, K. and Kline, D. (2001) *SQL in a Nutshell*, O'Reilly, Farnham.
Taylor, A.G. (2001) *SQL for Dummies*, Hungry Minds Inc.

8

PC databases and Access

8.1 Introduction

Database management systems (DBMS) are software packages that manage large and complex file structures. At the time of writing there are two major types of database management system, those based on the relational model and those based on the object-oriented model. The former are by far the most common. However, some modern DBMS enable both models. Previous to this, hierarchical and network databases were common database management systems. Nowadays, however, these technologies are considered somewhat out of date. Nevertheless, details of hierarchical and network databases, such as IMS and IDMS, can be found on our companion web site, along with sections on hierarchical and network data models on which they are based.

DBMS make large databases available to a single user or a large number of users. The sharing of data can reduce the average cost of data access as well as avoiding duplicate, and therefore possibly inconsistent or irreconcilable, data. The various users that access the database may be department managers, clerical staff and data processing professionals. Databases can hold large amounts of data and the operations required on them can be complex. Correspondingly, DBMS are large and complex pieces of software.

Users of databases do not directly access the database. Instead they access the DBMS software. This translates the data requirements into accesses to the database itself, makes the accesses on computer storage devices, such as disks, and returns the results to the user in the form that the user requires.

Users see only subsets of the overall database, that is, the subsets that concern each particular user. These subsets are sometimes known as **external views**. The subsets that different users see can be very different and also very different from the data structures actually held on computer storage devices. Thus there is said to be strong **data independence** in a database environment. This data independence also means that when there are changes to the way the data is held on the database, even the devices themselves, this will not be seen by the users. Another advantage of data independence is that it enables **control** over the database. As we saw in Chapter 3, the database administration team can control access and ensure privacy and security requirements are fulfilled. Another gain is that the data need only be held once, even though the data is used by a number of users possibly in different ways. Thus there is far less **data redundancy** in a database environment, and there should be no data redundancy which is not known about by the database administrator.

Users may access the database using query languages, such as SQL, which was discussed in the previous chapter, or other query languages. Computer programmers and analysts may access the DBMS via programs written in a conventional computer programming language, such as Cobol or C++. In this context, these computer languages are often referred to as **host languages** in which SQL is embedded. A useful distinction is to look at conventional computer programming languages as being concerned with the *how* of a database operation, and a query language as being concerned with the *what.* We concern ourselves in this book on the likely ways in which users will access the database, not computer programmers. We will therefore not discuss conventional computer programming languages. Again, however, there are sections in the web site that deal with this.

Some ways to access the database are even more natural to the user. With the availability of a WIMP (windows, icons, menus and pointers) interface of the Apple Macintosh and MS Windows operating systems, the users can state their requirements through a series of menus. Alternatively they might complete soft copy forms. The most natural, natural language itself such as English, is still not a completely successful technology yet but it will surely not be long before most input to databases is made through dictating directly to the computer.

8.2 Microsoft Access on personal computers

In this chapter we look at databases on personal computers (PCs). In particular, we look at Microsoft Access, the database software that is part of the Microsoft Office suite of programs. The history of databases on PCs has been one of very rapid development. In the early days they were just the computer equivalent of a single user card index, for example, the patient records of a dentist. They were very restrictive in terms of the number of records that could be held, and they could also be restrictive in terms of their update, retrieval and sorting abilities. Nowadays they can match the most sophisticated DBMS used on large computers of a few years ago. This is due as much as anything to progress in hardware development, such as processing speeds, disk capacities, computer memory capacities and the like.

We will discuss the DBMS Oracle in the context of large computers, corporate and distributed databases in the next chapter, but there is even a version of Oracle available for use on PCs. Of course with distributed computing and client-server systems, the largest and most sophisticated database can also be accessed using PCs. It would be foolish to put numbers to speeds, maximum number of users, size of databases and so on as the technology changes so rapidly. All we can say for sure is that PC databases are likely to be smaller, with fewer users, using fewer tools, compared to corporate databases at any one time.

At the time of writing, there are three versions of Microsoft Access in common use, Access97, Access2000 and Access2002. We will discuss Access2000, being the most well used version. A discussion of Access requires a series of books, so we will look at aspects particularly pertinent to this book.

On opening Access, we see the screen as shown in Figure 8.1. It shows seven basic object types. 'Tables' are the relations, then there are options 'queries', 'forms' and 'reports' to help query the data in the database enter data conveniently or provide reports from the data respectively. The option 'pages', new to the 2000 version, enables the creation of web pages using the database. A 'Macro' performs a set of commands in sequence and a 'module' is a larger program in Visual Basic. These are used for more complex or non-standard uses for the database. The database will consist of a series of related tables, and associated queries, reports, forms and so on.

In Figure 8.2, we show the design form for designing a table. The table shown is that for the Order Details table that we used in Chapter 5 when we were illustrating the normalisation process. This table has a composite key (see the key icon to the left) of order number and item code. We have specified most fields as text and two fields as numeric. There are many other options, such as date/time, currency, automatically generated number (often used as a primary key), a yes/no alternative and hyperlink to a web address. You will notice that the Access interface has a 'look and feel' similar to other Microsoft products with a series of menus along the top (for manipulating files, editing and so on) and icons held in tool bars (for saving, printing, spell checking, creating key fields, accessing help facilities and so on).

Figure 8.1: Access basic options

For each field in the table we can define a number of properties (see Figure 8.3). The field size limits the number of characters for a text field, the format controls the display of the field in datasheet view (for example, currency, true/false type or percentage), decimal places is relevant for a numeric or currency field, the input mask is useful when, for example, including a plus sign and hyphens for an international phone number, a caption provides a label for the field, and a default value is useful when a field will normally have one value more than others and hence save some keying in. A validation rule ensures invalid data entering the database is less likely.

As we see in Figure 8.4, once we began to enter data in datasheet view, Access rightly prevented us from completing the data because rows of data would be formed with duplicate keys. According to the relational model, there should not be rows with duplicate keys.

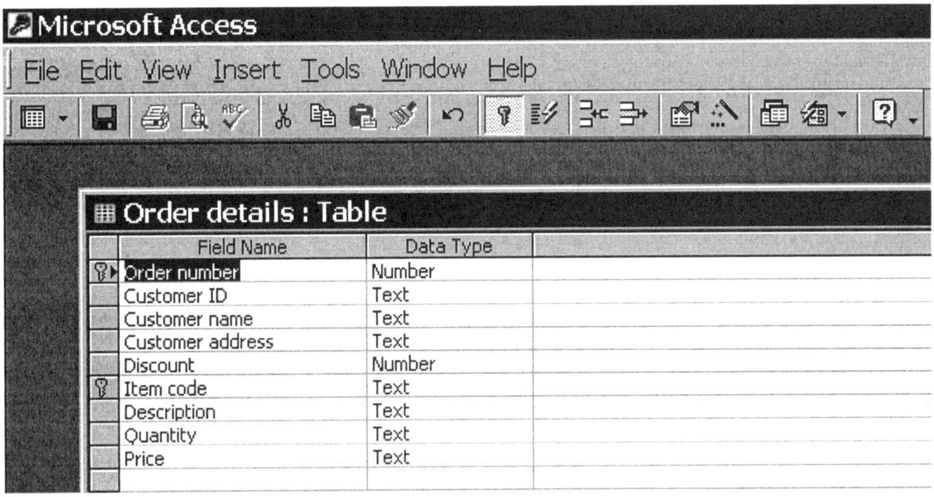

Microsoft Access

File Edit View Insert Tools Window Help

Order details : Table

Field Name	Data Type
Order number	Number
Customer ID	Text
Customer name	Text
Customer address	Text
Discount	Number
Item code	Text
Description	Text
Quantity	Text
Price	Text

Figure 8.2: Designing an Access table

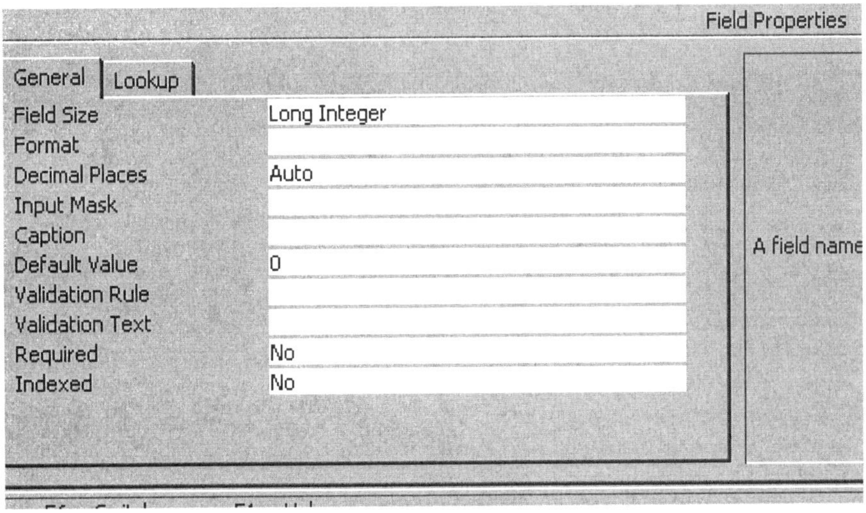

Field Properties

General Lookup

Field Size	Long Integer
Format	
Decimal Places	Auto
Input Mask	
Caption	
Default Value	0
Validation Rule	
Validation Text	
Required	No
Indexed	No

A field name

Figure 8.3: Field properties

New to Access 2000 is a wizard (tool) which analyses the tables on the database (Figure 8.5). In our order line table, the wizard has identified (through duplicate item codes and descriptions) data not in third normal form. The program will help us to create a new table of item code and description, linked to the order line table using the item code. Figure 8.6 shows the initial attempt at doing this with the relationship between the two tables being mapped.

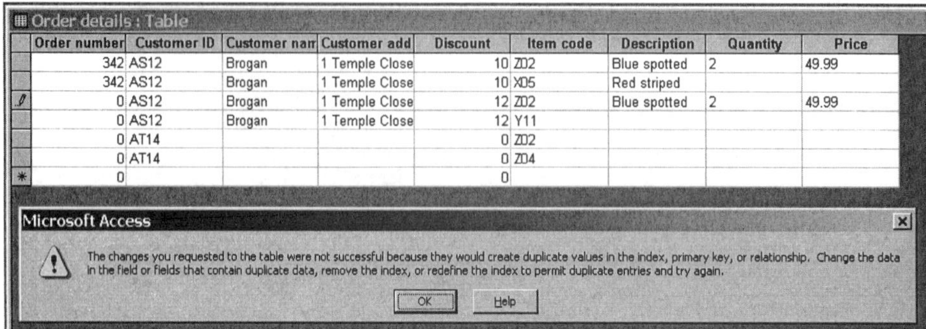

Order number	Customer ID	Customer nam	Customer add	Discount	Item code	Description	Quantity	Price
342	AS12	Brogan	1 Temple Close	10	Z02	Blue spotted	2	49.99
342	AS12	Brogan	1 Temple Close	10	X05	Red striped		
0	AS12	Brogan	1 Temple Close	12	Z02	Blue spotted	2	49.99
0	AS12	Brogan	1 Temple Close	12	Y11			
0	AT14			0	Z02			
0	AT14			0	Z04			
0				0				

Figure 8.4: Access warning message – duplicate keys

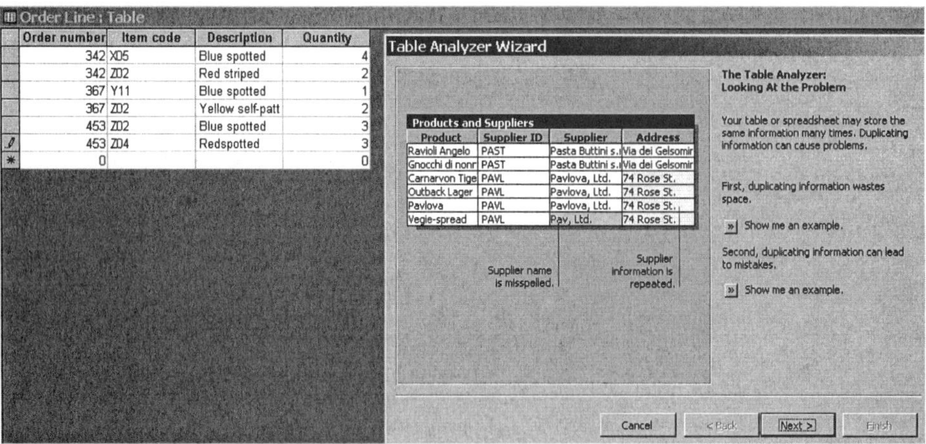

Order number	Item code	Description	Quantity
342	X05	Blue spotted	4
342	Z02	Red striped	2
367	Y11	Blue spotted	1
367	Z02	Yellow self-patt	2
453	Z02	Blue spotted	3
453	Z04	Redspotted	3
0			0

Figure 8.5: Access table analyser wizard

In Figure 8.7 we begin to create a query, again using an Access wizard, which is formed from data held in two tables: order details and order line. However, as the warning message informs us, we have not yet linked these tables together by a relationship. In Figure 8.8 we show how the relationship is formed using the field order number, to join the tables as it is in both relations, as our linking field. As shown in Figure 8.9, Access shows the relationship as one to many, with an infinity sign on the many side.

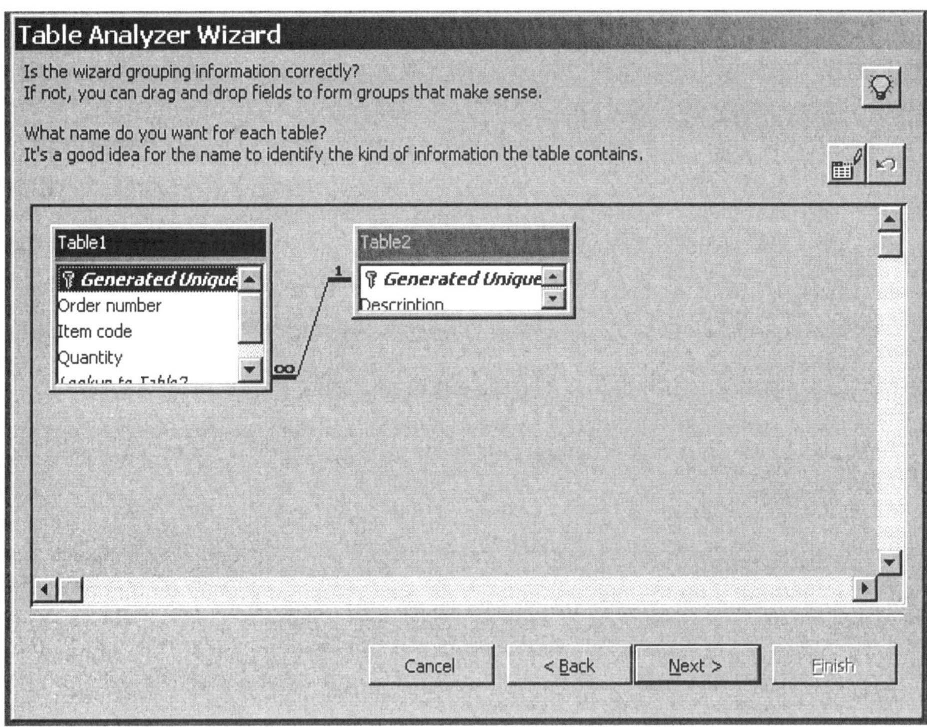

Figure 8.6: Access table analyser wizard creating a new table

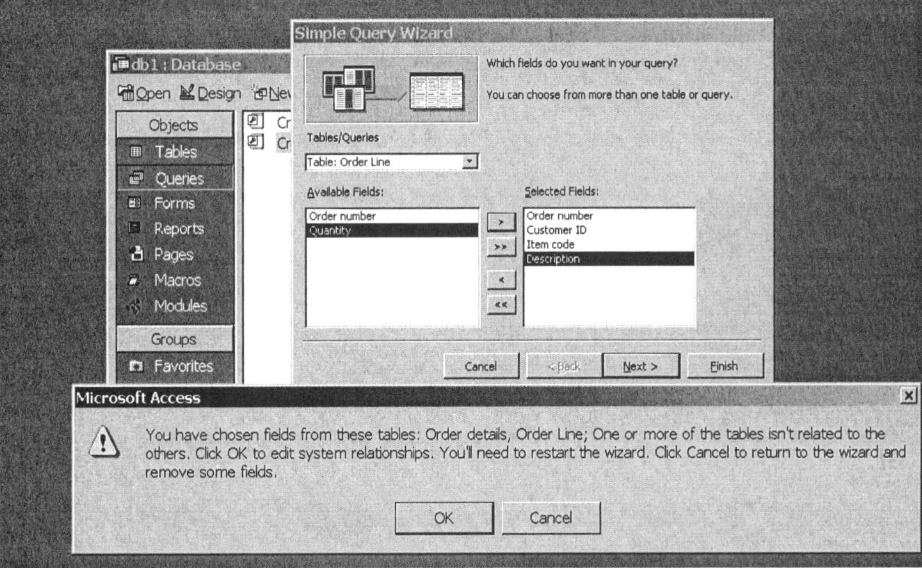

Figure 8.7: Creating a query

We notice in Figure 8.8 the possibility of enforcing referential integrity rules. The first of these states that you cannot enter data in the field that is used for the join in the related table, if the join field in the primary table does not have matching contents. The second rule prevents you deleting records from the primary table if there are matching records in the related table. Finally, you cannot edit primary key values in the primary table if related records exist. Like the rules for normalisation, these referential integrity rules help ensure that the database is well formed and easy to use.

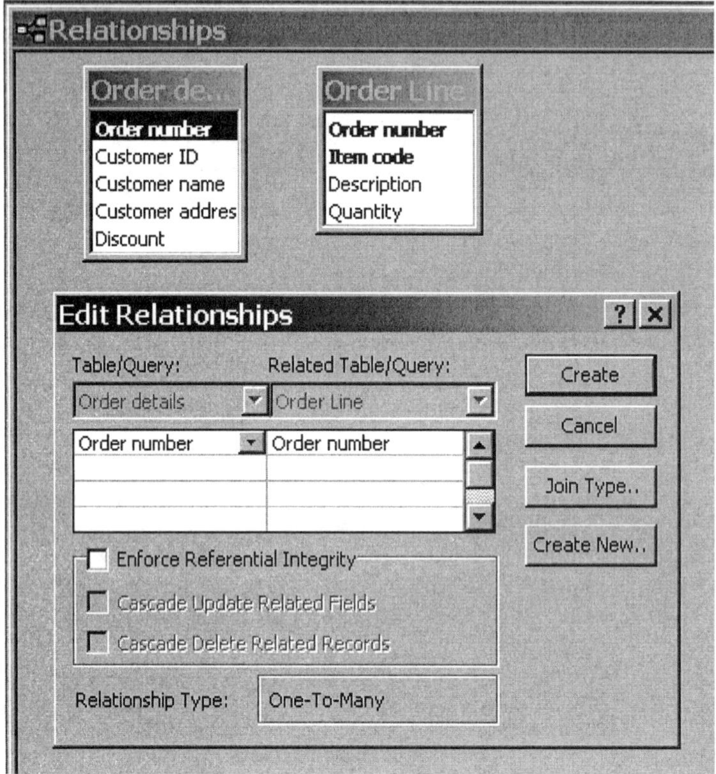

Figure 8.8: Establishing the relationship for the query

In Figure 8.10 we show the design for the query, including the opportunity to sort the query (sorting and searching are likely to be more efficient if the fields are indexed) and only show certain records in the criteria list. For example, we could have chosen to query only those customers who ordered a certain range of products. We did not choose to limit the number of records in any way and Figure 8.11 shows the full list. We can use SQL with Access as well as the query-by-example (QBE) method shown. Indeed, the equivalent SQL statement can be generated by Access, as shown in Figure 8.12. But constructing a query using QBE is more natural to the non-technical user and much easier than coding the equivalent SQL statement.

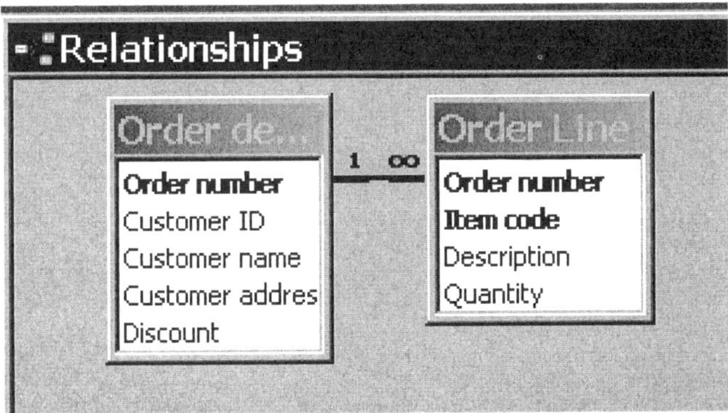

Figure 8.9: Access diagram of the relationship

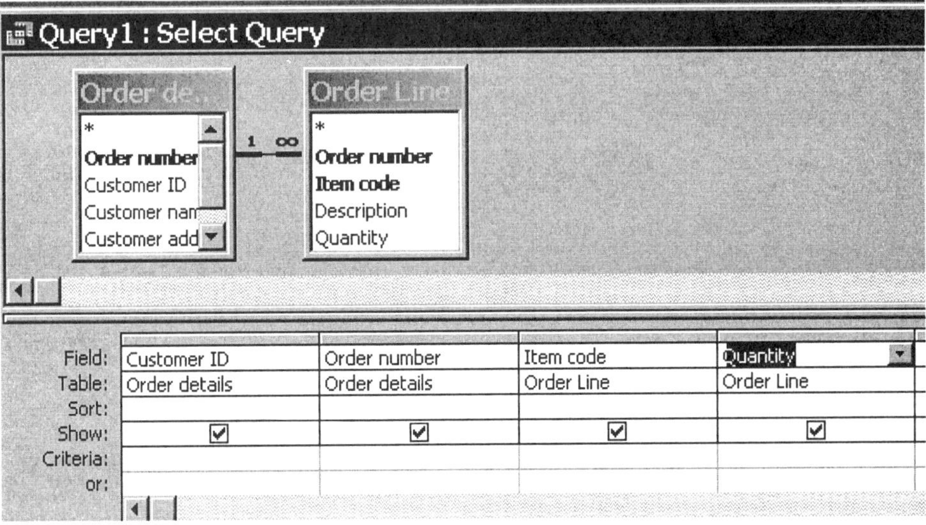

Figure 8.10: Access query

Forms for entering data can easily be created by using the form wizard. Figure 8.13 shows one stage in the process and Figure 8.14 shows the form created using one of the default styles. There are similar wizards for creating reports in all manner of styles and levels of detail.

Query order details : Select Query

Customer ID	Order number	Item code	Quantity
AS12	342	Z02	2
AS12	342	X05	4
AS12	367	Z02	2
AS12	367	Y11	1
AT14	453	Z02	3
AT14	453	Z04	3

Figure 8.11: Displaying the query results

Query order details : Select Query

```
SELECT [Order details].[Customer ID], [Order details].[Order number], [Order Line].[Item code], [Order Line].[Quantity]
FROM [Order details] INNER JOIN [Order Line] ON [Order details].[Order number]=[Order Line].[Order number];
```

Figure 8.12: The SQL statements for the query

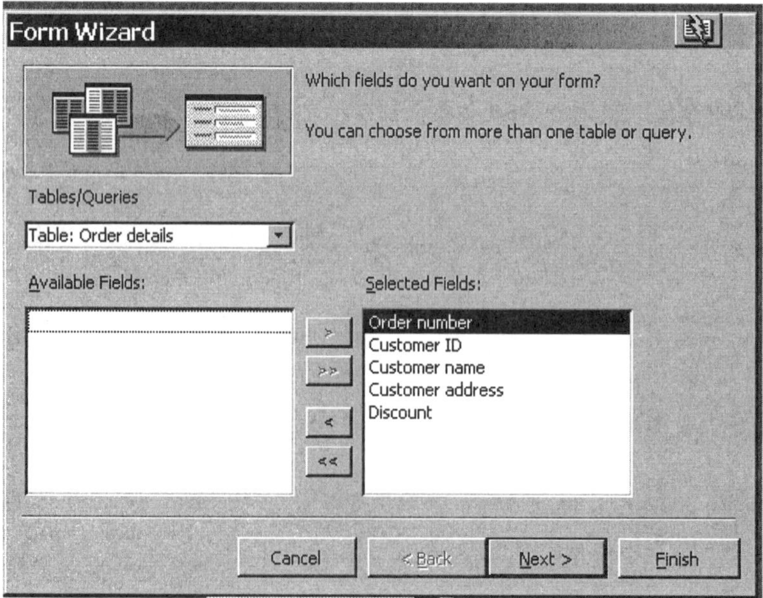

Figure 8.13: The form wizard

Access has a documentation tool as part of the analyser, and Figure 8.15 shows part of the automated documentation for the item table and Figure 8.16 that for the relationship between the item table and the order line table.

Access has a number of security features. A database can be opened read-only or exclusively (via a password). Access even enables encryption and decryption of the data.

As well as enquiries and reports, you can display data using charts, such as pie charts, line graphs, bar charts, column charts, area charts and so on. Figure 8.17 is a pie chart showing the different proportions of products ordered.

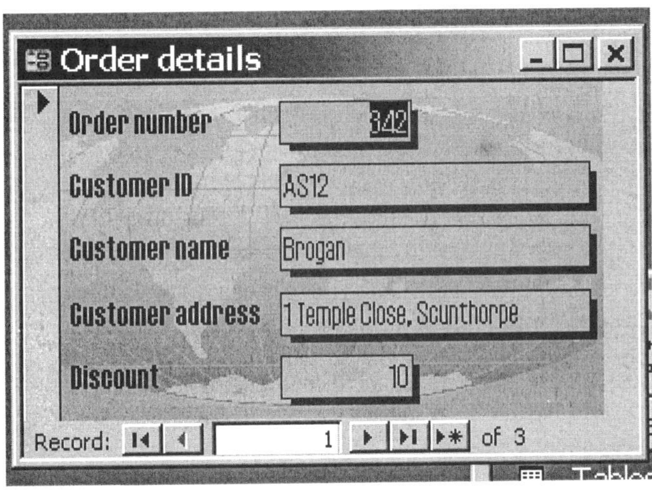

Figure 8.14: A wizard-generated form for order details

Macros are used to perform repeated actions such as opening tables and forms, regularly printing certain reports or answering particular queries, and finding particular records. Modules are programs written in the computer programming language Visual Basic for Applications. Compared to many computer-programming languages, VBA is much easier to use. It gives flexibility in using the database. When we add the much greater sophistications and individualised applications enabled by macros and modules, it is readily evident that Access is a very powerful database management system and yet available on personal computers.

Table: Item

Properties

Date Created:	23/05/2001 18:29:09	GUID:
Last Updated:	23/05/2001 18:30:27	NameMa
OrderByOn:	False	Orientati
RecordCount:	4	Updatabl

Columns

Name

Item code

AllowZeroLength:	False
Attributes:	Variable Length
Collating Order:	General
ColumnHidden:	False
ColumnOrder:	Default
ColumnWidth:	Default
Data Updatable:	False
DisplayControl:	Text Box
GUID:	Long binary data
Ordinal Position:	1

Figure 8.15: Access documentation tool – tables

Relationships

Relationships

ItemOrder Line

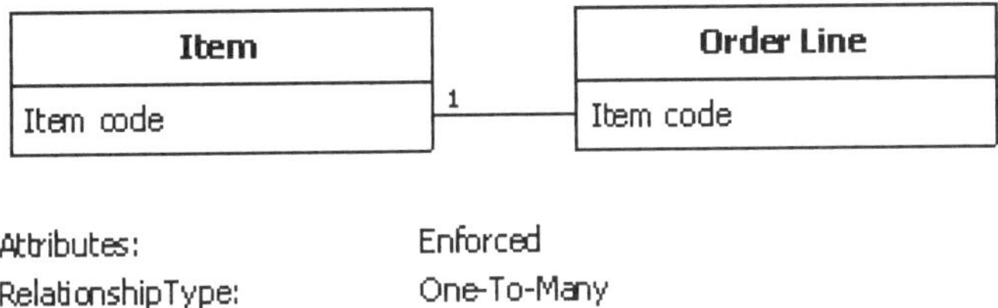

Figure 8.16: Access documentation tool – relationships

Order Line

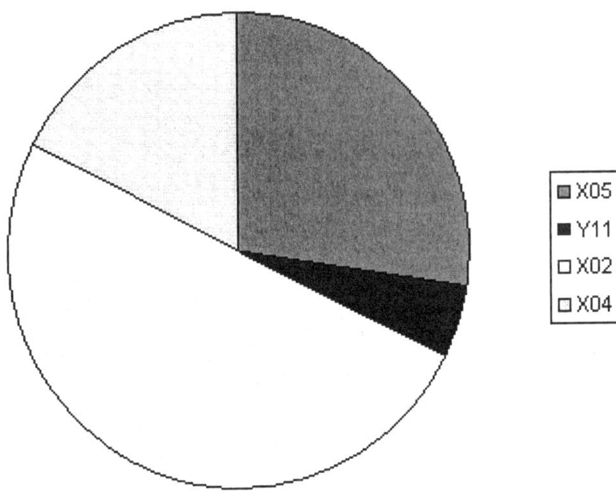

Figure 8.17: Pie chart

8.3 How to build an Access database

In this section we outline the processes involved when designing and building a database. It will be appropriate for smaller databases to be implemented on personal computers, hence we specify an 'Access database'. A database is a major integrated project and therefore it is appropriate to use a methodology of some sort. It is a good idea to plan and spend time on a thorough design as it is more difficult, though feasible, to make changes after implementation.

We would have started by agreeing the universe of discourse for the project, that is, the applications area or problem situation that we are addressing. Everything else will be external to this, part of the environment of the project. We may have outlined the various application areas in our information model. We may have done this through using the techniques described in section 2.5, maybe constructing a rich picture of the universe of discourse. We will have liaised with both business and information systems clients and managers, though in a small application area where an Access database may be appropriate, this group may consist of a very few people or even one – yourself.

Access is a relational database, so we will assume that we will follow entity-relationship and relational modelling that were discussed in Chapters 4 and 5. We might start with a pencil and paper and begin sketching our universe of discourse as a set of entities and relationships between them, maybe filling in some of the attributes, and at least think about the applications so that we ensure that as much as possible is thought of at this stage. It is easier to get it right now. We might suggest example tuples to test our understanding of the application area and database design.

Each of the entities is likely to become an Access table when we begin to implement the database on Access. We may think about which attributes will be used as primary keys for each of the tables. We will need to work on the relationships between tables and if some of the relationships are many-to-many, we will need join or junction tables to relate them. Again, a rough sketch can help the job of designing the conceptual model. We should think about normalising our relations, but as we saw, Access can help us even here.

We need to think about data entry. This will mean sketching input forms. We will try to keep them as simple as possible, but as we saw, Access will help us design these forms, even using the Access Wizard, which makes standard forms particularly easy to design. Check that standard data entry such as 'key in the customer sales orders' is catered for, and also (perhaps) less obvious tasks such as what to do if customers do not pay their bills. Each field on the tables needs to be specified, but there are standard data types such as numeric, date, switch as well as text. Our analysis may have detected homonyms or synonyms in our universe of discourse, and our models need to be consistent. Our investigation might have suggested events and operations to be effected on our database, and we will want to ensure these are feasible in our model.

Likely reports can be drafted now. Again, Access helps here, but it might be useful to sketch a few forms to get early reaction from users. Data in some reports may need to be grouped and sub-totaled. Some formulas may need to be designed where calculations are needed. Again, we might draft or design our queries using Access. We may suggest Access macros written in Visual Basic for Applications (VBA) that can automate the process of entering and retrieving data. This might be easier than writing SQL statements.

We will need to test and tune our Access database using sample and test data. There will follow a period of correcting and refining. This period will be less long if more thought is given to the earlier stages described in this section.

8.4 Conclusion

Microsoft Access is a DBMS designed for use on personal computers and smaller database applications. Larger DBMS, such as Oracle discussed in Chapter 9, are more appropriate for larger applications and are usually implemented on larger mainframe systems. Access is a relational system. It proves fairly easy to master the basics. Further, it proves a convenient implementation vehicle when developing applications developed using the approach described in this book.

Access2002 is part of the latest version of Microsoft Office (OfficeXP) just released at the time of writing. Many of the differences with Access2000 concern improvements in the user interface, a feature of this new version of Office. It is also more geared to web applications. Although there are many improvements, as far as this book is concerned, nothing has fundamentally changed in this version compared to Access2000.

Summary

- Database management systems (DBMS) are software packages that manage large and complex file structures and usually based on either the relational or object model or sometimes both models are catered for.
- DBMS provide data independence between the various user views of their data and data structures and how the data is stored physically on storage devices.
- Microsoft Access is a DBMS designed for use on personal computers and smaller database applications.
- Microsoft Access provides help to the user through its Wizard feature, which can be used when implementing standard applications. In particular, it helps the user implementing the tables, queries, forms and reports.
- More unusual or complex applications can be designed as macros or VBA applications. It is also to implement applications using SQL.

Exercises

1. For the entity-relationship diagrams that you created in exercises 3, 4, 6 or 7 of Chapter 4, implement these models in an Access database. It is not important which version of Access that you use. Follow the approach suggested in section 8.3 'How to build an Access database'. Did you change your model on implementation? If so, what was the reason?
2. Carry out exercises 6, 7 and 8 of Chapter 7, but this time implement the relations in an Access database and use the query facilities of Access rather than SQL. However, use Access to display the SQL statements. Are they the same as those you created in Chapter 7? If they are not, what is the reason?

Further reading

Oliver, P. R. M. and Kantaris, N. (2001) *Microsoft Access 2002 Explained,* Babani, London.

Viescas, J. L. (1997) *Running Microsoft Access 97,* Microsoft Press.

9

Corporate databases and Oracle

9.1 Introduction

In Chapter 8 we discussed PC databases. We created some tables and linked them to provide an illustration of the use of Access, mostly for ad hoc, stand-alone applications. The point was made that Access is capable of producing applications that only a few years ago would have required much greater resources, but the tremendous increase in power and capacity has brought that capability to the desktop. In addition, PC database software such as Access can be used to create multi-user systems and web-based applications of increasing sophistication.

And so the question remains, what can a large database such as Oracle do that something like Access cannot? Although Chapter 8 described Access development and argued that PC-based database systems proliferate, PC databases are not the major focus for this book. Most of our discussions take place with regard to the larger corporate environment. For example, Part I considers a database approach within the context of an information management strategy, assuming that a group of IT professionals exist within that environment dedicated to the development and maintenance of systems. Part II discusses the modelling of complex information systems. Many PC-based database systems do not need to be modelled in the same way. In many situations, this would be an unnecessarily complex and time-consuming way to develop applications using a PC database. Later in Part III we consider the implementation of a distribution strategy, database security practices and the design and development tools that are available for large-scale database implementation, but not normally for PC-based database applications. In Part IV we discuss the kind of database applications that large organisations develop and use.

Much of what separates Access and Oracle, therefore, is the difference between Chapter 8 and the rest of the book. For example, most of the tools described in Chapter 12 are not available for Access, many of the security issues discussed in Chapter 13 are not appropriate and the measures not applicable on a small scale, and the kind of implementation described in Chapter 10 relates only to large, complex organisations. And so this chapter begins by making clear the differences between a PC environment and a corporate database environment in the context of the book and with particular reference to Oracle – the leading corporate database provider. By way of illustration, a section on PL/SQL shows how a procedure using an Oracle database might be built. In reality it can be complex, and normally would require programming accomplished by IT professionals. This is much more likely to take place in a corporate environment.

9.2 Comparing PC databases and corporate databases

This book is therefore devoted to the design of an integrated information provision for, on the whole, larger organisations. It deals with database design and development, and applications such as customer relationship management, enterprise resource planning and data warehousing (all described in Part IV of the book). These are clearly strategic issues, of concern to and affecting the whole organisation, or at least a large part of it. Yet PC-based database applications developed in an ad hoc way by end-users proliferate in many businesses and homes today. So what is the difference?

- *Cost:* Cost is the first difference that might strike the potential buyer. MS Access often comes bundled with the rest of the MS Office software on a new PC. At the time of writing, the latest version of Access (2002) can be bought for under £300. In contrast, even a modest Oracle environment is a minimum of £30,000. Having said this, a personal edition of Oracle8 rivals Access for single-user applications. Indeed, Access itself can be expensive if the business needs an enterprise edition of MS SQL Server for multi-users.

- *Integratability:* Oracle enables a variety of database types and database applications to be integrated, as described in greater detail in Chapter 10. It is true that the latest version of Access can also do this to some extent, incorporating Oracle tables for example, using Microsoft's ODBC (Open DataBase Connectivity). However, Oracle is able to incorporate not just the tables but also database applications, and does so for all popular databases. This means that even transactions in an Oracle environment can span two or more database types so that a change to a customer order might initiate changes in tables of customer, agent and product data in Oracle, Sybase and DB2, for example. Consequently, although an Access database may be quite sufficient for, say, a clinician collecting and analysing blood pressure readings from clinic attendees, it is much less suitable for more complex applications. For example, Oracle would be able to integrate information systems after a merger or implement a purchasing system between a manufacturer and its various suppliers of raw materials.

- *Portability:* a different side to the same coin is that Oracle tables, and even rows of tables, can be used by all popular databases – including Access – subject to constraints (for example, on table size of the host database). In addition, Oracle runs on over 80 operating systems – anything that you are ever likely to come across – and is able to integrate systems across platforms. Again, this is discussed in further detail in Chapter 10. Access is built for a Windows environment. Users of other operating systems, most specifically Unix, are more likely to choose a product such as Oracle.

- *Volume:* In a straightforward situation Access can handle up to 50 users at the same time, and although the capacity for over 250 concurrent connections are claimed by Microsoft, practical experience suggests that in a database of some complexity, anything over 10 may cause difficulties. However, this is good performance for what is basically a desktop database, and adequate for many applications. In addition, well-written code and a sleek design can enable many users to use a single concurrent connection, thus multiplying the number of concurrent users without increasing the number of concurrent connections.

  On the other hand, Oracle can handle thousands of users concurrently, all performing different operations on the same data given a complex data design. Access can be used for web databases where the sites have a low hit rate and no high peaks. However, where user access is high, there are big peaks or use is unpredictable, or if availability is critical, then a larger-scale database is preferable.

Oracle can deal with terabyte-sized databases but can also be scaled down for small, personal database environments. The limitations of Access in a truly database environment inevitably leads to the creation of a number of databases, which of course compromises the integrity of corporate data and causes major problems for back-up and security because these facilities are comparatively unsophisticated.

- *Tools:* Tool support for database development is thoroughly explored in Chapter 12. The tools available for Oracle reflect corporate intentions and enable co-ordinated, large-scale development involving large, multi-disciplinary project teams, or focus on critical functions in large organisations such as human resources and supply chain management. A single developer creates the majority of Access databases – frequently a contractor or an end-user. The developer takes advantage of the speedy developmental tools of the PC and Windows environment to produce what is very often a stand-alone system of one or two tables. In this case, there is no requirement for a co-ordinated work group with auditing and change control procedures, and a lengthy modelling phase with full, active consultation with a range of business users or stringent security measures and business rules to enforce. There is no need to tune the database or optimise queries for maximum performance for that kind of system and in fact the system itself may be quite short-lived. We would expect an Oracle database, based on the organisation's underlying data model, to have a very long life span, and upgraded as new versions of Oracle are released.

- *Security:* Chapter 13 looks at security issues in some detail, and the comments there relate to large-scale database systems. With a large number of users, complex database architecture and a variety of operations possible with an Oracle database, the security measures must be equally sophisticated. Access has some security features, including password protection, and that is adequate for many systems. However, the password protection in Oracle systems is much more sophisticated and operates across platforms and systems, as already discussed. In fact, security is particularly emphasised in Oracle9i, which has been released at the time of writing, and it is advertised as being 'unbreakable'. However, it is in backup and recovery that the difference is particularly obvious, since Oracle can give online and partial back-ups and can recover from major failure, sometimes isolating a problem and leaving other users unaffected.

- *Data management:* Oracle has a read-only data dictionary that complies with the ideas in this book regarding the management of data; that is it contains all the data items and their tables, views and indexes as well as a variety of other metadata (data about data). The Oracle data dictionary also incorporates data integrity constraints such as the range of an employee's age or possible dates for a subscription renewal. Security aspects are included so that it is clear who has been granted what operations on what data. The data dictionary also stores a history of the use of the data. This is important to enable recovery from failure, and is part of the reason for Oracle's greater security. It is Oracle itself that makes changes to the data dictionary in response to data definition statements that create a table, row or column, or alter its data description in any way so that it remains a true representation of the database itself. The data dictionary is of vital importance to the role of data administrator, as described in Chapter 3. Access does not have a data dictionary of this comprehensiveness and will tend to be used in an environment where there are few or no IT professionals managing the data. Of course, this is perfectly acceptable in many environments, including home, small businesses and for dedicated end-user developed applications in large businesses.

- *End-user development:* Access has very good wizards (which support a user creating a database who is not technically knowledgeable) and a graphical user interface that allows non-IT professionals to generate quite sophisticated user interfaces quickly and easily. This is the appeal of Access to many end-users. It is useful for prototyping or rapid application development where feedback from the user can be quickly incorporated in the final design. The point should be made that Oracle's ability to interface with a variety of other databases allows developers to, for example, create forms in Access and use them on Oracle data. Further, Access database tables can be used in an Oracle environment.

It can be seen from the description above that the corporate database environment described, using Oracle as an example, is the kind of database environment that this book is mostly about. With Oracle we have all the functions of a full-scale database management system (DBMS) with the ability to add tools that enhance corporate information provision. Oracle will maintain overall high performance with large numbers of users using different applications. Access provides a database development environment, rather than a database management system in a true sense. It is of particular appeal to small teams or individuals creating simple systems for Windows applications where there is a small set of users. It is also appropriate where it is used as a design tool for use in rapid application development. In this case it may be followed by implementation of the operational system using Oracle or similar.

9.3 Programming in PL/SQL

Oracle has a procedural language extension for SQL that allows the developer to add procedural code to SQL statements for data manipulation. In other words, the programming constructs of sequence, iteration and selection are added to the non-procedural capabilities of the query language. The judicious use of PL/SQL improves performance by including procedures and functions, database triggers, packages and methods, stored centrally as PL/SQL code for the efficient execution of common operations.

The following example assumes some knowledge of programming and so the terminology of programming is not defined. Some readers may browse this section only or even skip it. However, this section is included because any successful IS professional in an Oracle environment must have a good working knowledge of PL/SQL in order to use it effectively.

As illustrated in Figure 9.1, PL/SQL programs are built in blocks. Blocks may be nested and each block consists of an optional series of data type declarations and the executable code between a BEGIN and END statement. Within the main body, there may (and inevitably should) be an exception block for dealing with errors.

The declaration part of a block allows the programmer to define variables and constants as characters, numbers, dates, Boolean operators and so on. For example, the program might require a counter, which would be declared as an integer variable. Alternatively, a tax rate might be included as a decimal constant. Once declared in the declaration part of the block, a variable can be assigned a value or otherwise manipulated in the executable part.

The basic elements of any procedural language are statements for sequence, selection and iteration. Each construct begins and ends with a reserved word. In PL/SQL selection statements are written as:

```
IF...THEN...ELSE...END IF;
```

From this basic selection statement, the simple IF...THEN...END IF; and the nested IF...THEN...ELSIF... THEN... ...END IF; can be used.

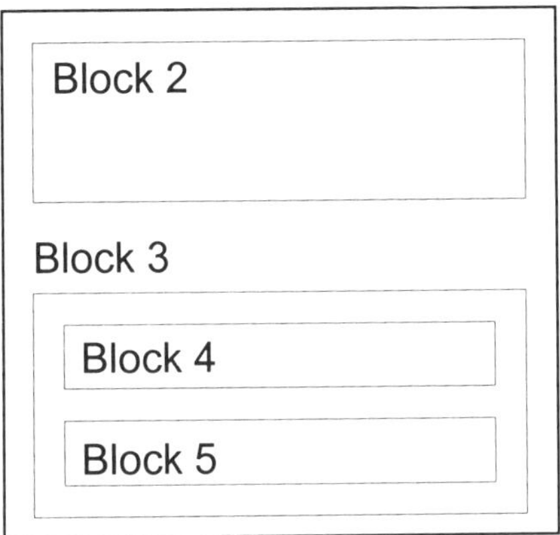

Figure 9.1 Block structure of PL/SQL

The three basic types of iteration are written as below. The counted loop (which performs an operation a set number of times) is written as follows:

```
FOR...IN...LOOP...END LOOP;
```

the condition at the end (which performs the operation at least once and until the condition is met) is shown as:

```
LOOP...EXIT WHEN...END LOOP;
```

and the condition before (which may not perform the contents of the loop at all if the condition is already satisfied when the code is encountered) is as follows:

```
WHILE...LOOP...END LOOP;
```

Structured programming almost, but not entirely, eliminates the need for a GOTO statement. Such a statement exists in PL/SQL but its use is infrequent.

All the usual arithmetic and logical operators can be used, such as + (addition) and < (less than). Some other symbols that are more specific to PL/SQL (although common to other languages) include := (assign to) and - - (comment delimiters).

Using cursors, the programmer can use the SELECT statement of SQL to identify any number of qualifying rows and then point to each one in turn for individual actions. Cursors are declared in the declaration part, and first opened and then advanced through the relevant set of rows. This ability to process the results of a query row-by-row provides the programmer with a powerful method of handling complex data relationships and processing complex user requirements.

Thus, like any other procedural language, PL/SQL is a series of statements made up of reserved words, operators, references to data and other declared data types, arranged in a logical way to perform a function. All the rules of good programming apply, and if you are familiar with Ada, C or something similar, and combined with an understanding of SQL, PL/SQL is easy to learn and use.

Perhaps the best way to illustrate PL/SQL is to look at an example. Here, a very simple example gives something of the flavour of procedural extensions to a non-procedural language.

The entity-relationship diagram shown as Figure 9.2 represents the relationship between owner data and pet data for a veterinary practice. It is a one-to-many relationship: that is, an owner may have more than one pet but the pet has to have one assigned owner who is responsible for paying the bills.

OWNER (<u>owner ID</u>, last name, first name, telephone, address)
PET (<u>pet ID</u>, pet name, pet type, pet sex, description, owner ID)

Figure 9.2: Entity-relationship diagram with associated entity descriptions

As discussed in Chapter 7, SQL is a data definition language as well as a data manipulation language. In Oracle8, a table can be created using SQL*Plus, a command line editor for Oracle's extended SQL and an integral part of the database. The example in Figure 9.3 shows the definition of the two tables described in the entity-relationship diagram of figure 9.2.

```
SQL> CREATE TABLE owner(ownerid CHAR(5) NOT NULL,
2 lastname VARCHAR2(30) NOT NULL, firstname VARCHAR2(30) NOT NULL,
3 telephone CHAR(12), address VARCHAR2(60) NOT NULL)
4 PRIMARY KEY (ownerid));

Table created.

SQL> CREATE TABLE pet(petid CHAR(6) NOT NULL,
2 petname VARCHAR2(30) NOT NULL, pettype VARCHAR2(10) NOT NULL,
3 petsex CHAR(1), descritpion VARCHAR2(60) ownerid CHAR(5)
4 PRIMARY KEY (petid)
5 FOREIGN KEY (ownerid));
```

Figure 9.3: Data definition statements for owner– pet example

The tables are very simple but by way of illustration, the tables are filled with data below.

OWNERID	LASTNAME	FIRSTNAME	TELEPHONE	ADDRESS
O1234	Louvieris	Hara	809678	20 Swift Lane
P5678	Huntley	Liz	902453	Fairholme
D9101	Dodd	Karen	876903	1 Rose Ave

PETID	PETNAME	PETTYPE	PETSEX	DESCRIPTION	OWNER ID
J90876	Jake	Dog	M	Tri-colour Border Collie	O1234
G76534	Angus	Dog	M	Black Labrador	O1234
H98043	Prudence	Cat	F	Tabby	P5678
V87065	Shoosh	Cat	F	Ginger, long-haired	D9101
D54378	George	Cat	N	Ginger & white, short-haired	D9101
J90871	Daphne	Rat	F	Brown	D9101

Figure 9.4: Populated tables for owner– pet example

The example in Figure 9.4 consists of PL/SQL code which illustrates the concepts including the use of cursors and three programming constructs.

```
DECLARE
-- Declare the name and type of variables needed --
-- %TYPE defines the type of variable at runtime so that table changes are
reflected --
 Petsearch      Owner.ownerId%TYPE;
 Thispetname Pet.petname%TYPE;
 Thispettype   Pet.pettype%TYPE;

 CURSOR petcursor IS(ownerpet VARCHAR2)
 SELECT petname, pettype
 FROM pet
 WHERE ownerid=ownerpet
 ORDER BY petname

BEGIN
…
…
--Assign value to petsearch —
 petsearch:='9101'
--Open the petcursor, identify relevant rows and point cursor at first row in
result table –
 OPEN petcursor(petsearch)
--Continue through selections from the result table… --
 LOOP
--Fetch one row at a time from the result table --
 FETCH petcursor(petsearch)
 INTO thispetname, thispettype
 EXIT WHEN petcursor%NOTFOUND;
--…until no more remain --
 END LOOP;
-- Ensure that cursor is closed --
 IF petcursor%ISOPEN THEN CLOSE petcursor END IF;
…
…
END;
```

Figure 9.5: PL/SQL code fragment for owner-pet example

9.4 Conclusion

The term 'corporate database' describes the information provision found in large organisations in information-rich sectors such as banking and retailing. The underlying data structure is complex, the volume of data is large, the number of users is great and there is a huge variety of integrated applications. The organisation relies on its data to survive, and the need for security is high. Although PC databases proliferate in large organisations, they generally form part of the sub-culture of that organisation. They may be used to develop end-user systems or as design tools, and may be ad-hoc, short-life, non-critical systems, not integrated with the rest of the organisation's data bank.

Summary

- Access is capable of producing applications that only a few years ago would have required much greater resources, but the tremendous increase in power and capacity has brought that capability to the desktop.
- Compared to a corporate DBMS such as Oracle, it is limited in terms of integrating with other databases, portability with other DBMS, volumes of data, numbers of users, tools supplied, security features, and data dictionary facility. On the other hand, it is also cheaper and easier to use.
- For most applications, Oracle requires programming skills.

Exercise

1. In which of the following computer applications might you use Access or Oracle DBMS (give reasons for your answer):
   a) A car parking system for a university
   b) Developing a timetable for classes at a university
   c) A postgraduate admissions system for a management school at the university
   d) A students admissions system for all students applying to the university
   e) A general administration system for the university.

Further reading

Allen, C. Oracle (2000) *PL/SQL 100,* Osborne/McGraw-Hill, Maidenhead.

Feuerstein, S. and Russell, D. (2001) *Oracle PL/SQL Best Practices,* O'Reilly, Sebastopol.

Lewis, J. (2000) *Practical Oracle8i,* Addison Wesley, Harlow.

Loney, K. and Koch, G. (2000) *Oracle8i: The Complete Reference,* Osborne/McGraw-Hill, Maidenhead.

Pribyl, B. and Feuerstein, S. (2001) *Learning Oracle PL/SQL,* O'Reilly, Sebastopol.

10 Implementation environment

10.1 Introduction

Most organisations will use databases on personal computers, such as the Access databases discussed in Chapter 8. They may well also have a corporate-wide database, such as an Oracle database described in Chapter 9. However, when describing corporate data as a 'pool' of data and discussing the advantage of storing elements of data only once, the impression is given of a single data store located centrally. Yet many organisations are not organised and managed centrally. Organisations are frequently sub-divided into departments or groups. The groups may be geographically dispersed, perhaps across national boundaries. Additionally, companies typically grow through acquisitions and partnerships. The decentralisation of the organisation may lead to a state where the strategy for information systems within an organisation disintegrates into a large number of different systems with no one user having access to another's database. Depending on the particular circumstances of the organisation, many of the advantages of a database approach could be lost.

The alternative strategy is to enable a planned fragmentation and replication of the database. Here, several computers each holding parts of the database or duplicates of the data are interconnected by a communication network. This is a distributed database system.

The chapter begins with a definition of a distributed database. We then go on to discuss the strategy of distribution with its central question around the appropriate extent of distribution. Date's (2000) principle and objectives of distributed databases are outlined, before a consideration of distribution issues. A discussion on client/server systems concludes the chapter.

10.2 What is a distributed database?

A distributed database can be seen as a 'virtual' database, the component parts of which are stored at several physical nodes or **sites**. The difference between a centralised and a distributed database should not be visible to the user.

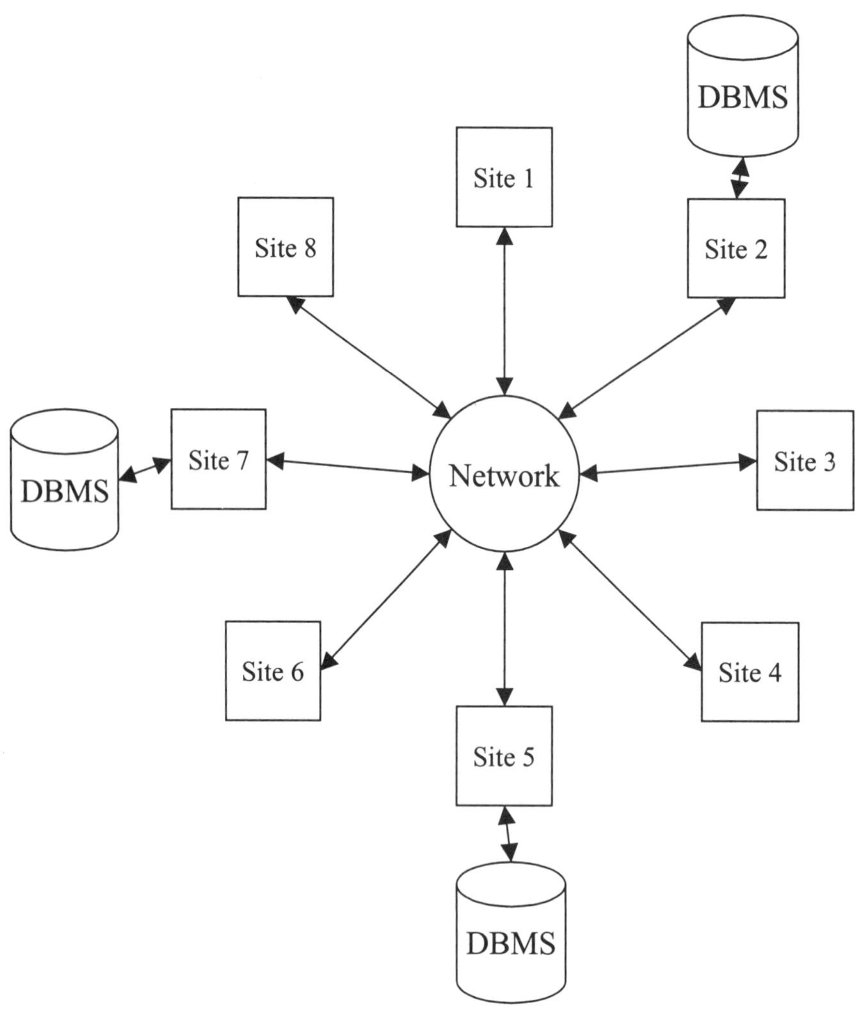

Figure 10.1: A distributed DBMS

Notice that in the example topology shown in figure 10.1, three sites 'host' the database but data is available to all the sites as required through the network. The best design would normally be one that has data stored and managed at the site that uses it most.

The sites of a distributed system may be **homogenous** or **heterogeneous**. A homogenous system has sites with identical hardware and software configurations. A heterogeneous approach allows different configurations at each site. A heterogeneous system may evolve from organisation expansion, particularly from mergers and acquisitions, or in partnerships across organisations and therefore a heterogeneous approach may be appropriate in some environments. However, standardisation of hardware, operating systems, networks and DBMS ensure a robust system.

If the distributed system is heterogeneous, then a gateway, or '**middleware**' is required to provide a consistent interface. Middleware is a term for any software that allows communication between DBMS of different types, for example, Oracle and Sybase, although the term is also applied to software that communicates between any applications and may be known as application integration tools or portal frameworks.

A distributed database system needs a network that communicates data and requests to and from the individual sites. Computer networking is an important topic and more detail can be found in the references at the end of the chapter such as Tanenbaum (1998). The connection might be via a **local area network** (LAN), a **wide area network** (WAN), or a combination of these.

A special case of distributed database is provided by the **mobile technologies**. It is likely that the recent advances in mobile technologies and changes in the way organisations conduct their day-to-day activities will lead to more use of mobile platforms for databases. Examples of mobile computing include home quotations and sales for various products and services such as installing a new central heating boiler or measuring for a fitted carpet. Other applications of mobile computing include journalism, monitoring financial markets, town planning and construction site visits. In each case, users of fixed-location data are in some way isolated, geographically dispersed or on the move. An alternative approach in a mobile environment is through an intermittently synchronised mobile database. Here, the user occasionally connects to the central database to download and receive updates, with most of the transaction processing occurring at the mobile unit.

10.3 Distribution strategy

Decisions about whether or not to distribute has been a concern for many decades. During the late 1960s and 1970s, the technology dictated a centralised approach. By the 1980s and 1990s and with the rise of relational databases, a distributed approach was more easily achieved and was seen as potentially cost saving. However, now the choice can be made based on a variety of issues that include cost, performance and availability but also incorporate management structure, organisational goals, new ways of working and organisational culture.

There may be a tendency for the strategy of distribution to develop from the bottom, up, as each group lays claim and isolates 'their' data, losing the advantages of the database approach. A better strategy is to enable a planned geographic distribution of the database where the users are interconnected by a network. In this situation, each group of users or individuals can have their data held on their local computer but all other users who have right of access can use this data. Therefore, data can be held where it is collected, validated or most used.

Such a strategy may be particularly suitable to organisations that are themselves dispersed and therefore a distributed database system is more natural. The management of each part of the organisation may need their independence. It may also be suitable for organisations seeking to integrate a number of databases that already exist but where it would be legally, politically or otherwise impractical to centralise, for example when crossing national boundaries. A distributed database approach also supports an organisation that tends to grow incrementally, for example, by buying out its competitors or suppliers or by the addition of new branches or warehouses.

10.4 Principle and objectives of distributed databases

The advantages of a distributed database over a centralised approach are commonly said to include cost, performance, scalability, reliability and availability. The management difficulty of distribution is how to get the advantages of the database approach together with the advantages offered by distributed data and processing. Date (2000) states that 'to the user, a distributed system should look exactly like a **non**-distributed system' and goes on to identify twelve objectives leading from this principle. Date's fundamental principle and the associated objectives offer a framework for the understanding of distributed databases. The objectives are:

- *Local autonomy:* local data should be owned and managed locally, with local accountability and security. Local operations should remain local, and no site must depend on another for successful functioning. Local autonomy ensures low coupling between sites and minimises network traffic.

- *No reliance on a central site:* there should not be any reliance on a master site for some central service as the central site would make the system vulnerable at a single point and there is the possibility of bottlenecks. Local autonomy should lead to no reliance on a central site.

- *Continuous operation:* there should never be a need for a planned system shutdown because with local autonomy and no reliance on a central site, new sites can be incorporated and software may be upgraded without disrupting the general service.

- *Location independence:* as already discussed, users should not need to know where their data is physically stored. This is desirable whether centralised or distributed, to gain the database benefits of flexibility and robustness.

- *Fragmentation independence:* Date considers that it should be possible to divide each data grouping for storage to reduce network traffic. Fragmentation independence is a natural occurrence in a well-designed relational database as rows and/or columns separated from the table still have context.

- *Replication independence:* where the same data is required at more than one site, it is necessary to replicate the data to maintain the benefits of distribution. However, this 'controlled redundancy' has the overhead of increased 'housekeeping'. True independence 'allows replicas to be created and destroyed at any time in response to changing requirements, without invalidating any … user programs or activities'.

- *Distributed query processing:* the query optimising strategy should take account of the distribution of data.

- *Distributed transaction management:* in distributed databases, control of concurrency and recovery need to be extended to take into account the several *agents* at different sites that might constitute a transaction. This requires multi-version locking and a two-phase commit and rollback protocol.

- *Hardware independence:* hardware independence comes from software compatibility. Although organisations may use a variety of hardware components, the DBMS will normally be the same and there should be a 'single-system image' for the user.

- *Operating system independence:* in the same way that hardware independence is sought, so a user view of the single system should not be affected by having different operating systems. Operating system independence is normally achieved by using the same DBMS on the different platforms.

- *Network independence:* the system should support a wide range of different network types.

- *DBMS independence:* although it may be usual for an organisation to have copies of the same DBMS on each of the platforms, it should be possible to have a variety of DBMS, integrated by the support of the same interface.

The objectives do not form a checklist, in that they overlap and each objective will be of greater or lesser importance depending on the organisation and context. The principles also describe an ideal case, which is not to say that advantages cannot be gained from distributed database systems that do not entirely conform. Client/server database systems, described below, for example, do not conform to Date's objectives but offer considerable advantages to some organisations.

10.5 Distribution decisions

In this section we look at some of the more complicated and interrelated issues involved in the implementation of a distributed database system. Such systems are complex because relations in the same database can reside at a number of sites. Relations can be fragmented and replicated, making data dictionary management and query processing problematic. User transactions involving data resident at several sites will require much processing at these different sites with added difficulties of concurrency control and synchronisation between the sites. As data copies may continue to be updated at a number of sites, even when a site is down, its recovery requires information from these other sites to ensure consistency; and the support of the various forms of transparency adds another translation mechanism that will be costly to maintain.

Even building a system log becomes more complex as a single transaction may use data from a variety of other sites. The decision usually concerns price against performance. Distribution can mean better performance but centralisation tends to reduce costs. Cost and performance will depend upon the complexity of the transactions and the network traffic, which in turn depend upon the management decisions that are made surrounding capacity, data usage, network type and topology, hardware, software and middleware.

Distribution decisions concern the following issues:

- *Migration.* Organisations may be moving from a centralised approach to a distributed database system, or may begin a distributed database approach in a 'green field' environment. If it is possible to start from scratch, then a corporate data model can be enabled using the latest technologies and standards. However, it is more common to move to a distributed database from an existing system. A gradual migration from centralised systems or piecemeal systems is likely to be very expensive, time-consuming and error-prone. However, many organisations have undertaken the task, often implementing changes in structure and integration of systems in business improvement or business reengineering programmes. A migration might be undertaken by first distributing the processing, and then the data in logical groupings to the various sites. A distributed database system should model the structure of the organisation to some extent, and this would suggest that different configurations are required for different environments. Although most organisations are at least logically distributed and, most likely, physically distributed as well, other businesses are centralised physically and controlled from the centre, and therefore a distributed database system would not be suitable.

- *Data location.* Decisions about where to locate the data and the data dictionary, and whether to replicate either or both will have a major effect on the speed of the system. A rule of thumb is that data should reside where they are most used but associated questions complicate the issue. For example, data sets may be fragmented but if they are decisions are needed regarding horizontal and vertical fragmentation and the level of redundancy required. The decisions about data directly affect performance, and will be guided by the performance criteria that are identified.

- *Control mechanisms* relating to recovery, concurrency and synchronisation can be centralised, distributed or both in a distributed database system. Distributed control, in principle, increases efficiency and survivability of a system. However, there will be a trade-off with other issues. For example, it may be considered politic to have centralised control over integrity or the level of security required may make centrally controlled access most sensible.

  One of the advantages of a distributed database system is its reliability but this can only be provided at the cost of frequent backup and complex recovery and restart mechanisms, which have to cope with synchronisation of multiple updates. Other security issues become even more important.

- *Transparency.* There are different degrees of transparency to the user. The higher the level of transparency, the greater the likelihood of a user-friendly system. However, the different users may suggest different choices at each site, and this will also have technical and cost trades-off.

- *Organisational issues.* A distributed database system is likely to have more impact on the organisation than a centralised database system. As well as the data administrator and database administrator teams of centralised systems that we discussed in Chapter 3, there needs to be local database administrators at each site. (Indeed, if there is total autonomy, a global database administrator may not be necessary.) Implementing such a system also requires people who do not normally work together to co-operate. There may also be conflict of interests over the ownership of data in a distributed database system.

- *Mobile computing.* Many of the problems associated with mobile computing are the difficulties with distributed computing already discussed, such as optimisation of queries, transaction management and security. However, the difficulties are exacerbated in a mobile environment where the extra dimension of location must be managed. Location may change during the course of a query or transaction and communication failures may be more common.

- *User acceptance and education* is vital in conventional database systems but there may be even greater pressures in a distributed environment such as the resentment felt by users who see their data being used by others. Although distributed database systems do permit greater freedom to local management, it is essential that they are restricted to components from an approved list of well-tried solutions and are tested on the network.

- *Risk.* There will be a number of implementation risks as with any new venture. For example, there is a risk that the distributed database applications will not perform properly, there may be delays or unbudgeted expenditure, and the benefits may bring increased complexity and technical demands or non-compliance with legal or other requirements. The distributed nature of the system may also lead information systems professionals to disperse with a resultant loss of focus, concentration of knowledge and expertise, and the synergy that can result from a carefully selected and well-managed information systems group.

- *Suitability* of distributed database systems for the organisation comprises a number of aspects. The first relates to the amount of potential and actual interaction between sites in terms of information flows and also how operations carried out or decisions taken at one site affect others. The second relates to the degree of centralisation of management and authority. The third relates to how much the data needs to be accessed from more than one site. If most data needs to be accessed by most people, then a centralised DBMS may be a better solution. Finally, it concerns how up-to-date the data needs to be. Again, if it has to be completely up-to-date then a centralised DBMS may be a better solution. As with conventional databases, it is essential that senior management perceives its value and that this in turn is seen by the rest of the organisation through senior management commitment and involvement in the distributed database project.

There should be some desired mid-point between total centralisation and total decentralisation that supports user needs and yet minimises cost. A further point is worth noting here. We tend to assume that physical distribution of data requires a physical distribution of the information systems function. However, organisations have found the distribution of information systems resources, as epitomised by the 'information centre' of the 1980s, expensive and inefficient. Many tasks, such as backup, can be performed remotely; enabling organisations to have the efficiencies of a centralised IS function without the disadvantages associated with centralised resources. Therefore, the model of distribution does not necessarily dictate the structure of the IS group.

There are also many technical issues that must be decided. Many apply to centralised database systems but can be more difficult in a distributed system because of the added complexity of some routines. Although the detail of these aspects is considered outside the scope of a management-oriented book, they are important because they affect the speed, accuracy and reliability of the service provided. The distributed database world is complex and therefore efficiency is particularly important. Such technological considerations include query decomposition and optimisation, consistency and synchronisation, and fault tolerance and recovery.

10.6 Client/server systems

The client/server configuration is characterised by the allocation of a number of specialised **servers** to deal with aspects of the system processing such as a **web server**, an **email server**, an **application server**, a **file server** and a **printer server**. All the sites that are connected to the server then become clients of the server when asking for services such as email or file maintenance. Clients are equipped with a suitable interface to communicate with the server, and have local processing power. Although the 'server' in question is, strictly speaking, a software component, it is often also a dedicated machine. However, individual sites can be both client and server.

A database can be distributed using client/server technology, as shown in figure 10.2, although the database is not distributed in the pure sense. In a client/server database system, the data resides on the server(s) and therefore is not 'local' but the processing is distributed around the clients. Date's principle is not fulfilled in a client/server environment, because the user needs to be aware of the location of the data. The flexibility, increasing standardisation and reducing cost of the client/server architecture make it an increasingly popular choice for organisations. In a relational environment, the DBMS resides on the server and the client has an interface for communicating with the DBMS. An **SQL server** will process the query or transaction and return the result to the requesting client. In this arrangement, the client and server are sometimes known as the **front-end** and **back-end** machines respectively.

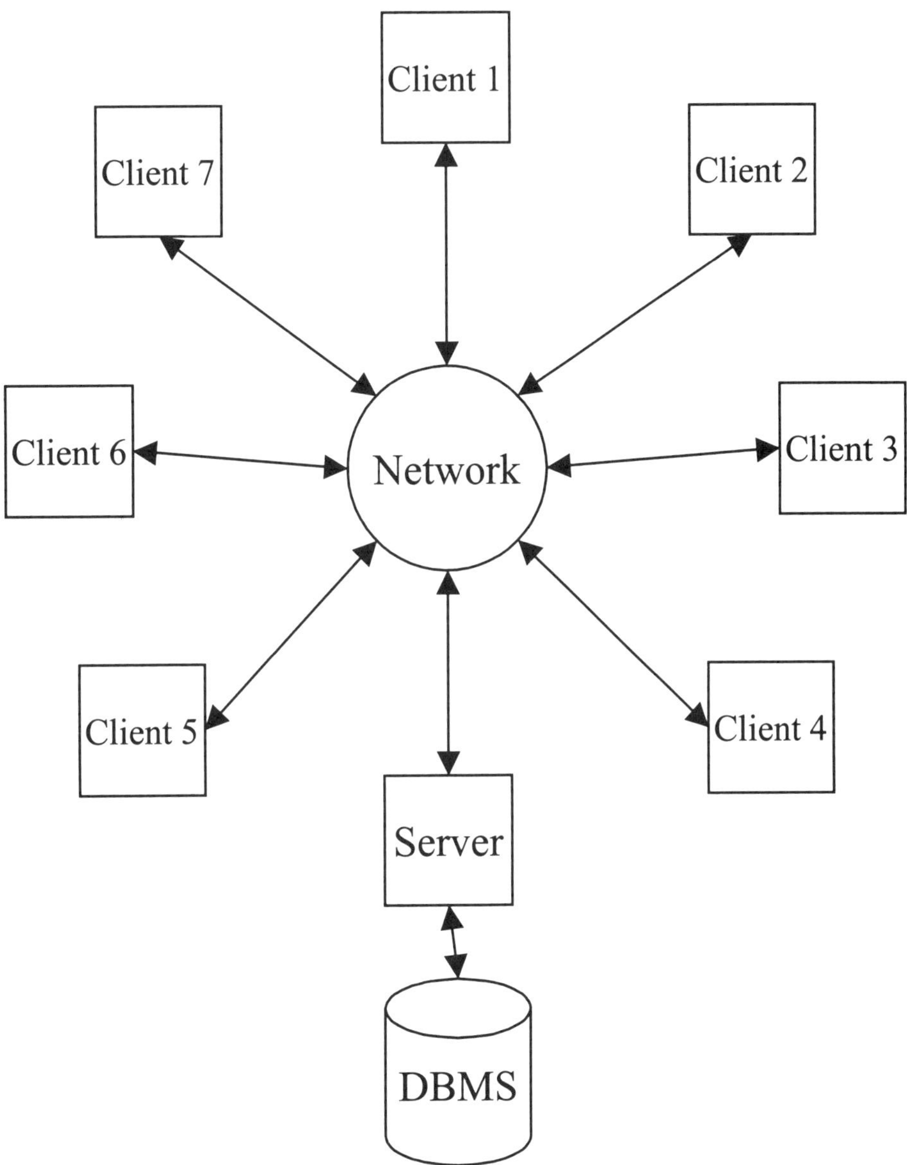

Figure 10.2: Client/server database implementation

Increasingly, the two-tier architecture described above is being replaced by a three-tier system that has the server acting as a go-between for the client and a host computer. This is a return to the centralised concept but has some of the advantages of a distributed database such as decentralised processing and may be the most cost-effective solution.

10.7 Conclusion

An ideal distributed database can be described in Date's principle and twelve objectives. However, decisions are made based on a variety of political, economic, social and technical issues, and many organisations choose a configuration that falls somewhat short of the ideal but which has an organisational fit.

Summary

- Many organisations are neither organised nor managed centrally. A distributed database is likely to be suited to them.
- There are different types of distributed database, but Date has suggested a set of principles and objectives that proves a useful basis for distributed databases. The central principle is that, for a user, the distributed database should appear no different than a centralised database.
- Nevertheless, there are certain additional difficulties and complexities that come with distributed databases, including data dictionary management, concurrent updating, security, and backup and recovery.
- Client/server systems relate to the configuration of servers (including file servers) and client systems (workstations) that use these servers.

Exercises

1. Justify Date's principle and each of his objectives suggested in section 10.4, particularly in the light of the popularity of client/server systems described in section 10.6.
2. For an organisation that you are familiar with, identify a political issue, an economic constraint, a social consideration and a technical limitation that would affect the strategy for the distribution of data and processing.
3. Find out about the distribution of IT facilities at your university or other institution. Would another type of configuration be more appropriate?

Further reading

Date, C. J. (2000) *An Introduction to Database Systems,* 7th edn, Addison Wesley, Harlow.

Goldman, J. E. and Rawles, P. T. (2000) *Local Area Networks: A Client/Server Approach,* Wiley, Chichester.

Johnson, E. J. (2000) *The Complete Guide to Client/Server Computing,* Prentice Hall, Englewood Cliffs, NJ.

Ozsu, M. T. and Valduriez, P. (1997) *Principles of Distributed Database Systems* 2nd edn, Prentice Hall, Englewood Cliffs, NJ.

Tanenbaum, A. S. (1998) *Computer Networks,* 3rd edn, Prentice Hall, Englewood Cliffs, NJ.

Tanenbaum, A. S. and van Steen, M. (2001) *Distributed Computing,* Prentice Hall, Englewood Cliffs, NJ.

11 Internet environment

11.1 Introduction

In the early stages of development, the Internet was viewed by many organisations as a billboard. The perception of the Internet as a vehicle for advertising is reflected in most organisations' first use of the Internet for basic marketing activities. Organisations automated their company literature.

Advertising and promotion is still an important role for organisations with an Internet presence but many other important roles have emerged. The rapid developments in Internet technology now allow many dynamic activities to take place, from the processing of an order for a bookseller and the issue of travel details for a ticket-less airline, to auctions, teleconferencing, literature searches, programme broadcasting, community-building and multi-user gaming.

In e-commerce, the Internet has reshaped the retail industry, allowing big companies to introduce new services to their customers (such as Tesco's online grocery shopping in the UK), new companies to emerge to challenge the traditional retailers (such as amazon.com), and small specialists to have a worldwide customer-base (such as www.organicsdirect.co.uk). Traditional industries are challenged by new initiatives. For example, Stephen King and the electronic publication of his latest novels has provided an alternative to traditional book publishing and the Napster music community has changed the future of music publishing. The Internet is changing the way organisations and individuals around the world communicate, negotiate, deal, and gather and use intelligence.

This chapter first defines the terms used in an Internet environment, and describes the technology architecture that supports an Internet environment. The focus of this book, of course, is databases, and so a section follows on database applications in an Internet environment. Sections on Hypertext Mark-up Language (HTML) and Extensible Mark-up Language (XML) describe the development of Web user interfaces, and a final section on Active Server Pages (ASP) describes the use of ActiveX Data Objects (ADO).

11.2 Internet concepts

The first task is to distinguish between the Internet and the World Wide Web (WWW or 'Web'). Often, these two terms are used synonymously. However, the term 'Internet' describes the worldwide network of computers, and the World Wide Web, is a subset of the Internet comprising web pages linked by hypertext. So, the Internet provides the infrastructure for activities such as email, file transfer and remote access and the World Wide Web is a collection of web pages, often linked together and arranged into websites.

The Internet was developed in the late 1960s by the US government's **Advanced Research Projects Agency** for defence purposes and to aid collaborative research in universities and was given the name, ARPANet. The World Wide Web was the invention of an academic now at Massachusetts Institute of Technology (MIT), Tim Berners-Lee. The Internet is considered by some to be a freethinking, multi-cultural and inclusive community, with no requirement for regulation of any kind. However, attempts have been made to standardise and direct the development of the Internet. The **World Wide Web Consortium** (W3C) was created in the mid 1990s to 'lead the World Wide Web to its full potential by developing common protocols that promote its evolution and ensure its interoperability'.

Although the idea of managing and controlling the Web is problematic, the **Internet Corporation for Assigned Names and Numbers** (Icann) is currently the main organisation that decides what domain names can be used and who can use them. Domain names can be generic, such as .com, .net, .org, .info and .biz, or geographic so that organisations in Belgium may have .be and in Italy .it. Alternative naming systems are available from rival organisations such as new.net who offer .shop and .web domains.

The **Internet Democracy Project**, another organisation based in the United States of America, exists to encourage non-governmental organisations to collaborate and 'enforce Internet governance structures that preserve and promote the principles of a civil society'. However, regulation of the Internet relies on co-operation between governments, industry and civil organisations, and, ultimately, conforming user behaviour. The battle for control of the Internet continues.

The many nodes and routes through the Internet mean that the Internet stays operating even in the event of a breakdown or disaster because communication can be re-routed. The Internet uses public telecommunication networks around the world, adopting the **Transmission Control and Internet Protocols** (TCP/IP) to assemble and reassemble messages between Internet addresses. TCP/IP uses the client/server approach; that is, every machine connected to the network is either a client (such as a home user) or a server (such as a web server or an email server). Since the client or server capabilities are provided by software rather than hardware, any machine may be both a client *and* a server. Similarly, an individual machine may act as a server for more than one type of activity, for example as both an email server *and* a file transfer server. This approach is described further in Chapter 10.

Some other protocols with which Internet users may be familiar use TCP/IP but provide a higher layer for specific tasks such as the **Hypertext Transfer Protocol** (HTTP) and the **Simple Mail Transfer Protocol** (SMTP). In this way, the facilities of the Internet with which we are increasingly familiar such as email, chatrooms, Internet Relay Chat (IRC) (e.g. mIRC, Pirch and Virc), telephony and surfing are provided to any user with access to the Internet.

As more organisations and individuals seek the benefits of the Internet, so the limitations have become more important. One of the major limitations of using the public telecommunications networks around the world is the limited **bandwidth** available. As more applications need speed to be effective, and technologies converge so that individuals can order pizza via the television or buy shares on a mobile telephone, so the need for extra bandwidth has become crucial. One solution is a **broadband** network, implemented using the new advances in cable, wireless and fibre optics. At the time of writing, broadband solutions are costly and not widely available. However, in early 2001, a private apartment block became the first in the UK to be supplied with fibre optic cabling, with speeds of up to 2,000 times the speed of a standard home user dial-up modem, and costs will reduce as more organisations adopt the new technology.

Figure 11.1: A search using the Netscape browser and Google search engine

Access to the Internet requires an **Internet Service Provider** (ISP). An ISP has a server, or more properly, a cluster of servers, that serve requests between the user and the rest of the Internet. For example, if a user requests the Tesco website, the ISP locates the address and displays the document for the user. If the user goes on to make a purchase, the ISP communicates between the retailer and consumer.

Netscape Navigator, MS Explorer and Opera are examples of a class of software known as 'browsers'. **Browsers** allow the user access to the web. Search engines, such as www.google.com and www.altavista.com search the web for pages based on search criteria entered by the user. For example, the search illustrated in Figure 11.1 for '<<abyssinian kittens>> using the Netscape Navigator browser and the Google search engine found nearly 4,500 pages that satisfied the criteria. The search items chosen, the order in which they are entered and the use of operators, quote marks and other constraints have a significant effect on the success of a search. For example, the search for <<abyssinian kittens for sale>> in the UK returns only 55 sites, a further search for <<abyssinian "kittens for sale">> in the UK returns 25 sites and a final search, shown in Figure

11.2 for <<abyssinian "kittens for sale" +London>> returns only addresses.

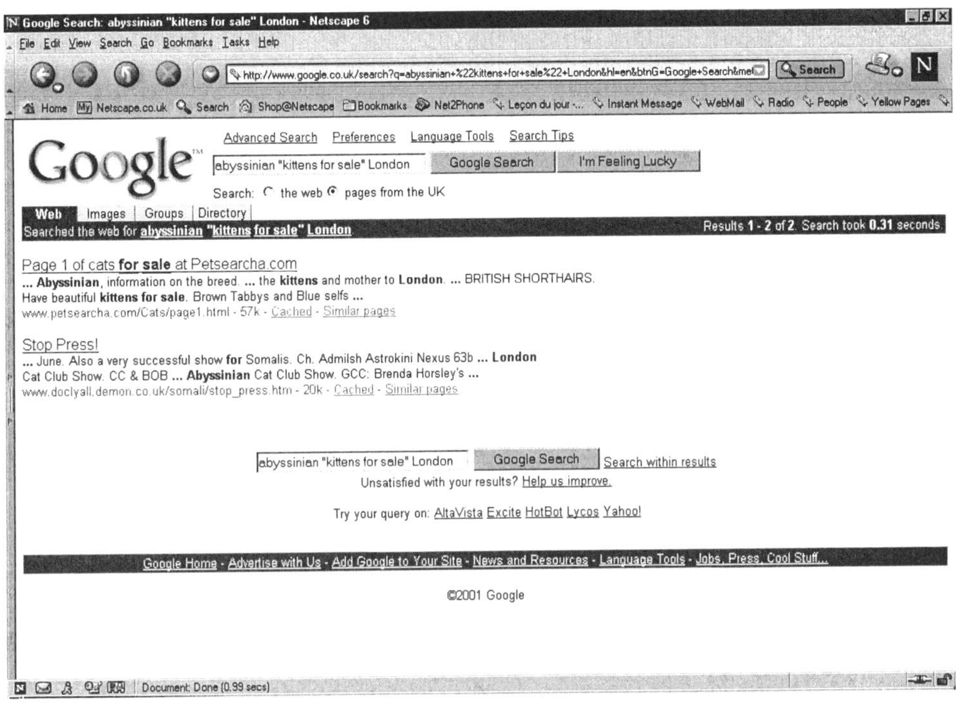

Figure 11.2: Refining the search

An **Intranet** is a private Internet within an organisation, protected from the outside world by a **firewall**. A firewall is software that examines each incoming or outgoing Internet activity and applies the organisation rules to determine whether the activity can take place. For example, an employee may be able to access their email from home but not anyone else's email, a journalist may be able to retrieve a copy of the latest company report but not get any research data about the development of a new product, and an employee may be able to access the World Wide Web to gather competitor intelligence but not to download games. The speed of an Internet connection is dependent on network traffic outside the control of an individual user or organisation, so that even an Intranet may be slower than a dedicated company network.

Extranets have largely replaced dedicated **Electronic Data Interchanges** (EDI) between organisations. Using Internet protocols and routing, an Extranet is like an extended Intranet, protecting the organisation and its associates from the wider Internet by a firewall. The use of Internet technology allows even small organisations to engage with others, and is more flexible and adaptable than a dedicated network. A good example of an Extranet is that between Tesco and Proctor & Gamble. Proctor & Gamble are as aware as Tesco of sales of Proctor & Gamble products in each of the Tesco stores but cannot see the same data for a competitor such as Unilever. Other examples include GlobalNetXchange (GNX) and the World Wide Retail Exchange (WWRE), bringing together retailers and manufacturers to negotiate contracts, for example. In this way, Extranets support business-to-business (b2b) activities.

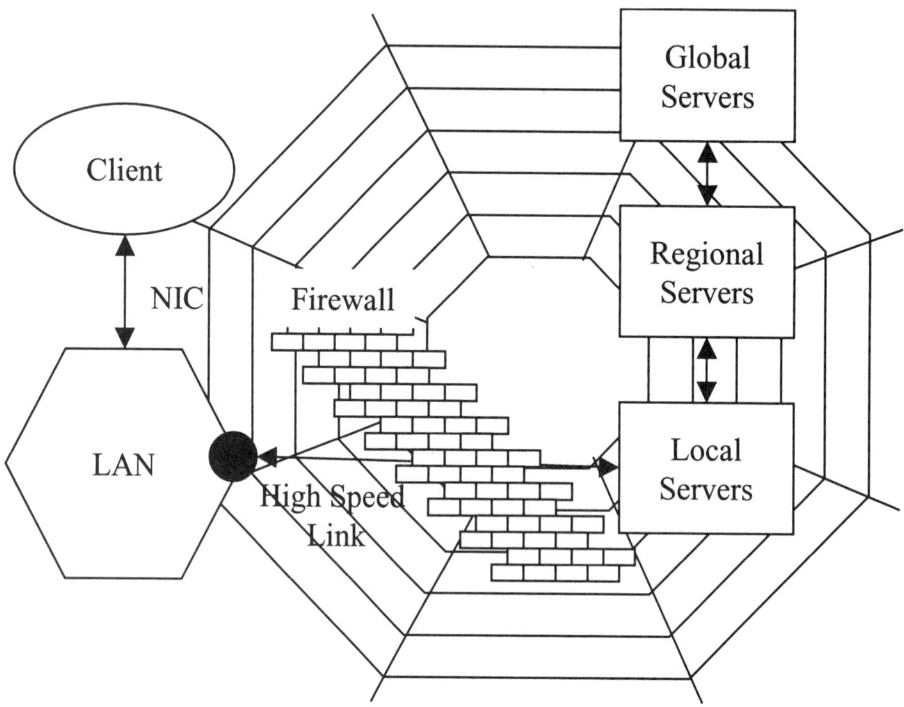

Figure 11.3: Access to the Internet

To summarise using an example: a home user with a browser acting as a client would probably access the Internet via a telephone link and a modem. The home user may then link to a company Local Area Network (LAN) if working from home, or an Internet Service Provider (ISP) such as BTOpenWorld or AOL. Within an organisation, a user is more likely to connect to the company LAN by a Network Interface Card (NIC). From a server on the company LAN, a high-speed connection accesses local servers, which in turn have access to regional and global servers. The inclusion of firewalls at appropriate points isolates Intranets or Extranets from the wider Internet, preventing the user from actions deemed inappropriate by the company or the ISP. This simplified explanation is represented in Figure 11.3.

11.3 Database applications

The Web is not the ideal place for database applications. The Web is based on a networked file-based systems architecture that is both peculiar to the Web and has limited functionality. There is tremendous demand and incredible potential for a worldwide network that can support database methodology and technology. Database and Web technology mix well for both centralised and outward-facing activities such as enterprise resource planning (ERP), data warehousing, e-commerce and home working. These activities are all described in more detail elsewhere in the book but the focus of this chapter is on the interface between traditional database architecture and the architecture of the World Wide Web.

The later releases of databases such as Oracle8*i* and DB2 EEE allow corporate databases to be shared over the World Wide Web by providing an interface, known as middleware, between the Web environment and the database environment. As well as giving organisations the ability to create new applications (for example, those that support business-to-business (b2b) or business-to-consumer (b2c) activities) this method might also be used to breathe new life into so-called 'legacy systems'. **Legacy systems** are applications that have been created using earlier languages and platforms but still perform a useful, and sometimes critical, function. These systems must be updated to current technology to aid maintenance and upgrade. Applying Web technology to existing databases may, by making the data easily available and open to Web-based applications, extend the life of such systems and make upgrading a less complex task.

Database applications for the Web are a combination of the mark-up languages of the Web and the Data Manipulation Languages of the database environment, as explained in the following sections. This might mean a combination of HTML, XML and SQL with JavaScript for the fancy bits, or perhaps a Java-based interface that serves both environments using an object-oriented approach. From storing and retrieving elements in a small table to accessing the powerful capabilities of a relational database, using the Web environment provides a highly graphical and ubiquitous environment. An introduction to methods of accessing data through Web browsers are discussed in the following sections.

11.4 Data, documents and web pages

Standard Generalised Mark-up Language (SGML) is the meta-language for both HTML and XML. XML is appropriate for database applications on the web, but we need to look at HTML first in order to understand this database environment fully. SGML was developed from an early IBM mark-up language and first published by the International Standards Organisation (ISO) in 1986. The term 'mark-up' referred originally to typesetting, and gave typesetters information about such things as the size and type of fonts and the placement of text on a page. Specialised mark-up languages are an inherent part of word processors such as MS Word and Corel's WordPerfect, though the languages themselves are not visible to the user. Generic mark-up languages do not specify the actual font or point, for example (the elements that make the style of a word processed document difficult to import to another word processor) but do specify the structure of the document. So, for example, instead of specifying courier font in bold 16 point, a generalised mark-up would simply identify a heading. The definition of a heading is left to the associated document type definition (DTD).

The information, made available on web servers, is encoded using a generic mark-up language, Hypertext Mark-up Language (HTML). HTML has a series of tags to describe how the text is displayed. For example, text written between the tag <p> and the end tag </p> appears as a paragraph and adding <i> and </i> inside the paragraph tags makes the text of the paragraph italic. An attribute can be added to some tags, so that, for example, using a <font> tag, the attribute 'size' is added, thus <font size="4"> determines the size of the font in the text that follows the tag. The important anchor tag <a>…</a> uses the 'href' attribute to link to another page. For example <a> href=www.google.co.uk </a> creates a link on the page to the google search engine. By using predetermined tags and attributes, HTML documents display a variety of font types, sizes and colour, tables and graphics, video and audio clips.

The following is the HTML source for a home page called 'mad about mountains'. You can look at any web page HTML by choosing 'page source' from the view menu of any browser. Although at first seemingly long and complex, it is feasible to read through the code and look at the web page and see how the latter has been formed from the HTML code.

```
<html>
<head>
<title>mad about mountains</title>
</head>
<body background="bg.gif" bgcolor="ffffec">
<center>
<h1>mad about mountains</h1>
<img width=192 height=128 src="mt.gif">
</center>
<b><p>Welcome to Ann Bowker's Home Page with info on mountains and molehills
across the world</p>
<dl>
<dt><a href="skiddaw.htm">Skiddaw</a>
<dd>A Home Page for my home mountain<p>
<dt><a href="ldp.htm">The Lake District</a>
<dd>recent pictures from my digital camera <font color=red> ... <img
src="hot.gif"></font><p>
<dt><a href="http://web.ukonline.co.uk/mountains/wain.htm">Wainwright's Lakeland
Fells</a>
<dd> a cross reference linking to walks up every fell (eventually)<br>
- just 1 fell to visit with the digicam - Selside Pike which is still closed due to foot and
mouth<p>
<dt><a href="mar2.htm">The English Marilyns</a>
<dd>178 hills with a 500 foot drop all round -
 from Cornwall to Kent - from the Borders to the Isle of Wight<br>
<font color=magenta>now with links to online maps</font><p>
<dt><a href="http://www.geocities.com/Yosemite/1015/wmar.htm">The Welsh
Marilyns</a>
<dd>155 hills - from Bardsey Island to the Black Mountains
 - and a traverse of all the Welsh two-thousanders<br>
<font color=magenta>now with links to online maps</font><p>
<dt><a href="iomar.htm">The Manx Marilyns</a><br>
<dd>5 hills on the Isle of Man with a 150m drop all round<br>
<font color=magenta>now with links to online maps</font><p>
<dt><a href="http://www.geocities.com/Yosemite/1015/scot.htm">Some Scottish
Hills</a>
<dd> The Grahams and other Scottish hills<br>
<font color=magenta>latest addition <a
href="http://web.ukonline.co.uk/mountains/barra5.htm">5 islands south of
Barra</a><br>
.. slowly adding scanned slides of some of the earlier Grahams</font><p>
<dt>Alpine Interludes
<dd> <a href="http://www.geocities.com/Yosemite/1015/zerm.htm">A visit to
Zermatt</a>
<font color=magenta> mainly the Matterhorn</font><p>
... to the <a href="http://www.geocities.com/Yosemite/1015/dol.htm">Italian
Dolomites</a><p>
...... and <a href="zerm00.htm">Zermatt again - August 2000</a><p>
<dt><a href="http://web.ukonline.co.uk/mountains/blanca.htm">Costa Blanca</a><p>
```

```
<dt><a href="http://www.geocities.com/Yosemite/1015/">Walking the Mountains of the
World</a>
<dd>some of the world's best known and easiest mountains<br>
<font color=magenta>latest addition - <a
href="http://web.ukonline.co.uk/mountains/cam.htm">Mount Cameroon</a></font><p>
<dt><a href="poems.htm">poems</a>
<dd>six songs for Keswick<p>
<dt><a href="links.htm">Wander the Web</a>
<dd>links to more mountain and hillwalking sites<p>
<dt><a href="mamcd.htm">Mad about Mountains CD</a>
<dd>this website on CD with all the Lake District pictures since September 1998<br>
<font color=magenta>now with more than 3 years of Lakeland pictures and more than
400mb of mountain madness</font>
</dl>
<hr>
Mail me at <a href="mailto:bowker@keswick.u-net.com">bowker@keswick.u-
net.com</a><p>
<hr>
<center><a href="http://home.earthlink.net/~swfry/pk2pk/p2p.html"><img
src="ban1.gif" ALT="Member of Peak to Peak Trail and Wilderness Links"></a><p>
This page listed by<p>
<a href="http://point.lycos.com/categories/index.html"><img src="top5icon.gif"
ALT="Lycos Top 5%"></a><p>
<a href="http://www.stpt.com/">Starting Point</a><p>
<a HREF="http://www.mcp.com/nrp/wwwyp/">WWW Yellow Pages</a><p>
<a HREF="http://www.linkstar.com/home/partners/ann-bowker">LinkStar</a><p>
Last update: 3rd December 2001<p></center>
</b>
</body>
</html>
```

In the example above, the document is identified as being written in <html>. Any word processor can be used to create HTML code. You can also see the beginning and end tags for the page title (which appears in the browser header) and headings, with the start tags for the body of the page and attributes to determine a background image and background colour. The page also includes images and links to other pages as well as the text. The web page as a browser would see it is shown as Figure 11.4.

HTML is not dependent on the machine used to display the contents of any document. An HTML document looks mostly the same whether displayed on a Mac or a PC, for example. The display is dependent on the browser used. Although it is possible to write HTML using any editor or word processor, it is now common to use packages such as Microsoft FrontPage, Macromedia's Dreamweaver or Adobe's GoLive to create and edit web pages, adapting the HTML generated for more complex activities.

As in the example above, web pages can include a mixture of media formats including video, sound and graphics as well as text. Web pages are arranged into coherent websites. A website will have a home page and a number of sub-sections. Home pages often include access to a site map and a search facility to allow users to navigate around the site. Navigation between pages in a site or the site and the wider Web is achieved using hyperlinks. A hyperlink states the Uniform Resource Locator (URL), or web address, of another web page. A link might also be made to a document in Portable Document Format (PDF). The most commonly used package to create and view PDF files is Adobe Acrobat, although other packages exist, such as Global Graphic's Niknak PDF Creator. The PDF file format ensures that the document looks the same to everyone viewing it, with embedded fonts and fixed positions of text, graphics and breaks. This is a common format for displaying company literature such as annual reports or policy documents on the Web.

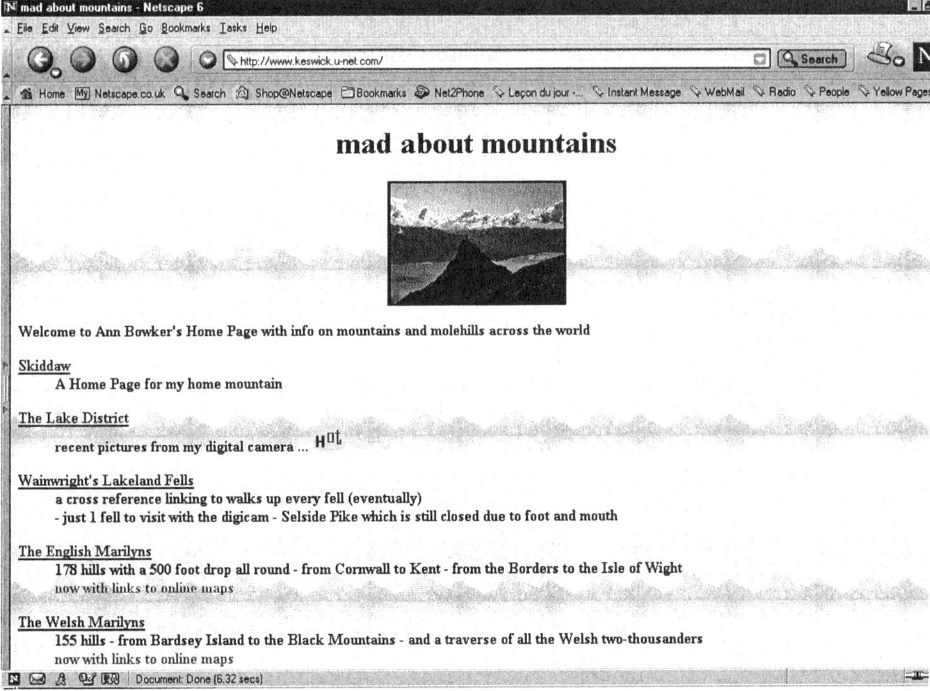

Figure 11.4: 'Mad about mountains' web site

The Web can be seen, from the above description, as a series of static pages, rather like a library. However, the Web has evolved from the billboard described in the introduction to this chapter into a dynamic environment by the use of scripting languages, further mark-up languages and databases. The reason for this is evident when we consider the strengths of the Web together with the advantages of databases. Compare a search using AltaVista at www.altavista.com with an SQL query. If we search for the 'price of database products' we get over 8 million references, the overwhelming majority of which have no relevance to the information sought. This is because a file system, which easily stores data about the size and type of file, makes it difficult to search the content with context.

While it is true that even the largest and most heterogeneous corporate database can be more focused in querying than a Web search engine undertaking the simplest of searches, a database system is concerned with the value of the data items and queries such as the example above return concise and accurate answers.

Other problems of providing database functionality using Web technology include the maintenance of websites and integration of systems. For example, it is difficult to keep track of changes that are made to site content, particularly when many users can make changes. The kind of performance that is required by database applications on the Web is the performance that database systems have been providing organisations before the advent of the Web. Therefore it is necessary to have either an interface so that the database can operate within a Web environment, a Web environment that describes the meaning and structure of the data, or a combination of the two.

11.5 Extensible mark-up language

Hypertext Mark-up Language (HTML) describes a web page in terms of the way it is displayed. Extensible Mark-up Language (XML), however, describes a page in terms of the meaning and structure of the data it contains. XML therefore provides a method of sharing both the data and format between users. The potential of such technology is increased when considering the possibility of using intelligent agents (or 'bots') to do the collecting and comparing. Imagine a lecturer wanting to put together a textbook from a variety of sources or an investor keeping an eye on a share portfolio.

XML allows the Developer to define tags and attributes. In other words, it is extensible. For example, a tag <order> might contain <order_lines> to describe the structure and contents of a customer order. XML's main advantage is the ability it gives to integrate disparate systems; therefore XML is likely to be an important development for e-commerce, since it provides a way of structuring data that simplifies data interchange between actors such as consumer, vendor, supplier and financial services provider. However, consumer, vendor, supplier and financial service provider would all have to agree to the definition of tags and adopt a series of document type definitions (DTD) and this is proving to be one of the barriers to the success of XML.

Let's look at a small example. A DTD for an order might include the line:

```
<!ELEMENT ROUTE_ID (#PCDATA)>
```

This defines a new tag <ROUTE_ID> and declares it as '#PCDATA', that is, formatted text. The tag <ROUTE_ID> can now be used in an XML document to structure a customer order. An excerpt from the XML document might be:

```
<ROUTE_ID>OXFORDSHIRE</ROUTE_ID>
```

In this way, the DTD is rather like a database schema and the XML contains the values. All that is required for any user to access the data in the XML document is access to the DTD, the URL for which is written in the XML document.

A complete DTD appears below.

```
<!ELEMENT ORDER (ORDER_NO, CUST_NO, ORDER_DATE, ORDER_LINES+,ROUTE_ID >
    <!ELEMENT ORDER_NO (#PCDATA)>
    <!ELEMENT CUST_NO (#PCDATA)>
    <!ELEMENT ORDER_DATE (#PCDATA)>
    <!ELEMENT ORDER_LINES (LINE_DETAILS+)>
        <!ELEMENT LINE_DETAILS (ITEM_ID, DESC, QUANTITY)>
            <!ELEMENT ITEM_ID (#PCDATA)>
            <!ELEMENT DESC (#PCDATA)>
            <!ELEMENT QUANTITY (#PCDATA)>
    <ROUTE_ID>OXFORDSHIRE</ROUTE_ID>
```

Notice that the '+' after ORDER_LINES indicates a repeating group – a one-to-many relationship with ORDER. The space after an attribute name indicates a mandatory, one-to-one relationship. This now allows the following XML document to be understood.

```
<?XML VERSION="1">
<!DOCTYPE ORDER SYSTEM "HTTP://WWW.MADEUP.CO.UK/DEFINITIONS/ORDER.DTD">
<ORDER>
	<ORDER_NO>123456</ORDER_NO>
	<CUST_NO>7890</CUST_NO>
	<ORDER_DATE>06-NOV-2001</ORDER_DATE>
	<ORDER_LINES>
		<LINE_DETAILS>
			<ITEM_ID>Y123</ITEM_ID>
			<DESC>RED STRIPED</DESC>
			<QUANTITY>999</QUANTITY>
		</LINE_DETAILS>
		<LINE_DETAILS>
			<ITEM_ID>Z456</ITEM_ID>
			<DESC>BLUE SPOTTED</DESC>
			<QUANTITY>555</QUANTITY>
		</LINE_DETAILS>
	</ORDER_LINES>
	<ROUTE_ID>OXFORDSHIRE</ROUTE_ID>
</ORDER>
```

Notice that the first two lines indicate that the document is in XML and the DTD can be found at the location shown.

XML could replace databases in many simple cases, for example, in company reports and policy statements, many government documents and research collaboration project data. Using XML ensures ease of sharing. However, the sophisticated search and retrieval capabilities of a database still make a combination of HTML and XML with a database backend the most appropriate choice for many organisations.

Although, like HTML, XML can be written using any text editor, XML editors, such as Vervet Logic's XML Pro or Altova's XML Spy, make the generation and maintenance of XML much easier.

11.6 Active Server Pages

Microsoft **ActiveX Data Objects** (ADO) provide a high-level interface between the Internet and databases that are compliant with **Open Database Connectivity** (ODBC). Access and Oracle are both examples of databases that conform to the open philosophy. The vehicle of the ADO hosting environment is the **active server page** (ASP). An ASP is a combination of a mark-up language, a procedural language (in particular VBScript and JScript) and perhaps a non-procedural language (such as SQL) held in a document with an ASP extension (for example whatsnew.asp or theses.asp). The code, or script, is contained within opening and closing tags, <%...%>. The tags are delimiters for the **server-side script** and can appear anywhere within the document, including inside or around HTML statements.

When a client requests the webpage, any ASP scripts are executed at by the server before delivery of the page. Therefore, every time you request an active server page, the web page that is displayed has the potential to be different from the last time you requested that same page, i.e. the structure remains the same but the data is different. Thus, as a database of research papers is updated, so when you access them each week via a browser, the list of papers changes, and if you refresh the home page of an auction site, you find that the date, time and number of users online has changed since you first requested the page.

HTML is used to format and display the data in the ASP, as in a non-active webpage with an HTML or HTM extension. When the source of an ASP is viewed by a user, only the HTML will be displayed, since the ASP script is executed on the server side.

Finally, you can see that the whole is rather like the PL/SQL explained in Chapter 9. In PL/SQL we have a language that combines procedural logic and SQL. Using ASPs, it is possible to do the same in a Web environment. The advantage is that the ASP remains functional whatever the volume and volatility of the database, providing a dynamic interface with the user.

Summary

- The Internet is changing the way organisations and individuals around the world communicate, negotiate, deal, and gather and use intelligence.
- Corporate databases can be shared using the Internet technology, for example by using an extranet. This allows access to permitted organisations, and this has largely replaced electronic data interchange for the sharing of data.
- Hypertext Mark-up Language (HTML) has become a generic language on the web and enables the specification of a web page in terms of the way it will be displayed.
- Extensible Mark-up Language (XML) describes a web page in terms of the meaning and structure of the data it contains and is more powerful for the web developer.

Exercises

1. Using a browser and a search engine, find some Belgium truffles for sale locally. Gradually refine your search until you get only a few sites returned.
2. View the source code of pages from a favourite website to determine the language(s) in which it is written.
3. Distinguish between the Internet, intranets and extranets.
4. Why has the Internet largely replaced dedicated electronic data interchange (EDI) systems?
5. Briefly describe the reasons, other than advertising, why an organisation might want to use the Internet.
6. Discuss the role of databases in the Internet.
7. Why might database applications and the Web be considered 'uneasy bedfellows', and how might greater harmony be achieved?

Further reading

Matthews, M. S. and Poulsen, E. B. (2001) *FrontPage2002: The complete Reference,* Osbourne/McGraw-Hill.

Powell, T.A. (2000) *HTML: The complete reference,* Osbourne/McGraw-Hill.

Powell, T.A. (2000) *Web Design: The complete reference,* Osbourne/McGraw-Hill.

Useful websites include:

The HTML Writers' Guild is a community of Web designers. The site offers support, online classes and discussion at www.hwg.com

The Internet Corporation for Assigned Names and Numbers (Icann) at www.icann.com

The Internet Democracy Project at www.internetdemocracyproject.org

The Internet Society at www.isoc.org

The WWW Consortium at www.w3c.org

The UN-sponsored organisation with a mission to 'provide an open XML-based infrastructure enabling the global use of electronic business information in an interoperable, secure and consistent manner by all parties' at www.ebxml.org

12

Tool support with Oracle

12.1 Introduction

Many information systems, as demonstrated in earlier chapters (in particular Chapters 8 and 9), have at their heart a DBMS. The product providers of DBMS and their partners have responded to prevalent information management pressures and technological advancements by also providing a set of supporting tools. The information management pressures requiring tool support include the increasing requirement for corporate integration of information systems, the 'applications backlog' (that is the number of applications in organisations awaiting the attentions of the IT professionals), information systems failures, increasing end-user development, the introduction of e-commerce and 'runaway' projects (that is, projects that are delivered late and over budget and sometimes never delivered at all). In this chapter we describe some of these tools, in particular those used with the Oracle DBMS.

The technological advances that have increased the level of support available to developers and end-users include improved graphical user interfaces, Internet developments (Chapter 11), object-oriented technology (Chapter 6) and data warehousing (Chapter 14). Consequently, suppliers of DBMS and third party providers have developed tools to support analysis, design and development, performance monitoring and tuning, networking and enhanced querying, among others.

The apparent separation of DBMS from support tools is, in fact, misleading since many DBMS are supplied with the support tools described below. Further, sometimes they come with different packages of products. Oracle Corporation, for example, produce Oracle8i Personal Edition, Oracle8i Lite, Oracle8i, and Oracle8 and Oracle8i Enterprise Edition to accommodate a variety of user types from single, mobile users to large scale implementers. Oracle examples will be provided in this chapter, as these are presently the most commonly used. These are normally supplied as options.

12.2 Analysis and design tools

There are a number of tools supporting database analysis and design. They may be known as Computer Aided Software Engineering (CASE) tools, integrated workbenches, designers, developers and so on. They may support the entire life cycle of database applications development from enterprise-wide information systems strategy development through analysis and design to construction of individual application areas (see Chapter 18).

They may be used to support the use of a branded IS development methodology, such as SELECT's SSADM Professional, which helps the developer following Structured Systems Analysis and Design Method (SSADM), an approach to IS development. SELECT's object-oriented Enterprise is useful to developers using an object-oriented approach. Oracle Designer is designed to help users following any information systems development methodology.

These tools allow both IS management and the development team to monitor and control the IS development process. Tools to support analysis and design include diagramming tools for business process, data structure or object modelling, translation tools that transform a logical design (that is, as mapped on to a database management system) into a physical design (that is, the database held on file storage devices), code generators, SQL editors, web page designers, form creators and report writing tools.

Critical to any analysis and design tool is a **central repository** that enforces methodological correctness (such as ensuring that all entities have a unique name in an entity-relationship model), incorporates business rules (such as 'a STUDENT may enrol on only one COURSE'), maintains consistency and accuracy, and provides change control procedures throughout the development process to ensure a high quality product. The repository is, in effect, the **data dictionary** for the analysis and design and may be also known as the data encyclopaedia or catalogue. The central repository supports the analysis and design of data structure and data flow, and forms the design of the implemented data dictionary. The central repository therefore contains metadata; that is, data about data.

Analysis and design tools may support the concepts of reverse engineering, allowing the development team to take existing database tables and structures (perhaps used by legacy systems) and incorporate them into the new design. This facility may be particularly helpful where an upgrade of the DBMS has taken place. If the tool is closely associated with the DBMS, as Oracle Designer is to Oracle DBMS for example, then application upgrades can at least be partly generated from the tool itself.

Oracle Corporation's Designer provides an example of the features and functions of a CASE tool. Designer supports the development activity throughout the whole of the information systems development life cycle. The central repository contains the metadata, as described above, which implicitly enables the enforcement of business rules. For example, it is possible in Oracle Designer to request a report of data items appearing in data flows that do not appear in entity descriptions, or entities that lack a unique identifying attribute. Further techniques help to enforce consistency such as the use of a matrix to ensure that each entity has an operation to create, amend and remove its contents.

Diagramming tools for Oracle Designer include those to draw data flow diagrams (a common technique for designing IS processes), entity-relationship diagrams, function hierarchy diagrams and object models. Thus either an object-oriented or data structured approach can be taken. However, a business process model alone, such as a set of data flow diagrams, will not suffice, particularly if intending to generate code from the design. Oracle Designer includes tools for generating the code for required forms and reports using a highly graphical, non-procedural method. Code for implementing applications in the programming languages Visual Basic or C++, for example, or PL/SQL, can be generated from the design.

Reports can be generated from the data, either screen-based or printed, according to the user request. Thus customer statements or student profiles, for example, might be created. Reporting constitutes a large part of most database applications. As with forms, reports can be generated by using SQL extensions available for the DBMS, employing report-writing tools such as Oracle Reports or using the facilities of a multi-purpose tool such as Oracle Designer.

Each designer has his or her own area in which elements of the design are created and tested. A common area for use by the team allows for the system build and testing, and provides a shared communication area to allow for integration of both effort and components. Oracle Designer includes version control (that is planned, accountable, incremental and recoverable development). Enhancements and modifications to the application make changes in Designer to the analysis and design, thereby ensuring correct change control procedures and version control.

A number of reports can be generated from the central repository to aid presentations to clients and users. For example, in Oracle Designer it is possible to generate a **system glossary**. Tools may also include word-processing and presentation tools for feedback, though MS Word or PowerPoint are also commonly used for this purpose.

Tools such as those described in this chapter help to enforce company standards for things such as naming conventions and screen layouts. These standards may result in benefits such as increased speed of production, maintainability, inter-changeability of IS personnel on projects, enhanced company image and user acceptance. Oracle Designer, for example, allows for the building of a Common User Interface that can be applied to all Oracle applications.

12.3 Development tools

As the power and capacity of computing has increased, so the need for efficiency in the execution of code has diminished and efficiencies are sought in the *production* of information systems instead. Furthermore, as efficiencies in the execution of code cease to be a driving force in many applications and the code generation becomes more intuitive and less scientific, so end-users are better able to develop applications for their own purposes, without the need of a database specialist. The search for speed in development and the growth of end-user development has led to the creation of many tools in support, both for the experienced programmer and for the less experienced end-user.

Tools, as described above, integrate part or all of the life cycle for database applications development, which is described in Chapter 18. However, some development tools support only a phase or stage of the development. Many tools are employed on large information systems developments, where the central repository helps to co-ordinate and regulate project team activities. Individual development tools might be used on smaller projects using a rapid application development (RAD) approach, or may be used for implementation following analysis and design. New tools to support development are being marketed, it seems, almost every day. A range of support tools is discussed here to indicate the number and variety available.

All DBMS include methods to allow developers to structure, store, retrieve and manipulate the data in the database, and some of these features, such as the facilities offered by SQL and its extensions, come as standard. Individual tools offering a Graphical User Interface (GUI), such as Oracle8's Oracle Database Configuration Assistant, enable the developer to create a typical database structure. Once the data structure has been created, Oracle Corporation's application development tool, Oracle Developer, allows the user or programmer to quickly produce forms, reports and graphical applications using a non-procedural, or fourth-generation language (4GL). A further Oracle product, Oracle Developer, produces Java code using coding 'wizards'.

Similar tools are available for the networking aspects of the system to be developed (Chapter 10). These include Oracle's Net8 Assistant. Many of the advantages of a database approach are reliant on the ability to connect users to the database and connect databases to each other, and all DBMS allow operation of the database within a multi-user environment. The additional support tools available for networking are principally concerned with establishing and tuning these connections, since many efficiencies in maintenance and operation can be gained through an optimised network to support the database and its users. For example, Oracle Names eliminates the need for client configuration files, Advanced Security includes network encryption and Oracle Connection Manager allows connection multiplexing.

Experienced developers can also use specialist development tools, such as Oracle Forms. This is an interactive tool for on-line data entry forms, such as order forms and job applications, and may be used where Oracle Designer or Oracle Developer has not been used for the earlier stages of development. This tool allows the developer to create the layout, data and processing requirements using wizards. However, the forms generated by Oracle Design and Oracle Developer make it easier to enforce standards in form and format that may have the benefits of consistency already discussed.

Not all data within a database need be textual. Increasingly, organisations have a requirement to store and manipulate images, sound and video data. Oracle8, for example, provides extensions to SQL to fulfil such requirements. Oracle8i has the *inter*Media option that supports multimedia document management on the Internet.

Though the most popular DBMS are based on a relational model, tools may be provided to allow for object-oriented development. For example, Oracle enables programmers to create and use object structures through Object Views, even though Oracle was originally designed as a relational DBMS. Development support tools are also available to retrieve and incorporate data from alternative electronic sources, such as different DBMS or other systems. Extraction and consolidation routines are also necessary for data warehousing. There are also tools supporting data warehousing and data mining, but we discuss these specifically in their context in Chapter 14.

12.4 Query tools

To support the end-user, query tools allow one-off, tailor-made interrogation of the database. SQL provides the main interface between user and data. However, some supplementary tools enable Query by Example (QBE) (see also Chapter 8) and a highly graphical interface especially designed for the end-user. SQL is used more by IS professionals.

Though aimed at the end-user, query support tools are more likely to satisfy users that already understand the logical design of the data in the database, that is the design as seen by the users. Table names may not always be as descriptive as they need to be and what might appear to the user as quite simple queries might entail a great deal of processing in their execution. Alternatively, an end user model can be created from the underlying data structure to support individual user reporting requirements. Users are, of course, restricted to their authorised user view of the data.

An example of a support tool for querying the database is Oracle Reports, a wizard-based product for creating reports in plain text or for Internet access, with some drill down capability. Oracle also produces Oracle Discoverer, which has the added advantage of offering the user some indication of the complexity of the query and its impact on performance, thereby helping to alleviate some of the difficulties of user-created queries.

Tools are available to allow the end user to operate in many different languages using Oracle's National Language Support (NLS).

12.5 Internet tools

Early Internet applications were coded in HTML and later Java. However, Internet applications can now use Internet application generators such as Oracle Corporation's WebDB, which enables application and site development in HTML for the Internet in a browser environment that interacts with an Oracle database.

Traditionally, a client/server environment meant a two-tier organisation, with a large proportion of the application processing undertaken by 'fat' clients. However, since the increase in the use of the Internet, a three-tier approach, as described in Chapter 10, enables a more efficient use of resources by moving the processing away from the client to the middle tier. Once implemented, a three-tier approach may aid the integration of organisational information systems and encourage component-based applications, thereby realising further efficiency gains. Oracle Application Server (OAS) is an example of this approach.

12.6 Interfacing tools

Support tools are available to interface between two or more DBMS. Interfacing tools may be known as middleware, mediators or gateways. Gateways allow communication between two different DBMS, for example Oracle and Informix. Gateways must translate communications between the differing products to provide an unchanged user view, so that the user is unaware that some of the data requested is assembled from a different DBMS. The translation of communications is not necessarily an easy process, since dialects of SQL may vary to such an extent that some SQL queries in Oracle may mean something different in Informix. The problem is made more complex if the DBMS do not share the same underlying model, and there are no support tools available that can guarantee security and integrity in this situation.

There may also be a requirement to move data between databases that have the same DBMS. Though essentially a much simpler operation than communication between differing DBMS, it is still necessary to have tools to replicate, export and import. Movement of data may be necessary when replicating data and metadata over a variety of sites, as in a distributed database, or for the development of a data warehouse or data mart. Tools available from Oracle Corporation include Basic and Advanced Replication, Transportable Tablespaces and Advanced Queuing.

12.7 Performance tools

When a database is not responding quickly enough for the user, then it is suffering from poor performance. This is not necessarily due to inefficiency, since a database can perform efficiently but fail to meet user requirements. It might also perform satisfactorily for the user without being tuned for maximum efficiency. Poor performance may be a general complaint from the user or can be experienced on one particular type of transaction, or at particular times of the day, month or year. Performance problems, then, may be caused by many different factors including hardware constraints or breakdowns, communications difficulties, poor data or application design, poor query construction and inadequate prioritising.

In looking at performance issues, it is possible to consider the SQL statements as well as the running of the database. Queries generated in SQL navigate the database and return the requested results. SQL statements are not necessarily created with performance in mind, however, though they may be executed efficiently. Queries may be optimised by using a set of weighted rules, for example to select the order of tables in a query or the choice of indexes for a particular search. An alternative method of optimising considers the cost of the query in terms of access requirements, and selects the most cost-effective path. Cost-based optimisation, based on a combination of rules, logic and statistics, is the more sophisticated. The optimisation tool is invisible to the user, and may not always follow the most efficient execution path. However, tools such as Oracle's Explain Plan, or ExplainSQL make apparent the execution path followed, and allow the developer to restructure SQL statements to lead the optimising tool towards a better solution. Further tools, such as Oracle Call Interface (OCI), allow experienced programmers to improve performance or add functionality to applications written in a host language such as C or Java by executing SQL statements that have been pre-parsed with performance in mind.

Performance tools are provided to monitor and control the performance of the database and include statistical and analysis routines, and facilities to reorganise the data and optimise queries. The way the data is organised by Oracle on physical storage such as disks may also need to be reorganised over a period of time as changes in data structure and content may lead to fragmentation and consequently poor performance. Employing a volume manager, for example Veritas Software's Volume Manager or HP's Logical Volume Manager, may make such improvements in performance.

Oracle also offers the concept of 'database parallelization' to improve the performance of querying, tuning and maintenance of very large databases. Using database parallelization, tasks are decomposed and executed apparently in parallel using partitioning, optimisation routines and process assigning. Database parallelization allows, for example, multiple table or index scans, or parallel backups and index builds. The partitioning option also allows individual partitions to be maintained separately, leaving the remaining partitions in place for undisturbed user and application access.

12.8 Management tools

Management tools associated with a DBMS provide support for the database administration staff. Many tools for developing and maintaining the database are included with the DBMS. Further support tools for data and database administration include backup and recovery routines, audit trails and recovery logs, encryption and decryption, and central and distributed data dictionary management.

The DBMS will normally be supplied with some, but not all, of these tools. For example, an Oracle DBMS is supplied with the Oracle Enterprise Manager (OEM), which uses agent concepts, web browser technology, a graphical interface and wizards. OEM supports the management of many database administrator functions including transactions, security, database design maintenance, storage, scheduling and execution, and backup and recovery. Further Oracle options, known as 'packs', enhance the facilities to monitor, analyse, diagnose and optimise data organisation and use, including impact analysis and capacity planning. The monitoring of the database is an important management task, as it highlights performance difficulties, patterns of usage and trends to aid tuning and assess future requirements. Tools may support periodic or ad hoc monitoring.

Backup and recovery is specifically discussed in Chapter 13. Some tools enable the automatic creation and updating of a duplicate database where speed of recovery from a disaster is critical. For example, Oracle's Recovery Manager (RMAN) provides automatic incremental backup and recovery.

12.9 Conclusion

DBMS, particularly multi-user, multi-site DBMS, have a wide range of features and options for analysis, design, development, querying, interfacing with other systems, networking, security, performance and management of data-based systems. Some are provided as standard, other tools are optional extras and third party suppliers provide further tools. This complex collection of software components is used throughout the organisation for the development of information systems from individual, ad hoc, stand alone decision support systems through to large, integrated, enterprise-wide solutions, DBMS and support tools together providing a powerful database solution.

Summary

- There are software tools available that support database applications development. They are sometimes provided with a database management system, such as Oracle.
- These tools are known variously as computer-aided software engineering (CASE) tools, integrated workbenches, designers, developers' toolkits and so on.
- These tools vary from basic drawing aids to application generators.
- Tools may relate to a particular development approach, such as SSADM, as well as a particular DBMS, some specific to the Internet and yet others related to performance and management issues.

Exercises

As with many areas discussed in the book, the best way to learn about tools is to use them. Use whatever tools available to you to help automate as many aspects of your case study as possible.

1. 'The selection of appropriate tools is as critical to the success of a project as any other phase of development'. Discuss.
2. Why is there a proliferation of tools to support database and other information systems development?
3. Compare and contrast using PowerPoint or similar presentation software to produce entity-relationship diagrams against using a development tool such as Oracle's Designer or Select SSADM.
4. Conduct some research (the Internet is a good place to start) to compare the tool support offered by Oracle with support available to Sybase.

Further reading

Most of the material on support tools is contained in general books on databases or books on specific DBMS. For general database books try:

Date, C. J. (2000) *An Introduction to Database Systems*, 7th edn, Addison Wesley, Harlow.

For tool support for a particular DBMS see:

Greenwald, R., Stackowiak, R. and Stern, J. (1999) *Oracle Essentials,* O'Reilly, Sebastopol.
Rodgers, U. (1999) *Oracle: A Database Developer's Guide*, 2nd edn, Yourdon Press, Upper Saddle River.

The O'Reilly Series of Oracle books provides a look at aspects of Oracle development. For example, try:

Odewahn, A. (1999) *Oracle Web Applications: PL/SQL Developer's Introduction,* O'Reilly, Sebastopol.

13 Security issues

13.1 Introduction

The benefits of a database approach are based on the expectation that the database contains data that is accurate, consistent, complete and secure. However, the maintenance of data in a volatile environment is problematic. Data may be deleted, created or altered because of fraud, sabotage or due to lack of training. Inappropriate users may read sensitive data out of ignorance, mischief or for personal gain. Data may be lost or corrupted, for example through power failures or a fire. Security of data can be achieved by:

- Limiting who can access the data
- Restricting what they can do
- Monitoring what is done
- Having the ability to recover from any loss.

Sensible data security begins with policy. Policies are then implemented during the development, maintenance and enhancement of the database in appropriate design, and during the day-to-day operation of the database in procedure.

Issues of security are of paramount importance to management in a database environment. However, the level of security that is appropriate depends upon the type of data, type of users and the environment. There may be legal requirements, issues of national security, safety or confidentiality and sensitivity concerns, as well as business issues that make a high level of security appropriate. We give examples of each of these:

- *Legal requirements:* In the UK there are legal requirements preventing the access of medical records by anyone other than a clinician. Many accounting activities are covered by legislation relating to the ability to conduct an audit trail and the requirement not to amend an invoice after its creation.

- *National security:* A simple inventory can threaten national security if it shows the stock level and location of military equipment, for example.

- *Safety:* Contraindications to prescribed drugs may risk lives if accurate data is not available.

- *Confidentiality and sensitivity:* Employees' personnel details, sales projections and data about products in development are only appropriate for a small number in the organisation.

- *Importance to the business:* Financial transactions for a bank or flight reservations for an airline cannot take place without the data being available 24 hours a day, every day. Increasingly for on-line customers, high security promotes trust and, for example, may be an important factor in the development of an on-line brand.

In some cases, security becomes so important that more than one site may be maintained to mirror the transactions and provide instant backup and recovery without loss of any time or data. Some environments require only a very low level of security. However, in many cases the level of security required is somewhere in between, and differs between users and data elements so that security classification need to be specified.

As appropriate in the context of this book, the emphasis in this chapter is on security of data rather than either applications or hardware and the emphasis is on logical rather than physical security, and of the database rather than the operating system or the network. The chapter discusses access control, operation control, monitoring and feedback, and backup and recovery in terms of policy development, design and procedure.

13.2 Access control

The first line of defence for any data is to limit the number and type of users. As figure 13.1 shows, the implementation of security policies restricts who has access to the database. Users can also be given limited access to resources such as disk space. It is not necessarily straightforward to establish policies relating to who should access the data in what way. Although access control is considered a task for the database administrator and access control is a function of the database management system, the decision is very much a management decision and the database administrator is simply implementing policy based on business imperatives.

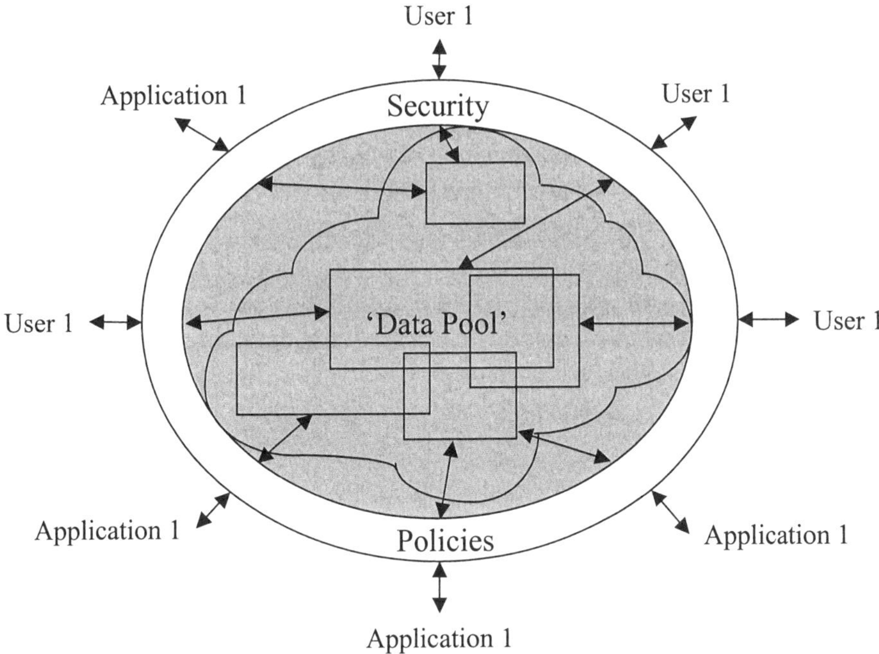

Figure 13.1: Users and applications access depends on security policies

Users may be protective of data in their business area, and for good reason. Organisations often have legitimate objectives that conflict. For example, it is quite reasonable to want to satisfy customer orders quickly and just as reasonable to want to limit the amount of stock held. The balance of stock against demand is a matter of business strategy, that is, the level of service that the organisation offers the customer. It is not a decision for sales or warehouse. Therefore, the policy relating to access reflects business strategy.

Access for a particular user or application in a relational database can relate to a series of tables, a single table, a subset of rows and/or columns down to a single data item. Statements enforcing access policy are stated in the data definition language and form part of the data dictionary description. In an object environment, it is rather more complex, with users granted access to objects so that, for example, an advertising executive might be able to see only the accounts that he or she manages, and not those of any colleagues.

Once access rights have been decided for a user or group of users, there must be a means of checking an access request against the access rights for that user. This is known as **authorisation**. To authorise a user, the system needs to know the identity of the user. Typically, the user is given a User ID for identification and a password for security. Access requests are checked against the user list. This is known as **authentication**. Further safeguards, such as the required length and format for the password, and regular changes of the password can be enforced by the DBMS. For example, Oracle8 requires all passwords to be at least four characters long and to be different from the user ID. Though it is usual to have a user ID and password, other devices, such as fingerprint readers and retinal scanners are available when the need for security is high. All multi-user DBMS support access control.

Data encryption is a method of protecting data directly, rather than seeking to prevent access to the data. Sensitive data, such as credit or debit card details or passwords, are encoded into ciphertext and only authorised users have the decoder or decryption key. Encryption is mostly concerned with the safe communication of data, since this is when data is most vulnerable, particularly in wireless communication, such as that between a mobile unit and the network in a distributed database system. Providers of encryption solutions include Encryption Software, Vasco Data Security and RSA Security. However, some DBMS providers' products, such as Oracle Corporation's Web Application Server or Informix Software's Enterprise Gateway include encryption of passwords and sensitive data. Governments around the world are challenging the right of users, particularly on the Internet, to use high levels of encryption because of the possibility of masking criminal activity. One solution is to require all users of encryption to lodge a data recovery key with a public authority, though at the time of writing this has not been agreed.

Despite the barriers to access outlined above, systems may still be vulnerable to access by unauthorised users. Passwords may be decoded or otherwise circumnavigated. Access may be gained via a legitimate PC, particularly if connected remotely. Where unauthorised users seek access intentionally, the term **hacking** is generally used, particularly when there is malicious intent. As security procedures become more sophisticated, so too do hackers. Criminal acts may be involved, such as fraud, and law enforcers throughout the world are establishing international standards to deal with violations across national boundaries. Where access barriers are breached, monitoring and control of operations offers the next line of defence.

13.3 Operation control

In the same way that access control reflects business strategy, so the policy relating to allowable operations is guided by business rules. For example, it should be impossible for a student to enrol on more than one course or for an accounts clerk to delete an invoice. Such rules can be implemented in the application logic. However, an advantage of the database approach is the availability of large amounts of data for ad hoc queries, rather than limiting the user to only data that an application can deliver. Operation control is about limiting the number of allowable operations that an authorised user can make.

Clearly, some users may have the authority to read, create, delete and amend any data item in the database. The database administration team requires this level of access in order to fulfil the requirements of the database administration role. However, most users will be limited in terms of the data items required and the operations they need to perform on those data. For example, a sales person should not be able to alter the production schedule and will not be able to read personnel details. An order-processing clerk will not be able to change an invoice once it has been created and may not be permitted to delete the details of a supplier.

Data may be read, inserted, deleted or updated. New tables may be created or deleted. The operations allowed by a user or an application are known as **privileges**. These are granted or revoked by the database administration team, for example when a new employee joins an organisation or an employee leaves. It may be that the authority to set privileges is delegated to the data owner.

Privileges may be derived individually depending upon the individual user requirements. Privileges may also be grouped into **roles** so that, for example, all sales employees or all board members have the same privileges. Finally, privileges may be associated with an application. When a privilege is granted to a user, a role or an application, it is known as **discretionary access control**.

In some environments, **mandatory access control** assigns a classification to data, such as top secret or public, *and* a clearance level to users, giving a user access to all data at the level they are cleared for and the levels below. Discretionary measures are often the only methods used to control access to data, although mandatory and discretionary methods can be used to complement each other. User or user group privileges are defined and revoked using a Data Definition Language (DDL) such as SQL. The SQL commands of GRANT and REVOKE handle privileges. In SQL, views are also to be used to limit users' access to data. However, SQL views do not allow for great sophistication in the discretionary access control.

Where unauthorised requests are made, it is most usual to prevent the operation and issue an error message. It may also be appropriate to record the attempt, and even prohibit any further access by that user.

13.4 Monitoring and feedback, backup and recovery

Monitoring is important for a variety of reasons from a security standpoint. Unauthorised users may overcome the barriers and gain access to the database, authorised users may operate in an unauthorised way, there may be legal requirements to have an audit trail or failures may require a reinstatement of the database to a previous state.

The DBMS keeps track of all operations that change values in the database in the **system log** or database journal. With the addition of user log-in and read-only information, it becomes possible to monitor each user and conduct a **database audit** in the case of any problem being detected. A database audit uses the system log to identify who did what, when, as well as allowing recovery to an earlier version or state of the database. It is worth noting that where a group of users has been given the same user ID and password, it is possible only to associate a group of users with a single transaction rather than an individual. Again, the value of the data decides whether the cost of individual user identification is appropriate.

The need to recover to a previous state can be triggered by many things including hardware, software or network failures, programming errors including the failure to adequately deal with exceptions and various physical disasters. Even an authorised user working within their privileges may require, for example, a table that they accidentally deleted to be recovered or a version of the table to be reinstated. An indication of the complexity of recovering from disaster is given when considering that several users and several applications can be using the same tables.

Some systems need to be available 24 hours a day, seven days a week. Others provide an opportunity for backup or recovery outside office hours. Some businesses will lose money as soon as the database system is not available. For others, for example a data warehouse, the impact may not be felt even after several days. If the required level of availability is high, the cost to the business of downtime is high and therefore the time available for backup is limited, it may be necessary to have a duplicate database system running the same transactions at a distant location. This failsafe option is chosen by some organisations as a high security measure.

Backups may be of the entire database, or of a portion of the database. Partial backups can take place while the database is available to users. However, it is most usual to require a period of time off-line in order to backup. Most DBMS provide some automatic backup. For example, Oracle8 will automatically reinstate the database after a failure, providing that there has been no damage to the data. Backup and recovery procedures should be tested, as they will be used. The period between backups and the method of enforcement will vary depending on the value of the data in either a business, legal or privacy sense. Since the system log is so important, the log itself needs to be backed up regularly.

13.5 Conclusion

The emphasis in this chapter has been on protecting the data held in database systems from unauthorised users and prohibited operations. Providing a high level of security is complex and costly. Therefore, organisations choose a level of security that is legal, ethical and reflects the business value of the data. For many organisations, there will be a variety of security levels required for different business areas. For example, a research and development area may need more protection from intruders than an inventory management area, and employee details may be more sensitive than company contact details. Security policy, then, must take many contextual issues into account and will be different for each organisation.

Summary

- The benefits of a database approach are based on the expectation that the database contains data that is accurate, consistent, complete and secure. Security issues help to ensure this is delivered.

- Security includes limiting who can access the data, restricting what they can do, monitoring what is done and having the ability to recover from any loss.

Exercises

1. In the following situations, who does the data need to be protected from, and why?
   Criminal records
   Research and development
   Individual tax returns
   Credit ratings
   Personnel records
   Individual cheque account details
   Customer details
   Student results
2. What constitutes a good password? What should you avoid when deciding on a password? How do the passwords that you use measure up? Whose responsibility is it to ensure that passwords are effective?
3. What are the issues that make it difficult for governments, individuals and businesses to agree on the use of encryption? How can the difficulties be overcome?
4. What are the issues that make it difficult for government and business to agree on methods to deal with hacking? What is the way forward?
5. For your university, hospital or other organization, decide on what level of security in general terms is necessary for your database and in particular decide who can access the data, restricting what they can do, monitoring what is done and having the ability to recover from any loss.

Further reading

Atluri, V., Sushil, J. and Binto, G. (1999) *Multilevel Secure Transaction Processing,* Kluwer Academic Publishers.

Lubbe, J. (1998) *Basic Methods of Cyptography,* Cambridge University Press.

Nasr, J. and Mahler, R. (2001) *Designing Secure Database-Driven Web Sites,* Addison Wesley.

Pipkin, D. (2000) *Information Security,* Prentice Hall.
Spooner, D. L., Demurjian, S.A. and Dobson, J. (eds) (1996) *Database Security,* Kluwer Academic Publishers.
Theriault, M. and Heney, W. (1998) *Oracle Security,* O'Reilly.

Part IV: Applications

In Part I we considered the database applications in the context of the organisation. In Part II we looked at developing the various models, which can represent a stage towards developing the database. In Part III we described how our database applications are implemented. We are now in a position to look at various database applications. We first look at data warehousing and data mining. These are very large database applications that became possible following the improvements in technology. We then look at enterprise resource planning systems, such as SAP, which enable an integration of the various applications (and their databases) in the organisation. Next we consider databases relating to e-commerce applications. Chapter 17 briefly describes a number of other database applications, such as public databases, geographic information systems, marketing information systems, computer supported co-operative working, document management systems, call centres and knowledge management systems.

14

Data warehousing and data mining

14.1 Introduction

Data warehouses are really special cases of databases, and many of the issues of development and maintenance are the same. However, a data warehouse differs from a 'conventional' database in its objective, and this is reflected in a different set of functions and performance criteria.

A database contains operational data relating to the present state of the organisation. It is a 'snapshot' of the organisation. As it is live, speed, backup and security in general, are major concerns. A data warehouse, on the other hand, contains historical data from a variety of disparate sources, much internal but some external. The data, which chiefly come from data sets used by a variety of operational activities on multiple databases, is 'cleansed' so that it is complete for its intended purpose, consistent and integrated. The data is then used for decision-support activities.

A live operational database may be used for operational decision making. A typical example would be a customer who wants a quick decision on a loan application or an insurance quote. However, tactical and strategic decision-support activities are now less often conducted on live, operational systems since the goal of a decision support system is more long-term and concerned with identifying trends and patterns in historical data. In addition, system administrators are naturally concerned with the speed of operational systems and ad hoc, processor-intensive analyses may slow up an operational system. Operational systems may not need the historical data or the overhead required for decision support. There may also be issues of security that require data for analysis to be isolated from the operational system.

Often, decision support systems are for one-off or occasional decisions such as the development of a new product or the siting of a new warehouse. For applications such as these, the data might be gathered from a variety of operational systems and translated into a consistent size, type and format for analysis. A data warehouse provides a robust, static data 'pool' dedicated to the support of all decision-making. Therefore, rather than have a myriad of small decision support systems, an organisation with a data warehouse has a single data repository to support decision-making activities.

14.2 Data warehousing

Organisations store vast amounts of data that, while used for operational tasks, could be analysed for tactical and strategic purposes. In addition, there may be cost savings in isolating the operational data from the decision support data. A data warehouse is large – they are usually measured in terabytes (a terabyte equals a thousand gigabytes) or even petabytes (a thousand times more or 10^{15}) – due to the multiple sources and the addition of data over a period of time. Of course, the capture and management of such large quantities of data, perhaps collected and maintained for different purposes, presents a difficult challenge.

Because of the greater volume of data, a data warehouse needs to be structured differently to a conventional database. The model is multidimensional, that is, the data is stored in matrices with three or more axes. The axes might be those of store, product and time. For example, a clothes retailer's sales may be represented in terms of stores, fashion items and seasons. This multi-dimensional array is known as a **hypercube**. For the large amount of data and processing necessary (operational applications very often use a very few data items only), query performance is particularly important.

The hypercube supports **on-line analytical processing (OLAP)**. This can enable analysis and ad hoc querying of multi-dimensional data. Its features include quick access, fast calculations, complex analyses, the ability to 'drill down' into the data to obtain greater detail, 'roll up' to summarise the data, 'slice and dice' that is, take parts of the data only for analysis. Of course its strength is the ability to do this on huge volumes of data.

Data warehouses, as well as conventional databases, may be **distributed** (Chapter 10). An alternative is to have a **federated warehouse**, that is, a series of autonomous data warehouses. A closely related concept is the **data mart**. A data mart is defined as a subset of the data warehouse, supporting for example a particular department. A data mart, in restricting the user to a particular type, class or location of data, allows the development of a data warehouse in stages or a speedier response to business demands for decision support.

It is not usually necessary for data warehouses to be up-to-date, though it is desirable that the data is 'non-volatile', that is, it does not change much over time. A significant amount of time and effort goes into loading, refreshing and purging the data warehouse and so how up-to-date the warehouse needs to be is an important management decision. However, data warehouses, like all database systems, do require extensive development and maintenance. In addition, data warehousing sometimes uncovers problems in some of the operational systems that feed the warehouse.

It may also be that the data warehouse needs data that is not stored by any operational system. This may be particularly true of any external data relating to, for example, government strategy, the market, the economy or the industry. However, even internal data may not be available or not available at the right level of detail and there is a decision to be made about whether to enhance an existing operational system. For data warehousing purposes, for example, an electronic point of sale (EPOS) system may not record the *time* a purchase is made from a particular retail outlet but if the time subsequently becomes of interest to a data warehousing activity it would be necessary to enhance the operational system accordingly.

An example of an application suited to data warehousing is the analysis of Internet access data. With the increasing use of the Internet, many organisations have an interest in who is going where, whether it is their employers or their customers. Using the data collected, organisations can make alterations to site structure and appearance to increase hit-rates, seek improvements in productivity or undertake more sophisticated customer profiling. The capturing of this data is now quite commonplace, and for organisations that are using the data, a data warehouse provides the basis for analysis.

Data warehouses may not be restricted to strictly internal use, and may be shared by suppliers, partners and even customers, particularly in business-to-business (B2B) exchanges. Examples of B2B exchanges include GlobalNetXchange (GNX) and WorldWide Retail Exchange

(WWRE) both bringing major food retailers closer to their suppliers, and Transcora, an exchange for food manufacturers. In providing information, it may be possible for elements in the supply chain to be better co-ordinated and more responsive. For example, if a component manufacturer is aware of the production details of a car manufacturer they supply, then their own business can be managed accordingly. If the awareness extends to an industry view, the benefits to the component manufacturer are even greater.

All DBMS providers can supply the additional software requirements of a data warehouse, including Sybase's WarehouseArchitect, Oracle Corporation's Oracle Warehouse Builder (OWB) and Informix Software's I-Spy.

14.3 Data mining

Although possible using operational databases, data mining is more usually enabled by data warehousing. The term data mining is used for the extraction and exploratory analysis of data that might allow further predictions to be made about an aspect of interest to the organisation such as factors affecting customer demand or most effective promotions.

For example, a typical UK supermarket carries around 25,000 stock keeping units (SKU); a large bookshop or music outlet might carry 250,000 SKU. Many retailers collect much customer data via scanning at point-of-sale and loyalty schemes. Imagine the data mining that can take place, allowing an organisation to target advertising, better negotiate with suppliers over promotions, improve merchandising and manage inventory, for example. Very successful applications of data mining might generate new business opportunities or suggest ways of gaining and sustaining competitive advantage. Data might also be used for identifying trends, segmenting and profiling customers and simulating the impact of alternative strategies. Again, this may better target advertising, help negotiation with suppliers or manage stocks.

Another common application concerns the use of Internet sites. Tools can be used to track all accesses to the web site: which parts of the site are people using, are they customers or employees, where in the site did they come from, and which parts of the site are not being accessed. The application may make alterations to the site structure and appearance to increase hit rates and the time people spend on the sites.

The concepts of data mining are, of course, not new. In the early days of business computing, automation of business processes meant the gathering and storing of large amounts of operational data which, when filtered, scaled and summarised, provided support for tactical and strategic decision making. More recently, the 24-hour availability of large amounts of data, the superior tools for analysis and the sophisticated data mining algorithms have made the advantages of data mining available to many organisations. Tools based on traditional modelling techniques such as correlation, regression and time series analysis may be used. Ideas from the fields of knowledge management (section 17.4) have also been adopted in data mining, and data mining may employ techniques from machine learning and artificial intelligence such as neural networks, genetic algorithms and fuzzy logic.

Taking the analogy of mining for gems of data further, some authors caution against 'data grubbing'. This describes the tendency to add data to the data warehouse without business reason, use data because it is available and over-analyse data so that it seems to give answers to questions that should never have been asked. Data grubbing is only really possible because of the powerful data mining tools that are now available, allowing complex calculations to be processed quickly and easily. Without an understanding of the underlying statistics, decisions can be made on scanty evidence. On the other hand, it is also true that there is an unpredictable pattern of usage and data held for 'no obvious reason' can become vital to provide an all-round view ready for decision making.

There may seem to be no real difference between data mining and a traditional decision support system. However, there is more of a suggestion of exploration and experimentation than a decision support system with well-defined terms of reference.

14.4 Data mining tools

Data mining is achieved with a variety of data mining tools. There are many tools available offering a variety of investigative techniques for segmentation and clustering, trend and deviation analysis, and dependency modelling. Tools include SGI's MineSet, Enterprise Miner, Clementine, Darwin, SAS and MarketMiner's Expert. Since data mining techniques are often used to learn more about customers, some providers of data mining tools market them as **customer relationship management (CRM)** software, such as Data Distilleries' DDSeries, Computer Associates' IntelligentCRM Suite or SPSS's CustomerCentric. We will look again at CRM in Chapter 16 when we discuss e-commerce. DBMS suppliers also provide software support for building and mining data warehouses, for example, Oracle's Data Mining.

14.5 Data warehousing tools

A database usually contains more than just a snapshot of system data. Historical data can be used for the identification of trends, segmentation and profiling, forecasting and simulation. Since the data used for data mining is not live data, support tools include tools to build a data warehouse from an existing 'live' database. Oracle support tools for data warehousing include a time series option for trend analysis, a spatial option for geographical information systems (section 17.3) and *inter*Media option for multimedia document management.

A data warehouse might be derived from enterprise-wide data stored on a variety of information systems. As with interfacing support tools, described below, gateways allow data from a variety of DBMS to be incorporated into a data warehouse. The data needs to be extracted from its source, converted for the format of the data warehouse, cleansed (that is, consistent and integrated), scaled or summarised as appropriate, stored and retrieved in order to be analysed. Data warehouses also require loading, backup and recovery procedures for their successful management, though sometimes it might be easier to reconstruct a data warehouse in the event of a disaster, rather than regularly backup.

The type of queries made of a data warehouse is different from the online transaction processing required of the operational database. Queries are complicated, and take a long time to return the results. Some of the most popular data mining tools include SAS, SPSS and Darwin. Specific OLAP tools include Oracle Express, Microsoft SQL OLAP services, Cognus Powerplay and Information Builder Focus.

Summary

- A data warehouse is a type of database and the development of a data warehouse is a huge undertaking for any organisation, involving many staff members and resources. However, a data warehouse differs from a conventional database because it is larger and the data is more diverse.
- The purpose of a data warehouse also differs from a database for operational activities, in particular, and this differing purpose is reflected in the structure and use of a data warehouse.
- The advantages of data warehousing include isolating decision support activities from the more volatile operational activities, providing a single source of data for decision support, faster querying of larger amounts of data and the opportunity for data mining.

- Data mining is the extraction and exploratory analysis of data that might allow further predictions to be made about an aspect of interest to the organisation such as factors affecting customer demand or most effective promotions.
- Both data warehousing and data mining are facilitated through the use of appropriate tools.

Exercises

1. Distinguish between databases, data warehouses and data mining.
2. How might data mining help a company selling on the Internet, a mail order business and a conventional manufacturing organisation?
3. Discuss the potential of data warehouses and data mining for the university, hospital or other organisation.

Further reading

Agosta, L. (1999) *The Essential Guide to Data Warehousing,* Prentice Hall.

Bashein, B. J and Markus, M. L. (2000) *Data Warehouses: more than just mining,* Financial Executives Research Foundation.

Dodge, G. and Gorman, T. (2001) *Essential Oracle8i Data Warehousing,* Wiley.

Inmon, W. H. (2000) *Exploration Warehousing,* Wiley.

Jarke, M., Lenzerini, M., Vassiliou, Y. and Vassiliadis, P. (1999) *Fundamentals of Data Warehouses,* Springer-Verlag.

Todman, C. (2001) *Designing a Data Warehouse,* Prentice Hall.

15

Enterprise Resource Planning (ERP)

15.1 Scale of ERP systems

The success of an organisation may depend largely on integrated systems, and in particular on the effective transfer of information throughout the supply chain. Enterprise Resource Planning (ERP) systems form a complex series of software modules used to integrate many business processes. Originally, these included production, inventory management and logistics modules for manufacturing organisations. Later, they developed from materials requirement planning and manufacturing resource planning systems to encompass the capabilities of money resources planning systems, so that ERP systems supported all the basic financial applications and other organisational functions, such as human resource management. Now they include strategic planning, sales and distribution, marketing, financials, controls, quality management, supply management, materials management, plant maintenance, production planning, workflow and human resource management, indeed, all the business processes and functions of the organisation. More recently still, modules have been incorporated that provide the capability for e-commerce. In this way ERP systems impact outside the organisation as well as within it, as they allow for communication with suppliers and customers. Indeed, they attempt to provide a complete IT solution for businesses.

Many potential advantages are obvious. The business gains from a fully integrated system that enables visibility and integrity of data throughout the organisation. Some of the potential disadvantages are also obvious; in particular, the complexity of integrating many or most of the organisation's applications and the consequent cost in terms of money and time to achieve this. There is therefore some risk associated with the implementation of ERP systems.

As we have said, the latest versions incorporate Internet technology to pull suppliers and customers closer together in the supply chain. An example might be a customer buying a new car from a dealer. The customer may be able to find where the car is in the manufacturer's production schedule and the suppliers of raw materials are able to predict manufacturer requirements based on dealers' forward orders.

Enterprise resource planning systems are supplied by SAP, Oracle, JD Edwards, Baan and PeopleSoft. The 'sales pitch' is obvious – there is support for every aspect of the business, each system is seen as the 'best of breed', top management can see the implications of one part of the business on others, and 'discipline' can be imposed on the workforce as all activities can be costed and controlled.

The market leader SAP has around 40% of the overall market, over 15,000 installed sites worldwide and over US$6 billion in development. The temptation to join this bandwagon has been difficult to resist. It is even possible to have such software configured for certain sectors, including universities, banks, airlines and retail. Along with the software itself, there is a huge business in training and consulting.

However, many organisations have found that it is not that simple. The long implementation time span, the huge investment, the impact of everything changing at the same time and the sheer direct and indirect costs are just some of the complaints offsetting some of the claims. Further, in order to make the likelihood of success greater, many firms change processes to fit the software that is, minimal customisation or 'vanilla ERP', and this causes problems. In practice, implementation of ERP systems have often coincided with downsizing (in all but ERP expertise) as companies try to alleviate costs, and middle management in particular suffers. Nevertheless, many businesses have found that their ERP implementation has proved to be a great success.

15.2 Database embedding an ERP system

ERP systems provide a dramatic realisation of the database approach that has only become possible in recent years. ERP uses a fully integrated, normally relational database based on a client/server model. In order for the modules to communicate, the database needs to be highly normalised and structured with centralised data architecture. It is very data intensive. The data is available to any of the application components of the ERP system.

The standardised aspect, necessary for a reasonable implementation timetable and to reduce the risks of incompatibility, opens the way for a potential criticism, that all businesses that use these systems might be similar in regards to their database and IT aspect. Therefore potential competitive advantage gains are more difficult to realise. On the other hand, the potential gains of 'best of breed', integration, and the gains of discipline, are apparent as well. Their databases are a centralised and growing repository of organisational information that becomes an immensely powerful resource. To some extent they have the advantages of databases, data warehouses and data mining, without the problems that comes from a lack of standardisation that usually is associated with some data warehousing.

The integrity, security, flexibility and independence of the data is critical to the integration of processes and the provision of the executive perspective, allowing multifaceted, ad hoc queries with 'drill down' facilities to get more detail from the database. The project and programme planning, monitoring and control represents a major information systems and management investment. These are all concerns of conventional database applications, but the scale of some ERP applications makes them particularly critical in that domain.

15.3 ERP and business process reengineering (BPR)

ERP projects may be linked to business process reengineering (BPR) initiatives in organisations, and there is some discussion as to whether the reengineering of business processes should lead or be led by the IT solution. We have seen that the potential benefits of ERP reflect the broad scope of the IT solution, including lower costs, improved customer response times and customer relationships, reduced stock holdings, increased product range and quality, better co-ordination of supply, demand and production.

But the implementation of ERP to this extreme implies a massive change in the way the business does its processing. Thus BPR may be caused by the decision to adopt ERP. On the other hand, business management may argue for change in the way it does its processing. This change may suggest a change in its IT as well. Thus ERP often follows BPR as well.

It is conventional thinking that IT change should follow business change and not the other way round. Reengineering determines what an organisation should do, how it should do it, and what its concerns should be, as opposed to what they currently are. Emphasis is placed on the business processes (and therefore information systems that reflect them and enable the change), but it also encompasses managerial behaviour, work patterns, values, beliefs, measurement systems and organisational structure.

The role of information systems and information technology – and ERP in particular – is seen as an enabler of change, supporting the running of the new processes that replace the old ones. On the other hand, as we have shown above, ERP systems are particularly costly to implement, and many argue that in order for them to be successful, they cannot be customised. In that case there will be at least some element of the business changing to suit the system as well. At the extreme, ERP systems model an 'ideal' organisation. It then expects the organisation that does not meet the ideal to change.

Summary

- Enterprise Resource Planning (ERP) systems form a complex series of software modules used to integrate many business processes.
- In the extreme, they include strategic planning, sales and distribution, marketing, financials, controls, quality management, supply management, materials management, plant maintenance, production planning, workflow and human resource management.
- ERP uses a fully integrated, normally relational database based on a client/server model. In order for the modules to communicate, the database needs to be highly normalised and structured with centralised data architecture. It is very data intensive.
- ERP projects may be linked to business process reengineering (BPR) initiatives in organisations, and there is some discussion as to whether the reengineering of business processes should lead or be led by the IT solution.

Exercises

1. What are the advantages of ERP systems when compared to a series of legacy systems?
2. What is the role of the database in an ERP system?

3. Argue the case for and against an ERP system in the organisation of your choice. Does your university, for example, have one already? If so, why was it adopted and what do users say about the system?

Further reading

Grint, K., Case. P. and Willcocks, L (1996) Business process engineering reappraised. In: Orlikowski, W., Walsham, G., Jones, M. and DeGross, J. J (1996) *Information Technology and Changes in Organizational Work*, Chapman and Hall, London.

O'Shea, J. and Madigan, C. (1998) *Dangerous Company: Management Consultants and the Businesses They Save and Ruin*, Penguin.

Parr, A. N., Shanks, G. and Darke, P. (1999) Identification of necessary factors for successful implementation of ERP systems. In: Ngwenyama, O., Introna, L. D., Myers, M. D. and DeGross, J. I. *New Information Technologies in Organisational Processes,* Kluwer, Boston.

Ptak, C. A. and Schragenheim, E. (1999) *ERP Tools, Techniques and Applications for Integrating the Supply Chain,* St Lucie Press.

Shtub, A. (1999) *Enterprise Resource Planning (ERP),* Kluwer Academic Press.

Web sites

SAP at www.sap.com
PeopleSoft at www.peoplesoft.com
J.D.Edwards at www.jdedwards.com
Baan at www.baan.com

16

Electronic commerce

16.1 Background

Electronic commerce (or e-commerce) describes the buying and selling of products, services, and information via computer networks, in particular, the Internet. It is often assumed that most transactions are business-to-consumer (b2c), but about 80% of electronic commerce activity is business-to-business (b2b). Other activity includes that between government-to-consumer. Again, e-commerce is a huge issue, so we will only focus on those aspects that are particularly relevant to the subject of this book.

16.2 Business-to-business (b2b) e-commerce

Supply chain management concerns the activities related to the flow and transformation of goods from raw materials, to semi-finished goods to finished goods delivered to the customer. Computer networks enable supply chain management to be improved even where there can be many business suppliers and customers. This includes procurement, production, inventory, marketing, and logistics activities.

b2b activities are usually conducted within a sub-set of the Internet. This is called an Extranet of businesses which have tied-in to the b2b e-commerce activity. It is therefore a development from the more traditional electronic data interchange (EDI). Electronic commerce is seen as more flexible, less expensive, quicker to set up and less complex. There needs to be a firewall (hardware and software), which allows only those specific external organisations that are part of the b2b network to access the Extranet.

One frequent activity in procurement is to ask suppliers to make bids for a contract to achieve a best deal amongst its suppliers. This is referred to as a request for quotations (RFQ). Another activity concerns auctions between businesses – auctions are also available in the b2c environment.

16.3 Business-to-consumer (b2c) e-commerce

On the b2c side, according to a survey by NUA Surveys in 1999, 179 million people were connected to the Internet by June of that year, representing 3% of the total population worldwide. Accessing the Internet has quickly become an everyday activity for millions of people around the world. In 1999, US online sales took place worth $31 billion, a little over 1.4% of total US retail sales. Only the previous year, the Internet had accounted for just less than 1%, representing a significant increase that is expected to continue. UK online retailing in 1998 reached £200 million. Minimum estimates for Christmas 1999 are given as around £200 million, again indicating a trend towards 'e-tailing'. In January 2002, Amazon.com reported its first-ever profit. The most popular purchases are books, videos, CDs, computing and electronic equipment, flights and holidays. However, almost anything is available by e-commerce from locations around the globe. Auction sites are also increasingly popular. In general, users are likely to be younger (20–40), middle class, white (in America), and well educated. But this is a generalisation and the appeal of e-commerce is widening into most groups.

16.4 Databases and e-commerce

Electronic commerce provides a good example of a database application, incorporating customer, product, order, fulfilment, payment and financial data to allow the buying and selling of goods and services using the medium of the Internet. Such applications include club memberships, mailing lists and library catalogues. Many databases are created for the e-commerce application, as Amazon's was (though book data was transferred from such sources as Books in Print), and it can be difficult to integrate the Internet and electronic commerce software with some existing databases. Many other Internet applications include a database for storing, retrieving, manipulating and displaying data.

The creation of a catalogue database is a typical example. Thus Amazon has a catalogue of books; RS Components a catalogue of electrical items; and Blackstar a catalogue of videos. Updating prices and adding new items to electronic catalogues is convenient and cheap and a major improvement on paper catalogues which are expensive and can only be updated infrequently. From the consumer's point of view there are improvements as well, for example, the ability to search the catalogue on product type, number, or organise products on price or manufacturer. Thus the end customer utilises the capabilities of databases.

Some 'malls' search through database catalogues of various suppliers and compares prices of equivalent products. This requires intelligent search software along with access to the catalogue and product databases.

E-commerce is based on Internet technology, combining networking, a client/server model and storage with software to provide the base of data, security and routing. Some telephony may also be incorporated.

Database vendors provide development tools for e-commerce such as Oracle's Designer. ERP software, such as SAP, may also contain modules for e-commerce applications. The 'glue' of ERP – the integration of applications – is also the 'glue' of e-commerce. Sales orders, payment, workflow, stock control, accounts, product list and other catalogues are a feature of e-commerce as well as bricks-and-mortar companies. Even though there are differences in form, for example, the medium of communication, electronic payment and virtual catalogues, many of the basics are not much different. Indeed some of the major work involved concerns the integration of e-commerce applications and databases with existing systems. Again, ERP software may be designed to integrate these legacy systems with the new applications.

For b2b e-commerce there are likely to be databases of catalogues, supplier and customer order information (as well as suppliers and customers), bidding information and so on.

Security is an overriding concern for organisations involved in e-commerce. Electronic transaction security protocols have developed to safely deal with Internet transactions, and many organisations have dedicated servers. Routers and firewalls provide a software barrier for security and encryption aims to ensure that intruders do not intercept data. Encryption methods try to ensure details such as credit card numbers, and customer addresses remain confidential. Various protocols relate to the authentication that both parties in the transaction are the people they claim to be. For e-commerce, robustness and reliability of hardware and software is critical to success. The size and growth of the transaction processing is difficult to predict, and 24-hour service requires a level of redundancy to support backup and recovery procedures.

Related to security are the privacy issues associated with the possibility of holding personal data on databases. Customers may wish to give their personal data (name-and-address information, for example) for one use only. The customer will want to know if these details will be used more than once or be released to other businesses, where the data is stored, and how the data might be used. There should be a policy available to customers stating how data is collected, what data is collected, that data kept is accurate and remains confidential. For example, data collected should relate only to the particular transaction, sensitive data should be checked carefully, the security procedures should ensure confidentiality and data not disclosed without permission.

16.5 Customer relationship management

Customer relationship management (CRM) represents an overt attempt of an e-commerce organisation to build a long-term association with its partners (business and consumer) thus enhancing the relationship. It is characterised by purposeful cooperation and mutual dependence. In an e-commerce context it is sometimes referred to as e-care, the support for customers that will hopefully lead to a long-term commitment and therefore be mutually positive. So, for example, in the b2c context a customer on logging on to a website might see a welcome which mentions the customer's name, a list of new products related to products that the customer has shown interest before, a list of special offers geared to the customer's previous purchases and so on. In this way the customer is more firmly tied into the site and more likely to be a loyal, long-term customer. In order to do this, amongst other things, it is necessary to create a database which records sales, problems and requests. In a b2b context, it suggests a dedicated service providing information for these important associates.

CRM also relates to customers in a general sense, so that, analysis software might inform on the use of particular pages, the source in terms of regions of the requests, and so on. E-commerce provides an opportunity to use these data mining techniques (see Chapter 15) to provide traffic reporting and user behaviour.

Summary

- Electronic commerce (or e-commerce) describes the buying and selling of products, services, and information via computer networks, in particular, the Internet. It is usually either business-to-business or business-to-consumer.
- Much of e-commerce concerns supply chain management that is, the activities related to the flow and transformation of goods from raw materials, to semi-finished goods to finished goods delivered to the customer.
- Customer, product, order, fulfilment, payment and financial data will be held in databases supporting e-commerce activities.
- Customer relationship management (CRM) represents an overt attempt of an e-commerce organisation to build a long-term association with its partners (business and consumer) thus enhancing the relationship. It usually incorporates data mining techniques.

Exercises

1. Look through some b2c web sites and suggest the databases that are likely to support them.
2. Discuss the role of databases in the Internet.

Further reading

Material is this area is constantly changing as more customers choose to buy a wider variety of goods on-line and the possibilities for e-commerce afforded by the emerging technologies and concepts increase. However, the following references provide some of the fundamentals of e-commerce:

Chaffey, D (2001) *E-business and E-commerce management,* Prentice-Hall.

May, P. (2000) *The Business of E-commerce,* Cambridge University Press.

Fellenstein, C. and Wood, R. (1999) *Exploring E-Commerce, Global E-Business and E-Society,* Prentice Hall.

Whitely, D. (2000) *E-Commerce,* McGraw Hill.

Web addresses

The updated figures mentioned in the text are available from www.nielsen-netratings.com and www.nua.ie. Sites for e-commerce in the UK include www.amazon.co.uk selling mainly books, CDs, DVDs and videos but incorporating a shop for other items and an auction, www.tescodirect.com and www.iceland-freeshop.com for largely grocery shopping and www.a2btravel.com for flights using the travel agents' Sabre database, holidays, car hire and entertainment. www.nufc.co.uk provides information on a great football team. Vendors of e-commerce systems include Enterprise Resource Planning (ERP) providers such as SAP at www.sap.com and J.D. Edwards at www.jdedwards.com, and database developers such as Oracle at www.oracle.com.

17

Other database applications

17.1 Introduction

Technological advances have brought greater power, capacity and interconnectivity to the desktop from the boardroom down to the shop floor. Today's client/server technology makes the storage and retrieval of data and applications independent of local processing capability. At the same time, development software has become more powerful and flexible, and may be applied successfully to a wide variety of real-world problems. The combination of increased processing capability and adaptable software makes it difficult to derive a classification of system types that neatly describes the distinction between one information system and another.

Therefore this chapter on database applications describes, not a series of database systems types, but a variety of IT solutions that incorporate a database. Some of the applications can be bought as dedicated software, such as geographical information systems, while others, for example, marketing information systems, are implemented using a standard DBMS such as Oracle. Applications range from specific problem-solving tools to enterprise-wide integrated environments. The following list is not exhaustive but represents a cross-section of current database applications. Each application is defined from a business perspective, and then described in terms of its features and the supporting technology.

17.2 Public databases

Much data is available to the general public through databases created and maintained by government bodies, public sector organisations, voluntary groups and individuals. A vast array of data sets are available, including electoral and census data, library catalogues, bibliographies, education figures, genealogy, astronomical data, legal material, medical facts and other scientific data. The data is used by individuals and businesses for a wide variety of purposes: from choosing a primary school to targeting marketing campaigns.

Public databases are non-commercial. The general public may access the data in a variety of ways depending upon the availability and medium of the data or on individual preference. Some items of data are available only by a written request; others can be viewed using CDRom or microfiche technology in libraries, government offices, schools and elsewhere. Many public databases are available on the Internet, allowing easy access from home and workplace at any time and from around the world.

Public databases are created and used by government offices to make data available to the public and to conduct analyses to meet their objectives. For example, UK census data is used by government to inform debate within government, and is available to the general public at the Office for National Statistics web site. Other organisations might use the data to perform further analyses. For example, the UK University League tables published by the *Times Higher Education Supplement* are created from data collected, stored and maintained by the Higher Education Statistical Agency. Where a third party becomes involved, there may be a charge for the analysis. Public databases provide useful data for many organisation types including those in retail, finance, politics and leisure.

Example public databases available in the UK on the Internet include government sites such as www.ons.gov.uk. The British Broadcasting Corporation at www.bbc.co.uk sometimes uses data provided on public databases for news items and features, and provides links to related sites. On payment of a subscription, sites such as www.thesis.co.uk provide analyses that use data collected by government.

17.3 Geographical information systems

A Geographical Information System (GIS) is a database application that captures, stores, retrieves, manipulates and displays human and physical geographical data. The possible applications for a GIS are numerous, and include deciding on store location for retailing, road planning for local government and vehicle routing for the wholesale distribution of goods. The data may be represented in a typical map format incorporating 3D and photographic images or displayed in graphs and charts. In the same way as any database may be queried, so a GIS may be used to find, for example, all the towns in the UK of between 80,000 and 120,000 inhabitants or the value of a piece of land. A tremendous amount of data is brought together in a GIS, providing a powerful and versatile tool for solving real-world problems in a wide variety of business environments.

A GIS is based on a relational database that manages multiple data sets. For example, store locations might be related to survey data to provide a customer profile for each store. A GIS can be ready-loaded with some basic geographic data but further data requirements vary from application to application. The required data may be created by the user, derived from public sources or from companies such as Ordnance Survey and AC Nielsen. Most GIS will combine some aspect of all three. Some GIS will integrate data from Oracle and other relational databases, allowing the organisation to incorporate data from other business applications. For example, timetables for bus routes or vehicle data for fleet management.

The GIS software provides tools for the input of geographical data, and the query, analysis and displaying or printing of information in a variety of formats. The input of data may not be an easy task, as geographic data exists on a variety of levels and it must be transformed to the same scale before it can be integrated. However, some data is available from third party companies in a plug-n-play format. A GIS may be used to answer simple queries such as the location of a postcode or the percentage of inland waterways. However, the querying capability of a GIS also provides the ability to help to predict outcomes and spot trends. GIS may be used to simulate the impact on traffic flow of a pedestrianised town centre or to monitor the growth of violent crime in a suburb, for example. The display of geographical information, a complex combination of multiple spatial data providing a rich description of geographical locations, may be based on a vector or raster graphics model. More recently, GIS are based on a combination, thereby realising the advantages of both models. The highly Graphical User Interface (GUI) for a GIS provides a user-friendly environment for managers, analysts and customers.

Much of the information provided by GIS is available in other formats from other software products, for example standard DBMS or spreadsheets. However, the ability to display information in a geographical format may be considered an improvement over the graphs and charts generated by other systems. Maps may be better appreciated by the human senses and can be used to make communication more effective throughout the organisation in reports and interactive displays. In some organisations the GIS will have very few users with specific requirements such as fleet management or site selection. In other organisations, the GIS may support the core activities with many users and a diversity of uses. To support this diversity, GIS might run on a variety of platforms including PC, Macintosh and Sun workstation. Adopting a client/server model in a multi-user environment, GIS may use Internet technology to allow internal and external communication of geographical information and analyses.

Examples of GIS software include MapInfo at www.mapinfo.com, GeoMedia from Intergraph at www.intergraph.com and ArcView from ESRI at www.esri.com. Data for GISs is available from companies such as ordnance survey at www.ordnancesurvey.co.uk and AC Nielsen at www.acnielsen.com.

17.4 Marketing information systems

A marketing information system (sometimes abbreviated to MkIS) uses the input, storage, retrieval, manipulation and dissemination capabilities of database technology to support marketing decision making. Examples of marketing decisions include the development of a new product or a new pricing strategy. When implemented using a standard DBMS such as Oracle or DB2, a MkIS has at its heart a database of internal data. From within the organisation, the marketer may be interested in sales and order data, payment records and production figures. Data may be aggregated and the marketer is unlikely to need to identify, for example, an individual customer's buying pattern but may use the data for customer segmentation.

Internal data is important in a MkIS. However, the data needed to support marketing decisions may be derived from an integration of data from both internal and external sources. For example, a customer loyalty scheme for a supermarket may rely on data collected at the point of sale. However, competitors' data, economic data and social trends may support an advertising campaign. Sources of external data include specialist market research agencies, academic institutions, trade and business associations, government departments and news agencies.

A MkIS may include components to assist in management, including sales forecasting and sales force automation, product management, including promotion and advertising, and market research including trend analysis. The querying capability provided by a database approach allows for ad hoc interrogation and reporting, particularly useful in dynamic decision making. A MkIS may use data warehousing and data mining technology, using data gleaned from around and outside the organisation, and perhaps including primary data, that is, data collected primarily for the purpose of supporting a particular decision.

The increased power and capacity of modern-day database technology allows the marketer to collect, integrate and analyse a far greater volume of data than ever before, allowing more sophisticated analyses, more refined segmentation and better decisions. For example, the Summer 1999 mailing to Tesco supermarket customers in the UK had 80,000 variations depending upon customers' buying patterns, so that, for example, vegetarians did not receive offers on meat and pet owners were targeted with pet product promotions.

For further reading, specialist database texts may contain chapters on decision support, and the marketer will find chapters in general marketing books on database technology. The reading list at the end of the chapter includes a standard database text, a standard marketing text and a marketing text focusing on data.

17.5 Computer supported co-operative working

It is clear that information technology can support individuals in organisations performing a wide variety of activities. However, many projects, from the development of a new product to the implementation of an information system, require a significant amount of group work. On large projects across organisational or national boundaries, group members may encounter difficulties in time, location, language and culture. It is likely that projects of this type, relying on close collaboration between disparate group members, are increasingly common, and Computer-Supported Co-operative (or sometimes collaborative) Working (CSCW) provides the required technology for co-ordination and integration.

The term CSCW is usually used to describe a research area that combines a technological solution with a multidisciplinary approach to group work. The term was first used in the 1980s and tends to be associated with research in the social sciences, with its emphasis on the cultural, political and social aspects of group work, as well as the technical support. The type of group work that may be supported by computer is diverse but can be described as any activity that requires a number of people to work together across boundaries of culture and/or discipline. Therefore, CSCW tends to be used by researchers and developers on collaborations between institutions or organisations in different countries. However, the term is of interest here as it provides the underlying concepts for some of the applications that use a database to support communication and co-ordination for group work.

Applications include Computer Aided Software Engineering (CASE), large-scale project management, Computer Aided Design and Manufacture and distance learning. All these applications depend upon communication technologies developed as a result of research into CSCW such as Computer Mediated Communication (CMC), workflow management, electronic whiteboards and teleconferencing, and use a data pool to provide a shared understanding.

The term 'groupware', which is sometimes used synonymously with CSCW, might be used to describe the enabling technology, with CSCW more usually applied to the area of discourse. In an environment where the emphasis is on facilitating the decision making within a group, CSCW is sometimes known as Group Decision Support Systems (GDSS).

Even something as simple as an e-mail list could be described as CSCW, as it provides a communication method irrespective of time and place. However, the most sophisticated CSCW applications include modules to allow teleconferencing, e-mail, workflow management and collaborative writing with shared workspaces and multimedia communication, representing a combination of database technology and other developed and emerging fields of computing including natural language processing, voice recognition, speech synthesis and virtual reality.

Examples of CSCW systems include software such as Lotus Notes, Microsoft Exchange and Novell's Groupwise5, though CSCW may be facilitated using a wide variety of software solutions depending on the application area. For example, Oracle Designer at www.oracle.com supports group software development and SuperProject by Computer Associates at www.cai.com.

17.6 Document management systems

One of the benefits of increased automation promised by the early information technologists was the concept of the paperless office. Though office automation systems failed to remove paper-based documents from the office, document management systems (DMS) provide the modern-day solution, using imaging and associated techniques to translate and create electronic documents. Any written communication might be considered a document, and there are many examples in all organisations from orders, delivery notes and invoices, through job applications and descriptions, policy documents and mission statements, to memos, newspaper articles, photographs, drawings and rotas. Any action associated with the creation, storage, retrieval or dissemination of a document is Document Management.

Databases contain data items, many of which are assembled or derived from documents. Documents such as invoices, orders, picking lists and despatch notes all contain data items that are logically identical. However, documents are important in all organisations, and critical to some. Documents might drive the workflow, as in order processing or have legal implications, like a signed and witnessed Statutory Declaration. Therefore, Document Management is an increasing concern of many businesses, particularly in those areas where the management of documents might be considered a critical success factor, such as in the legal profession, publishing and some government offices.

Document Management in its broadest sense might include paper documents but the term has come to mean management of the documents that are created in or translated into an electronic form. To emphasise the significance of technology, they are often referred to as Electronic Document Management Systems (EDMS). The management of documents is concerned with document creation and final archiving or destruction, as well as storage and retrieval. For example, a contract may be created during negotiation, referred to during its life cycle and archived on completion. A document is not simply stored but is indexed and fully searchable, not only by key word, but also on any word, pattern or character, and even elements such as sound waves in the more sophisticated DMS.

Documents are translated using scanners and associated techniques such as Optical Character Recognition (OCR) and Intelligent Character Recognition (ICR). Within a DMS, a profile is generated and maintained for each document that includes information for version control, access and change audit, levels of security and confidentiality, attachments and relationship to other documents.

The obvious possible benefits of efficient and effective document management include speed of communication and a reduction in paper. However, Document Management clearly has a role within Knowledge Management (see Section 17.8), as Document Management creates, maintains and provides controlled dissemination of a repository of organisational knowledge. The nurturing of organisational knowledge may have wider implications for a learning organisation.

Document Management Systems (DSS) software sits on top of the DBMS, providing the tools for Document Management. Examples include DOCS Open from PC Docs at www.pcdocs.com, EFS from Excalibur Technologies, several Documentation tools and Novell's Groupwise5. The Ovum report from 1998, *A how to guide to Electronic Document Management Systems*, is expensive but provides a thorough guide for business.

17.7 Call centres

Call centres are increasingly a feature of everyday life. A user may come across a call centre when ordering flowers, placing a complaint, asking for technical help over the telephone, when e-mailing a suggestion for improvement to a company web site or faxing some documents to help with an insurance claim. A call centre may also be responsible for a call from a bank to encourage a customer to take out a loan or from a telecommunications company to seek customer feedback on a new service.

Call centres were first created as a method of building and maintaining customer relationships using communication by telephone. However other channels, including the Internet, are increasingly employed. A call centre may, therefore, include technology to support a variety of methods used for communication between the organisation and its customers. Call centres are used by many types of organisation to reduce costs and enhance customer service, including extending opening hours and creating and using individual customer profiles.

A call centre may be centralised or distributed. If centralised, all the facilities and personnel are in a single geographic location. The site of a call centre will be influenced by economic factors, rather than necessarily being located at the organisation's headquarters. In employing a sophisticated integration of network and Internet technology, computing and telephony, the call centre may be situated anywhere around the world and still provide an apparently local service. A call centre may be stand alone, or be connected to other centres in order to route calls to personnel with particular skills, deal with overflow or provide choice to give the most efficient routing of calls. The technology can also be used to provide a distributed system, with personnel geographically dispersed, perhaps working from home. A call centre may have some entirely automated procedures such as a credit card company giving balance information to a customer over the telephone, or a bank responding to an e-mail request for a statement. Call centres are commonly outsourced; that is a third party may provide the functions of the call centre.

The technology used by a call centre relies on telecommunications provided by companies such as BT, AT&T and Nortel. However, database technology provides the underlying database of customer and product information for use by the centre. A call centre can process a large volume of customer contacts using a variety of media and methods. The data required at the point of customer contact will vary depending upon the application. For a mail order company, product and stock information is required. For a bank, transaction data and a customer history may be used in the interaction between the call centre and the customer. The call centre may access corporate databases, or more likely use data warehousing techniques,

17.8 Knowledge management

Knowledge management concerns getting information to the appropriate people, when required, helping them to share this information and experience, and enabling them to use it to improve organisational performance. Competitive advantage might be achieved through this knowledge sharing, encouraging innovation, building on past experience and creating new capabilities. Its aim is therefore to build on organisational memory through organisational learning.

Too often, organisations forget what they know, and one aspect of knowledge management is identifying its knowledge assets, and then to manage and make use of these assets by diffusion. In the long term, organisations try to change the culture so that knowledge sharing is the norm. In doing that, it needs to counteract the view that knowledge is power and therefore sharing it loses personal power. Reward schemes can help to make the sharing of knowledge advantageous to the individual.

From the organisation's point of view, knowledge management is about sharing best practice, but externally, it wants to make capabilities rare, valuable and difficult to imitate. Sun Microsystems, a company that sells hardware and software, makes available knowledge about new systems to staff out in the field for training purposes whilst they are at work. Staff are therefore up-to-date without the need to go to frequent formal training courses. Ernst and Young, a consultancy company, provides knowledge to its customers about auditing, tax updates, methods and tools. These customers pay for the particular service, belonging to the knowledge network. 3M a company relying on innovation, uses knowledge management systems to diffuse knowledge on best practices in their research and development and their technical communities. Their intranet site includes the ability to access library and information services, a corporate learning management system (including access to e-learning), a news management facility, a directory of e-business contacts, and communities of knowledge management and knowledge exchange.

But like other applications, at the core of knowledge management applications are consolidated databases supporting the data, information and knowledge handling. These databases and the web pages enabling access to them by authorised users can be regularly updated. Indeed, databases have been at the heart of all the applications discussed in this chapter.

17.9 Conclusion

In this chapter we have illustrated the power of databases through a brief discussion of eight database applications which add to those of data warehousing, data mining, enterprise resource planning, electronic commerce and customer relationship management discussed previously. Even so, we have only begun to discuss the applications of databases, for it is most likely that at the centre of any successful computer application there will be a database or databases of some sort.

Summary

- Information is available to the general public through databases created and maintained by government bodies, public sector organisations, voluntary groups and individuals. A vast array of data sets are available, including electoral and census data, library catalogues, bibliographies, education figures, genealogy, astronomical data, legal material, medical facts and other scientific data.
- A Geographical Information System (GIS) is a database application that captures, stores, retrieves, manipulates and displays human and physical geographical data. The possible applications for a GIS are numerous, and include deciding on store location for retailing, road planning for local government and vehicle routing for the wholesale distribution of goods.
- A marketing information system uses the input, storage, retrieval, manipulation and dissemination capabilities of database technology to

support marketing decision making. Examples include the development of a new product or a new pricing strategy.
- Computer-Supported collaborative Working (CSCW) provides the technology for co-ordination and integration for projects relying on close collaboration between disparate group members. Workflow management and collaborative writing with shared workspaces and multimedia communication, require databases and other technology.
- Document management systems use imaging and associated techniques to translate and create electronic documents. Databases contain data items, many of which are assembled or derived from documents to enable efficient retrieval of relevant documents according to various criteria.
- Although call centres originated with telephone calling, they now include technology to support a variety of methods used for communication between an organisation and its customers. Database technology provides the underlying database of customer and product information for use by the centre.
- Knowledge management concerns getting information to the appropriate people, when required, helping them to share this information and experience, and enabling them to use it to improve organisational performance.

Exercises

1. Attempt to find examples of the various database applications via the Internet and library search.
2. What other types of database application can you find in your library search?

Further reading

Beaudouin-Lafon, M. (1998) *Computer Supported Co-operative Work,* Wiley.

Bernhardsen, T. and Dangermond, J. (1999) *Geographic Information Systems,* Wiley.

Bielawski, L. and Boyle, J. (1996) *Electronic Document Management Systems,* Prentice Hall.

Bradshaw, D. (1999) *Next Generation Call Centres,* Ovum.

Burrough, P. A. and McDonnell, R. A. (1998) *Principles of Geographical Information Systems,* Oxford University Press.

Cusack, M. (1998) *Online Customer Care,* McGraw Hill.

Date, C. J. (2000) *An Introduction to Database Systems,* 7th edn, Addison Wesley.

Grimshaw, D. J. (1999) *Bringing Geographical Information Systems into Business,* Horizon.

Heywood, I., Cornelius, S. and Carver, S. (1998) *An Introduction to Geographical Information Systems,* Addison Wesley, Harlow.

Kotler, P. (1998) *Marketing Management,* Prentice Hall.

Lockwood, T. (1999) *Call Centres,* Fenman.

McKeown, M. (1999) *Call Centres: Strategies for Survival,* FT Business.

Probst, G., Raub, S. and Romhardt, K. (2000) *Managing Knowledge: Building Blocks for Success,* Wiley, Chichester.

Samli, A. C. (1996) *Information-Driven Marketing Decisions,* Quorum.

Sutton, M. J. D. (1996) *Document Management for the Enterprise: Principles, Techniques, and Applications,* Wiley.

Part V: Developing applications

In Part I we considered the database applications in the context of the organisation. In Part II we looked at developing the various models, which can represent a stage towards developing the database. In Part III we described how our database applications are implemented and in Part IV we discussed various database applications. It remains only for us to provide a description of the process of developing a database application such as ones described in Part IV. We suggest two general approaches, a formal information systems development methodology and then rapid application development. Finally we look at outsourcing, where the decision is made to develop and perhaps also run the application externally.

18

Information systems development

18.1 Introduction

Most information systems will use a database as the source of data. We have discussed some application types in Part IV. In this chapter we show how information systems are developed using these databases. This should be done in a fairly systematic way, perhaps using one of the methodologies available, at least as a guide. We first look at a generic approach, the information systems development life cycle. We then consider a 'brand name' methodology, SSADM. We consider rapid application development, an approach that emphasises both the speed of delivery of applications and an enhanced role for users. Finally we look at another alternative, that of outsourcing applications development to a supplier.

18.2 Information systems development life cycle

In this section we outline a generic approach to develop information systems. It is based on Avison and Shah (1997). As Figure 18.1 shows, it has six stages: feasibility study, systems investigation, systems analysis, systems design, implementation, and review and maintenance. In principle, each of these stages is completed before starting the next phase. In practice, of course, it is an iterative process.

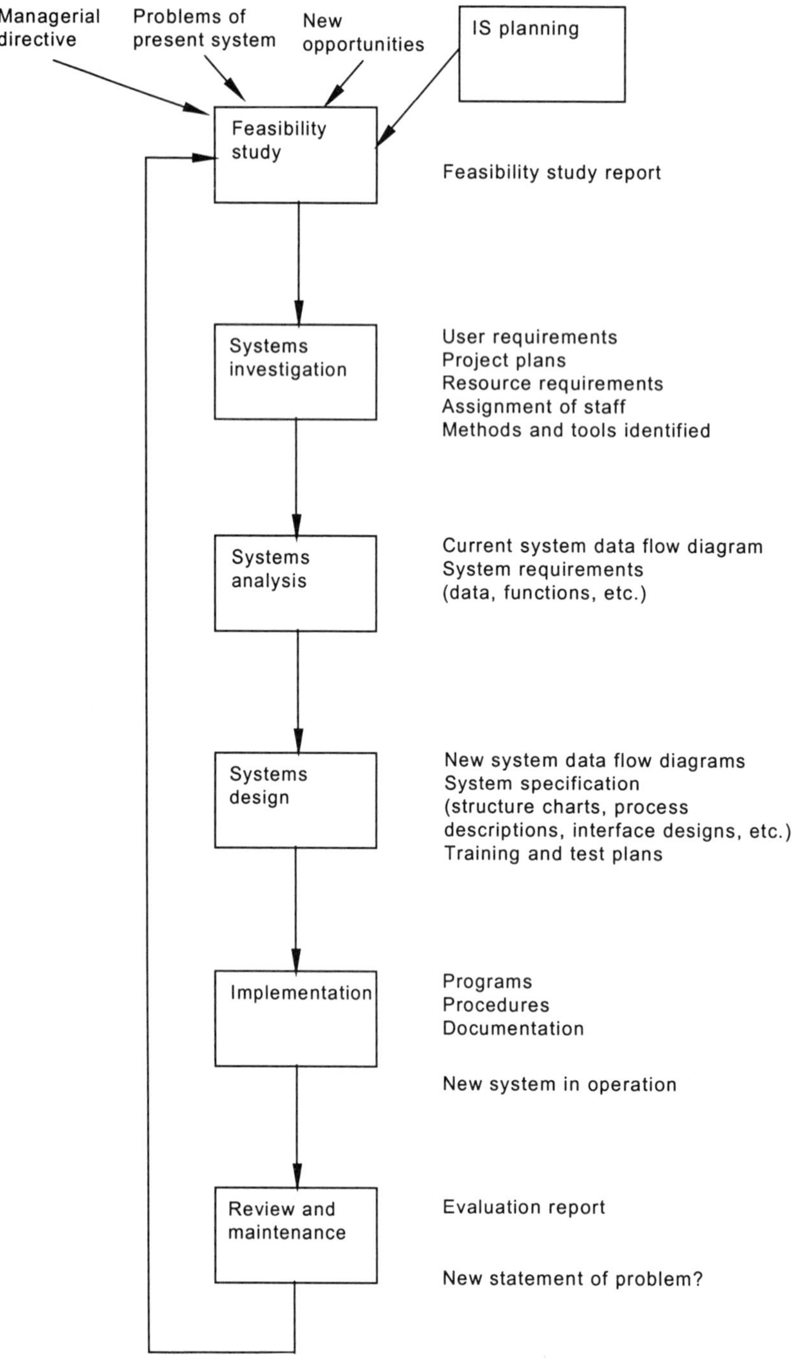

Figure 18.1: The information systems development life cycle (from Avison and Shah, 1997)

In the **feasibility study** stage the systems analysts and others in the systems development team who are the IS implementers are asked by the IS managers to identify the initial framework for the application. This will be done with the overall supervision of the systems planning team. An investigation is carried out to see whether it is feasible to carry out a project given the available organisational resources. The analysts will look in outline at the present system, new requirements, problems, new opportunities, and responsibilities. In this way, a feasibility study is really a scaled-down version of the systems investigation to come next. Alternative solutions with details of costs and benefits should be considered. The result of the feasibility study is a feasibility report, which is presented to the business client, perhaps in the presence of business users, in the organisation. They will choose one of a number of options regarding the project. This might vary from keeping the present system, choosing the recommended option or taking an alternative option. The one chosen is likely to be that which is seen to be technologically reliable, reasonable to schedule, economically worthwhile and organisationally acceptable, and therefore most likely to be a success.

Once the project has been given the go-ahead, then the subsequent stages must be planned in more detail. During the next **systems investigation** stage, the systems analysts need to know what information is required, when is it required, who wants this information, and what activities give rise to the data that is used to produce the information. This will require investigation of the problem domain in much more detail, picking out data types, volumes and so on, not only determining the data items required but also identifying the sources of the data and the users of the data. Hopefully, the data will already exist on the database. Otherwise it will be necessary to collect, validate and add data to the database. Techniques for systems investigation including interviewing personnel, using questionnaires, observing present practices, sampling, and looking at existing documents. Techniques are recommended at this phase, many of them aimed at keeping good documentation.

The next stage is to carry out a thorough **analysis** of the current system and to determine the requirements of the new system. Typically the analysts ask a series of questions at this stage. These might include 'how is it done at present?', 'when is it being done?', 'why is it done in that way?', 'why are there problems at the moment?', 'why do they occur?', 'how can these be solved in a new system?', 'what would be the future volumes and will the new system cater for these?' and so on. All this analysis should result in a detailed description of the system required by the client. The clients need to agree that this is an accurate description of the system that they require. Again, good documentation techniques can help communicating the results of the analysis to other technical people and users. Techniques include those of conceptual modelling, entity-relationship, relational and object modelling, discussed in Part II of the book. These help analyse the data needs of the new system as well as understand the present one, and dataflow diagrams and functional models to help analyse the process aspects.

The purpose of the **system design** phase is to produce a design of the system to be developed which meets the requirements that have been identified. This phase includes consideration of the different hardware and software alternatives. There may be a combination of application package solutions (perhaps adapted for the particular application) and tailor-made solutions. Decisions related to this might lead to extensive computer programming work or relatively minor modifications of the application package.

Of course in relation to this book, the decision might include whether to use centralised or distributed databases or whether to design a new database or adapt an existing one for this new application. The analyst will use some of the techniques of conceptual modelling, entity-relationship, relational and object modelling to help design the data needs. The role of the database administration team will be crucial in these decisions.

The logical design (the design 'in principle') is translated into a physical design through the specification of hardware, software, database, program and procedure specifications. A full technical specification of the system requirements must be produced so that the design also includes a report layout and contents, screen designs, and plans about how the system and database are to be tested. The design of the human–computer interface is particularly important, and there are many choices depending on the experience of the users and whether they are likely to be frequent users or not. Most people are now comfortable with the Windows, Icons, Menu and Pointer (WIMP) interface of the Apple Mac and Windows systems on PCs.

During the **implementation** stage, the information system is built and this will involve coding the programs, or at least modifying the application packages purchased, designing the operating procedures and producing the accompanying documentation. Testing the system is also undertaken to see whether the system meets user requirements and also to see if it is robust and performs efficiently. In addition, the installation of the tested system will be made after having converted from the old system to the new. Training staff in the use and operation of the new system will also take place at this stage. All the business users need to be comfortable with the new system. Equipment is installed and the changeover to the new system is made.

The **review and maintenance** phase consists of activities triggered by the identification of problems when using the now operational system or implementing changes to the system to reflect changes in the environment. The system will be evaluated and at some point in time, the system will become too expensive to maintain or fails to provide adequate business support. At that time the life cycle starts again.

Software tools are likely to be used by the analysts to help the process. Some of these were discussed in Chapter 12. The diagrams can be produced using CASE tools, which can also help to form the complete documentation. Project control tools can help control the project so that, ideally, the operational date is met without exceeding cost estimates. Testing tools can help test the programs. In some instances it might be possible to partly generate the application programs automatically.

18.3 Structured systems analysis and design method (SSADM)

In the previous section, we looked at a generic life cycle approach to develop applications. In this section we look at a 'brand name' methodology that is widely used, particularly by government departments and larger organisations in the UK. It was developed originally by Learmonth and Burchett Management Systems (LBMS) and the Central Computing and Telecommunications Agency (CCTA), which is responsible for computer training for the UK Civil Service. It has been in use since 1981 in a number of forms. At the time of writing, version 4.3/4+ is the most widely used. There are a number of texts on SSADM including Weaver *et al.* (1998).

SSADM has seven stages (numbered 0 to 6) within a five 'module' framework with its own set of plans, timescales, controls and monitoring procedures. The activities of each stage are precisely defined as are their associated end products (or deliverables), and this facilitates the use of project management techniques (the project management method PRINCE is recommended).

The SSADM modules are:

- Feasibility study (Stage 0)
- Requirements analysis (Stages 1 and 2)
- Requirements specification (Stage 3)

- Logical systems specification (Stages 4 and 5)
- Physical design (Stage 6).

The stages in SSADM are:

- Stage 0: Feasibility
- Stage 1: Investigation of current environment
- Stage 2: Business systems options
- Stage 3: Definition of requirements
- Stage 4: Technical system options
- Stage 5: Logical design
- Stage 6: Physical design.

SSADM provides detailed guidelines for conducting feasibility studies. It gives details of the steps and stages required. For the systems analysis stage, SSADM specifies the means of recording and analysing the results of the investigation. This is dealt with by Stages 1, 2 and 3 of SSADM. Stage 1 is concerned with the analysis of the current system; stage 2 with producing outline systems design and stage 3 specifies the requirements of the new system.

In systems design, various technical solutions that meet the requirements are evaluated and one is selected. A detailed logical design of the new system is developed showing, in non-technical terminology, how the system will function within the organisation. SSADM stages 2, 3, 4 and 5 deal with the activities of this phase of the life cycle. During the physical system design activities, the logical design is mapped to the specific hardware and software selected. Further, database definitions are specified, as well as the specification of programs and detailed manual procedures. This activity is dealt with by stage 6 of SSADM.

SSADM does not provide any direct support for the construction phase, although there is indirect support through the planning activities carried out in Stages 4 and 6 of SSADM. Similarly, SSADM does not provide any direct support for the systems implementation phase, which involves the transition from the old system to the new system. However, the plans for this activity are developed in SSADM stage 4. Finally, SSADM does not provide support for the production and review phases of the information systems life cycle.

SSADM is essentially a data-driven approach. Therefore, within this approach, data is modelled at an early stage. The final system architecture is based on the underlying data structures.

The feasibility study stage is considered optional in the SSADM approach, as this is considered to be something that is carried out during the information systems planning activities. In addition, projects are sometimes considered to be such a fundamental requirement that it does not require an assessment of feasibility. The following provides a more detailed look at each of the other stages:

STAGE 1 – Investigation of current environment
- Establish analysis framework
- Investigate and define requirements
- Investigate current processing
- Investigate current data
- Derive logical view of current system
- Assemble investigation results.

STAGE 2 – Business system options
- Define business system options
- Select business system option.

STAGE 3 – Definition of requirements
- Define required system processing
- Develop required data model
- Develop specification prototypes
- Derive system functions
- Enhance required data model
- Develop processing specification
- Confirm system objectives
- Assemble requirements specification.

STAGE 4 – Selection of technical options
- Define technical system options
- Select technical system options.

STAGE 5 – Logical design
- Define user dialogues
- Define update processes
- Define enquiry processes
- Assemble logical design.

STAGE 6 – Physical design
- Prepare for physical design
- Create physical data design
- Create function component implementation map
- Optimise physical data design
- Complete function specification

- Consolidate process data interface
- Assemble physical design.

The methodology recommends the use of entity-relationship diagrams, known as logical data structures in this context (along with a series of techniques to analyse processes). These are suggested for stage 1 but the entity model is emphasised particularly at stage 3 where it is seen as the essential basis of the logical design of the new system. Documentation forms for all the entities and attributes are completed. At stage 4 investigation and analysis are replaced by specification and design. The entity-relationship model is followed by normalisation of the relations to third normal form. As we saw in Chapter 4, the method suggests that events are traced through the data model to see if it is robust enough for all the possible transactions. Each function and process is also specified in detail.

There is also an optional prototyping phase. The methodology suggests demonstrating prototypes of critical dialogues and menu structures to users and this will verify the analysts' understanding of the users' requirements and their preferences for interface design. As well as verifying the specification, this phase can have other benefits such as increased user commitment.

At stage 4, the environment in which the system will operate, in terms of the hardware and software configuration, development strategy, organisational impact and system functionality, is determined. Stage 5 is carried out in parallel with this. The logical design is a statement of what the system is required to do rather than a statement about the procedures or program specifications to do it. The latter is the realm of the final stage 6, the physical design. In stage 5 the dialogue structures and menu structures and designs are defined for particular users or user roles. User involvement is recommended at this stage and the prototypes developed in stage 3 are referred to. Furthermore, the update processes and operations are defined along with the processing of enquiries, including the sequence of processing. In other words, it is at this stage that further detail about how the system will apply and control of the operations following each event will be defined. Detail such as the rules of validating data entered into the system, will be specified. All the requirements to start designing the physical solution are now in place. It is at the physical design (stage 6) that the logical design is mapped onto a particular physical environment. The roles of the technologist, the programmer and database designers in particular, are stressed in this phase, although the analyst and user should be available to verify that the final design satisfies user requirements.

The logical data model will be converted into a design appropriate for the database management system available. The database mapping will be a key aspect of final implementation and include not only the way data and data relationships are held on the database, but also key handling and access methods. Much will depend on performance measurement so that database access is efficient, and again this will depend on the actual hardware and software configuration (including database management system).

SSADM is used along with computer tools and there are many tools designed specifically for users of SSADM as well as those designed for other methodologies, which are also useful to followers of SSADM. There are, for example, a number of tools that help analysis and design, some generating code from the SSADM design, and drawing tools, to help draw entity-relationship diagrams and others, and all these can be very supportive of the information systems development process.

The successful implementation of the methodology relies on the skills of key personnel being available, though the techniques and tools are widely known and the project team method of working encourages good training procedures and participation. SSADM emphasises good documentation standards, clear and detailed guidelines and thorough quality assurance. The people involved will be similar to those mentioned in Section 18.2 (and Chapter 3) though the systems development team will be familiar with this particular methodology to develop information systems.

18.4 Rapid application development

The goal of rapid development of applications has been around for some time and with good reason, as the objective of speeding up the development process is something that has been on the agenda of both general management and information systems management for a long time. The need to develop information systems more quickly has been driven by rapidly changing business needs. The general environment of business is seen as increasingly competitive, more customer-focused and operating in a more international context. Such a business environment is characterised by continuous change, and the information systems in an organisation need to be created and amended speedily to support this change. Unfortunately, information systems development in most organisations is unable to react quickly enough and the business and systems development cycles are substantially out of step. In such a situation, the notion of rapid application development (RAD) is obviously attractive.

RAD is probably best known from the works of James Martin (for example, Martin, 1991, and see also Avison and Fitzgerald, 2002) who has defined a RAD methodology that we discuss in this section. RAD is actually a combination of techniques and tools that are, for the most part, already well known and dealt with elsewhere in this book. We identify the following as the most important RAD characteristics.

It is not based upon the traditional life cycle (Section 18.2) but adopts an evolutionary/prototyping approach. It focuses upon identifying the important users and involving them via workshops at early stages of development. It focuses on obtaining commitment from the business users. Indeed, it is to be hoped that business and IS visionaries will be present at these workshops, along with clients and users and IS management and implementer staff, including all the systems planning and development teams. It requires supporting tools to help speed up development. RAD has four phases: requirements planning, user design, construction and cutover.

RAD devotes a lot of effort to the early stages of systems development referred to as **requirements planning**. There are two techniques used in this phase, both of which are really workshops or structured meetings. The first is **joint requirements planning** (JRP) and the second is **joint application design** (JAD). In some other RAD methods, these are not separated, indeed, Martin points out that they may in practice be combined with some of the functions of JRP being subsumed into JAD.

The role of JRP is to identify the high-level management requirements of the application system at a strategic level. The participants in JRP are senior managers who have a vision and understanding of the overall objectives of the system and how it can contribute to the goals and strategy of the organisation. If this understanding does not already exist, the workshop may be used to help determine such an understanding or vision. The JRP is a creative workshop that helps to identify and create commitment to the goals of the system, to identify priorities, to eliminate unnecessary functions and so on. In JRP, the participants need to have a combination of overall business knowledge and specific knowledge about the area that the proposed system is addressing along with its requirements. They also need to have the necessary authority and seniority to be able to make decisions and commitments.

JAD is the main technique of the second phase of RAD known as **user design**. JAD adopts a top-down approach to user design and is based on the recognition that user requirements are difficult to understand and define, and that the traditional requirements analysis techniques of observation, interviews and questionnaires are inadequate. In JAD, the user design is achieved via the combination of the right people, the right environment and the use of good prototyping tools. The prototyping tool allows the quick exploration of processes, interfaces, reports, screens, dialogues and so on.

Prototyping may be of the overall system or be used to explore particular parts of the system that are contentious or present particular problems. The user design is developed and expressed using diagramming techniques such as entity-relationship modelling, functional decomposition and data flow. The participants in the workshop need to be familiar with these techniques, but the emphasis is on getting the requirements as correct as possible and to reflect the business needs. Therefore, the language used in the workshop and expressed in the diagrams is that of the business and the users, rather than the more technical language of information systems. The results of the user design are captured in a CASE tool which checks both internal consistency and that with other applications and corporate models. Where necessary, the terms used should be discussed and defined and entered into the repository of the tool. The use of a CASE tool enables the speedy, accurate and effective transfer of the results into the next phase, the construction phase.

The typical characteristics of a JAD workshop are as follows:

- *An intensive meeting of business users (managers and end users) and information systems people:* There should be specific objectives and a structured agenda, including rules of behaviour and protocols. The information systems people are usually there to provide assistance on technical matters, for example implications, possibilities and constraints, rather than decision making in terms of requirements. One of the most important people is the executive owner or executive sponsor of the system.

- *A defined length of meeting:* This is typically one or two days, but can be up to five. The location is usually away from the home base of the users, but most importantly, away from interruptions. The participants are expected to attend full time and cannot drop in and out of the meeting.

- *A structured meeting room:* The layout of the room is regarded as important in helping to achieve the meeting objectives. The round table principle is usually employed, and the walls of the room are typically covered in white boards and pin boards. When CASE and other tools are employed, these are usually placed at the side with the ability to display output on large screens and print when necessary.

- *A facilitator:* This is a person who leads and manages the meeting. He or she is independent of the participants, and specialises in facilitation. This person may be internal to the organisation or brought in from outside, and will understand the psychology of group dynamics and the tasks that the participants are undertaking. A facilitator is responsible for the process and outcomes in terms of documentation and deliverables. He or she will control the objectives; agenda, process and discussion, using a variety of techniques to help move the meeting forward and achieve the objectives. Techniques such as brainstorming, reflection exercises and cooling breaks will be used.

- *A scribe:* This is a person (or persons) responsible for documenting the discussions and outcomes of the meeting (including the use of CASE and prototyping tools when available).

From these characteristics it can be seen that there are a number of principles underlying JAD. First, the user design should be moved forward as quickly as possible. There may be a series of JAD meetings (ideally two, although more may be necessary) which either address different parts of the design area or more commonly take the design from overview to more detailed levels. Often further work is carried out between the meetings, such as the preparation of more sophisticated prototypes, but decisions are taken only at the meetings. The proponents of JAD argue that it replaces cycles of interviews and meetings on an individual basis that normally take many months. This can significantly reduce the elapsed time required to achieve the design goals. In the traditional approach, meetings usually consist of a small group or are held on a one-to-one basis. When analysts find a conflict or discrepancy between users as to requirements or interpretations, they have to re-schedule all these meetings again to try to resolve things. It may be necessary to cycle round the groups more than once. Typically, this takes a great deal of time, because setting up meetings is notoriously difficult in most organisations. JAD seeks to overcome these kinds of problems with one or two major workshops.

The second key element is getting the right people together for the workshop. The right people are all those with stakes in the proposed system, including end users, and those with the authority to make binding decisions in the area. This avoids all the time-consuming cycles that are encountered with traditional methods.

A third element is the commitment that the JAD meeting engenders. With traditional meetings, commitment is often dissipated over time and decisions may be taken off the cuff in small meetings where all information is not available and implications are not fully understood. With JAD, it is all out in the open and high profile. Decisions tend not to be taken lightly, but when they are made, they are made with conviction and commitment. In particular, because JAD focuses upon the benefits of the system for the business and users, the commitment is more marked and visible.

The fourth element is the presence of an executive sponsor. This is the person who wants the system, is committed to achieving it and is prepared to fund it. This person is obviously a senior executive who must understand and believe in the RAD approach and, due to the senior position can overcome some of the bureaucracy and politics that tend to get in the way of fast development.

Perhaps the most important single aspect of JAD is the facilitator. This person can make or break a workshop and is critical to determining whether the objectives are achieved. Apart from skills in handling JAD workshops, along with an understanding of group dynamics, it is the independence or neutrality of the facilitator, which is crucial. This enables facilitators to achieve more than any other stakeholder who might be regarded with suspicion by others. A facilitator is able to avoid, and smooth, many of the hierarchical and political issues that frequently cause problems, and will be free from the taint of organisational history and past battles.

In the **construction phase** the user designs are converted to detailed design and code generation. Information systems professionals using a CASE tool undertake this phase, and the key users then review a series of prototypes. Thus the screens and designs of each transaction are prototyped and the users then approve them. If they do not approve them, they will request changes and the process goes on through a series of iterations. By prototyping and the use of CASE tools, these iterations are achieved quickly and testing is enabled. Some of these key users will already have been involved in the earlier phase of user design. Construction is performed by small teams of three or four experts in the use of CASE tools. These experts are known as SWAT teams. SWAT stands for 'skilled with advanced tools' and the approach requires them to work quickly, making maximum possible use of re-usable designs that already exist. Teams are kept small so as to reduce the number of interfaces and interactions between people in the teams. One of the problems of traditional development is low productivity that, it is argued, results from the large teams of developers involved and the consequent large communications network and the number of communications. Normally there is a SWAT team member allocated to developing each transaction in a system. In practice, there is often only one developer for a particular part of the system and this reduces the number of potential interactions with other developers for the area to zero. Using this approach, it is argued that the core of a system can be built relatively quickly, typically in four to six weeks, and then it is progressively refined and integrated with other aspects developed by other team members.

Once the detailed designs have been agreed, the code can be generated using the CASE tool and the system tested and approved. Because of the way that the construction has occurred, there should not be any surprises to the users when they see the finished version. All associated documentation is then produced and database optimisation is performed.

The final phase is **cutover**, and this involves further comprehensive testing using realistic data in operational situations. The users are trained on the system, organisational changes, implied by the system, are implemented, and finally the cutover is effected by running the old and the new systems in parallel, until the new system has proved itself, and the old system is phased out.

RAD adopts an evolutionary, or timebox approach, to development and implementation. Typically, it recommends implementation of systems in a 90-day life cycle. The objective is to have the easiest and most important 75% of system functionality produced in the first 90-day timebox, and the rest in subsequent timeboxes. This forces users and developers to focus on only those aspects of the system that are necessary and probably most well defined for development in the first timebox. Everything else is left until later. The knock-on benefit of this is that with experience and use of the basic system, developed in the first timebox, users often find that their requirements evolve in different directions to those originally envisaged. In other words, the benefits of an evolutionary approach accrue. The other advantage of the timebox is that it creates a focus on achieving an implementation in the specified period. In order to achieve this, the functionality must be trimmed accordingly. No simply 'nice to have' but not strictly necessary features can be included, and the development must be made achievable. The timebox approach contrasts with the traditional approach where every conceivable requirement is implemented together and the resulting complexity often causes long delays in implementation.

18.5 Outsourcing

One way to avoid potential difficulties in developing your own applications as described above (but potentially attract alternative difficulties) is to outsource information systems development and possibly the running of operational systems once they are developed. The outsourcing of IT activities and services is increasingly being considered as a legitimate option in managing and organising IT in many organisations. The motivation is, in the main, efficiency gains, and it is often associated with two other 'mantras' – downsizing and sticking to core competences. In other words, it is argued that IT will be cheaper and more effective if carried out at an external specialist commercial company than in-house. Two leading outsourcing suppliers are EDS and IBM.

Some organisations simply require any new work to be given out to tender (including an in-house quotation which, it is hoped, might lead to in-house 'commercial realism'); others have moved all their IT activities to an external company (and there are many solutions within these extremes). Outsourcing reduces the risk of developing non-core competences at the expense of core competences, it enables talented staff to be involved in your information systems work without your organisation having to employ and keep these expensive individuals, it is a way of keeping your technology up to date and minimises overheads during slack times.

What, then, are the downsides? First and foremost, the organisation is in danger of losing control of their data and thereby their information, a major organisational resource. Many argue that it is essential that organisations retain ownership and exercise control of their key information. Further, keeping critical tasks internal is at least 'desirable'. This indicates a loss of control.

But there are other, long-term effects for the organisation. The experience of developing systems and running system is being lost for the future. The outsourcing supplier's expertise and learning are increasing, not yours, with the result that the organisation is increasingly dependent on the supplier. There is a danger that the organisation fails to manage the supplier sufficiently well with the result that service levels decrease. Further, the supplier will be less concerned about your issues, such as strategic alignment of IS/IT, with the organisation's overall strategy.

Of course, there may well be financial and other advantages in outsourcing some activities. An obvious example is companies outsourcing the development of their web sites. In this case, the motivation is often speed. But it is perhaps wise to keep some core staff in house to be aware of IT opportunities and negotiate with suppliers.

18.6 Conclusion

In this chapter we have looked at how we might develop the information systems applications discussed in Part IV of the book. One possibility is to use one of the formal methodologies. We discussed SSADM, but there are others such as Merise and Information Engineering. There are others devoted to particular database types, such as that of Mathiassen *et al.* (2000). Rapid application development provides a semi formal structure and framework to the quick development of applications, which is often essential, even if some ideals are ignored. Another possibility is to outsource all or some applications development to suppliers.

Summary

- The information systems development life cycle has six stages: feasibility study, systems investigation, systems analysis, systems design, implementation, and review and maintenance.
- SSADM is a formal approach used by many UK organisations to develop their information systems.
- The goal of rapid applications development is to speed up the development process. Important steps include joint requirements planning and joint application design workshops.
- Outsourcing enables application development to be carried out by a third party supplier.

Exercises

1. Compare the development of an information system using a formal approach with rapid applications development.
2. Argue for and against outsourcing of IS applications development.
3. If you were following the IS development lifecycle approach, when would database considerations be important?

4. Suggest other ways of developing applications. Which approach might be particularly appropriate for developing your university or hospital application? Explain why it is appropriate.

Further reading

Avison, D. and Fitzgerald, G. (2002) *Information Systems Development: Methodologies, Techniques and Tools,* 3rd edn, McGraw-Hill, Maidenhead.

Avison, D. and Shah, H. (1997) *The Information Systems Development Life Cycle: A First Course in Information Systems,* McGraw-Hill, Maidenhead.

Martin, J. (1991) *Rapid Application Development.* Prentice Hall, Englewood Cliffs, New Jersey.

Mathiassen, L., Munk-Madsen, A., Nielsen, P. A. and Stage, J (2000) Object Oriented Analysis and Design, Marko, Aalborg.

Plant, R and Willcocks, L. P (2000) Sourcing Internet Development. in: Willcocks, L. and Sauer, C., *Moving to E Business,* Random House, London.

Weaver, P. L., Lanbrou, N. and Walkley, M. (1998) *Practical SSADM Version 4+,* Pitman, London.

Willcocks, L., Fitzgerald, G. and Lacity, M. (1996) To outsource it or not?: recent research on economics and evaluation practice. *European Journal of Information Systems,* **5**, 3.

Index